The New Testament:
Book By Book

A 26 lesson outline series covering the entire
New Testament

I0168423

by
Roy E. Cogdill

Truth
Publications

Taking His hand,
Helping each other home.
™

ISBN 10: 1-58427-218-X

ISBN 13: 978-1-58427-218-2

Photo Credits: British Museum, 36, 93, 167: Ferrell Jenkins, 50, 56, 67, 187; H. Armstrong Roberts, 108; Southeastern Films, 130; Turkish Tourism & Information Office, 78, 192.

Truth Publications, Inc.
CEI Bookstore
220 S. Marion St., Athens, AL 35611
855-492-6657
sales@truthpublications.com
www.truthbooks.com

he New Testament: Book By Book

Part 1

Part 2

Introduction

Brother Roy E. Cogdill has written several books, including six or seven of the workbook variety. He has authored or co-authored several other books. Two of Brother Cogdill's books have been among the most widely used workbooks prepared by anyone in the church. Many years after their publication, the contents of these books remain so essential that public demand causes these two books to be kept in print. His book, *The New Testament Church,* has sold about a quarter of a million copies—though it is a book of 138 pages. About 50,000 copies of *Walking By Faith* have been sold.

Brother Cogdill is now at the peak of his analytic ability, and it is my judgment that this book, *The New Testament: Book By Book,* will be yet in use long after he has gone on to his eternal reward. This book is so designed to make an ideal six-month study for High School-age boys and girls, but it is more particularly aimed at adults who want to acquire an overall view of the New Testament. The amount of material contained in each lesson is great. A teacher may find it difficult to cover a lesson in one time period, but it can be done. In fact, it *has been done* by Brother Cogdill himself.

To me it is an honor to be permitted to introduce this new book to adult classes. It should be taught in every church across the land and around the world. One can never acquire a knowledge of a Biblical book in depth, until he first has acquired an overview of that book. This book is designed to give each one an overall survey of the New Testament so that each student may go on to more detailed knowledge. However, do not underestimate the thoroughness of this study. Coming from a brilliant mind which has been used for more than 50 years in Scripture study, the richness of the fruit of those decades of study will amaze you and improve your own knowledge greatly.

It is a pleasure now to present to a great multitude of Bible students this invaluable book. Generations yet unborn will benefit from the labor and wisdom of this our brother as he presents to us a sweeping scope of the grand plan of the Holy Scriptures which we call the New Testament.

—Cecil Willis

Introduction to the New Testament

A. The Relation Between the Testaments.

The New Testament, like the Old Testament, sets forth not only a system of doctrine and duty, but a historical record of facts, involving and demonstrating the will of the God of Heaven, and of the Lord Jesus Christ, and of man's duty toward God, his fellowman, and toward himself. The history of the New Testament is not independent of the history of the Old Testament, but is rather, a sequel to the old. During the period of Old Testament history, God's plan for human redemption, which had been formulated "before the foundations of the world were laid," was kept hidden in the mind of God as a mystery (1 Pet. 1:18-20; Eph. 3:8-11; Rom. 16:25-26), and it was not revealed for men to know and understand the provisions that God had made for human redemption, or the plan by which it was to be accomplished, until these truths were revealed by the Holy Spirit in the New Testament. Someone aptly has said that "the Old Testament is the New Testament concealed, and the New Testament is the Old Testament revealed." The two constitute the whole of Divine revelation and complement each other. We understand both only when we take into consideration their unity. It is important, however, to know that God's plan for human redemption existed in God's eternal purpose but remained a mystery in Old Testament days, and is now a revelation in the New Testament (1 Cor. 2:6-13; Eph. 3:1-7).

The Old Testament reveals the attributes of Deity; God's eternal self existence, His perfect holiness, the absolute unity of the Godhead, His unlimited power to rule over nations and men, the principles of righteousness as they relate to God and to one's fellowman, the necessity of holiness as a condition of receiving God's blessings, irreparable ruin as the final consequence of sin, and eternal life as the reward of the righteous. Some of the purposes and uses to be served by studying Old Testament scriptures today, and the reasons why they have been preserved, are set forth in the New Testament in such passages as Rom. 15:4; Heb. 2:1-4; Heb. 11; Heb. 12:12; Heb. 3 and 4.

Some other fundamental truths incorporated with the revelation of the Old Testament in promise, prophecy, type and shadow, and yet not as plainly revealed as they are found in the New Testament, are the resurrection of Christ from the dead, future rewards and penalties, God's universal provisions by His grace for the justification of all mankind, the atoning blood of Christ, etc.

The identity, person and office of the "promised Messiah" like unto Moses, whom God would raise up for His people in the latter days, as the mighty King of David's seed who would sit upon His throne and reign over His kingdom, to order and establish it with judgment and justice forever, and as that great High Priest after the order of Melchisedec, whom God would establish forever with a solemn oath, had all been promised, typified, and prophesied in the Old Testament scriptures, but are revealed in the New Testament.

The New Testament then, in the coming of our Lord as the perfect example of holiness in life, in His death for our sins, in His resurrection for our justification, in His ascension at the right hand of God as King and Priest, records the fulfillment of the primary message of the Old Testament, "the coming of Christ, our Savior." In the New Testament is also recorded the fulfillment of God's purpose from eternity, in the revelation and confirmation of the gospel through the work of the Apostles and prophets by the Holy Spirit, and in the establishment of the church purchased by the blood of Christ as a saved relationship for the children of God.

The word, "Testament," perhaps is not as clear and meaningful as the more preferable word ordinarily used, "Covenant." The "Old Covenant," was God's covenant or agreement with his people. It was sanctified by the sprinkling of the blood of animals when it had been ratified by the agreement of the people to hear and do all that Jehovah had commanded them therein (Ex. 19:7-8; Deut. 5:27; Ex. 5:24-26; Heb. 9:18-21). The New Testament is God's "Covenant" with His people today (Heb. 1:1). It has been sanctified by the blood of Christ (Mt. 26:28; Heb. 9:15; 10:4-10; 10:15-22). This new "Covenant" relationship with God can be ratified only by our individually believing in the promises and provisions of God's grace (Rom. 3:20-26; 5:1). Our faith likewise must pledge complete obedience to all He commands therein (Rom. 16:26; Gal. 5:6).

B. The Background of the New Testament.

It is impossible to understand many things in the New Testament and from them to learn what God would have us to know, without being acquainted to some degree with the conditions under which men lived in the New Testament day. These conditions, historical, political, economic and social, constitute the background for many things contained in the New Testament scriptures. The principles of righteousness are eternal and, therefore, remain the same under all circumstances, but the statement of those principles and their proper application is always affected by the exact situation existing. We want, therefore, in this beginning lesson of this series to acquaint ourselves briefly with the background of the New Testament scriptures. This background of New Testament teaching needs to be considered in the light of three primary influences affecting the lives and attitudes of the people in New Testament days.

1. *The Religious Background.* While the history of the Jewish people began with the call of Abraham (Gen. 12), we need, for the purpose of this study, to keep in mind particularly the period of Jewish history between the end of the Babylonian captivity and the reign of the Herods. Prior to the period of captivity, the Jews had

4

given only periodic devotion to the Law. In the 9th century B.C., the entire northern kingdom, Israel, had been alienated from God under the influence of Jezebel, Ahab's queen, and had been caused to worship Baal. During the 8th century B.C., the temple worship in the southern kingdom of Judah had fallen into neglect and disuse, and during the time of Manasseh and of Amon, the worship of foreign gods had been introduced. This condition was corrected by Josiah, who cleansed the temple, restored the worship of the Jews, and brought to attention the book of the Law (2 Chron. 34:1-33). As long as the Jews continued to live in Palestine and were surrounded by prosperous and powerful heathen neighbors, they were influenced by them, and periodically were led to turn their backs upon God.

During the time of their captivity, synagogue worship arose and continued as we find it in the New Testament day. During the Babylonian captivity, the Medes and Persians had conquered Babylon, and Cyrus, the ruler, had allowed the Jews to return to Jerusalem. Zerubbabel rebuilt the temple, Ezra re-established the Law as the constitution, and Nehemiah rebuilt the walls. Following the Persian period of rule, there was the Alexandrian period (332 - 301 B.C.). The coming of Alexander and the Grecians to Palestine meant that the Jews were subjected to Greek (Hellenistic) influences. Upon the death of Alexander a struggle arose for the control of the Grecian empire. The Syrians on the east and Egypt on the south were divided into separate kingdoms, and for about 100 years Palestine was under the influence of the rulers of Egypt (301 - 198 B.C.).

The Syrians won control in 198 B.C. and continued until 167 B.C., at which time Jewish rebellion was successful and the Maccabean period began with 167 B.C. When the yoke of Syrian rule had been broken, the sanctuary was again cleansed and re-dedicated, an event still celebrated in New Testament times (Jn. 10:22-23). In 63 B.C., the Roman forces under Pompey subdued Palestine. Except for the rule by the Parthians (41 - 47 B.C.), Jerusalem and Palestine remained under Roman government until the fall of the Roman empire. Under Roman rule, however, the Herods were made responsible for Galilee. The Herodian dynasty began with Antipater. His son was Herod the Great, who died on April 1, 4 B.C. He was a very unscrupulous man, immoral in character, and harsh and unjust in his treatment of the people. He sought to leave a name for himself by engaging in a great program of construction throughout Palestine. The Herods were all appointed by Roman authority. Herod the Great ruled as "king of the Jews." Matthew 2 records the slaughter of the children in an effort to take the life of Jesus, heralded as the "new born King." Upon his death, his son, Archelaus, ruled from 4 B.C. to A.D. 6 in Judea and Samaria. Herod Antipas was tetrarch of Galilee from 4 B.C. to A.D. 39. Jesus referred to him as "that fox" (Lk. 13:32), and he is the one responsible for the death of John the baptizer. The book of Acts records the reign of the last of the Herods, Agrippa I, King of Judea from A.D. 37 to 44 (Acts 12), and

Agrippa II, tetrarch of Chalcia and territories north and east of Judea from A.D. 48 through 70 (Acts 25 and 26).

It is well to remember in our study of the New Testament, however, that over the Roman province of Judea, as a direct representative of the Caesars, there was a procurator, Pontius Pilate, from A.D. 27 to 37, who pronounced the sentence of death upon Jesus by Jewish demand (Jn. 18:19).

Josepheus, the Jewish historian (Antiquities XIV, 115), testifies that the Jews, who had been scattered abroad through the ancient world, were to be found in "every place." Wherever the Jew went, his influence emphasized two things: the worship of the one true and living God, the God of his fathers, Abraham, Isaac and Jacob, and the Law, the standard of ethical conduct. They propagated both of these by word of mouth, and when the Old Testament was translated out of Hebrew into the Greek language by the seventy (commonly called the Septuagint), about 250 to 150 B.C., this increased the influence of the Jewish religion among the nations. Wherever they had gone they built their Jewish places of worship, the synagogues, as a meeting place, both in Palestine and in Gentile lands, for the reading of the Old Testament scriptures and as a place of prayer and worship.

The chief sects of the Jewish religion for 200 years or more before Christ came were the Sadducees and the Pharisees. The Sadducees were the priestly party and controlled the politics of the people under Roman supervision. They were not as numerous as the Pharisees, but through the exercise of political influences and wealth, they were powerful. The Pharisees, often referred to in connection with the life of Christ, were religious leaders, emphasizing the entire Old Testament scriptures, believing in the existence of angels and spirits, in immortality, and the resurrection of the body.

2. The Political Background. At the time the New Testament was written the Romans dominated the entire civilized world, with little exception. They had one vast empire under the Emperor, referred to in the New Testament as both "king" (1 Pet. 2:17), and Augustus (Lk. 2:1). This empire reached from the Atlantic ocean on the west, to the Euphrates River and the Red Sea on the east, and from the Rhone and Danube Rivers, the Black Sea, and the Caucasus mountains on the north, to the Sahara Desert on the south.

Rome, as a city, was founded in 753 B.C. By alliances with other cities and a long succession of wars, Rome won control of the Italian peninsula by 265 B.C. By 146 B.C. they had ended their war with Carthage and established control over Spain and North Africa. Macedonia had been conquered and made a Roman province, and with the capture of Corinth in the same year, 146 B.C., Achaia became a part of the Roman empire. In 63 B.C., Pompey organized Syria into a province and annexed Judea. Under the Caesars, many of whom were very wicked, bitter enemies of the Jews, and determined persecutors of Christianity, and in spite of such imperialism and injustice as characterized them, the Roman empire was extended through the world (Col. 1:5-6). Jesus was born in the reign of Augustus Caesar (Lk. 2:1); His public ministry and death occurred in the reign of Tiberius Caesar (Lk. 3:1); the great period of evangelism came during the reigns of Claudius (Acts 18:2) and Nero (Acts 25:11-12).

Palestine, therefore, was under a dual form of government, during the time of Christ; the Jewish government headed by Herod, and the Roman government represented in Palestine by Pontius Pilate. The right of inflicting the death penalty had been denied to the Jews by the Romans. This is the reason why there are two separate divisions to the trial of Christ recorded in the gospels, one before the Jewish courts and one before the Roman governor. The latter was necessary in order for the Jews to succeed in having Him put to death.

3. The Cultural Background. While the Romans had conquered the Greeks with military might, the Greeks, in a very real sense, had conquered their captors with their culture. The Greek language and Greek customs were spread out all over the eastern world. Greek teaching, culture and influences pervaded even the city of Rome itself. Paul wrote the letter to the Roman church in the Greek language. The Romans were greatly influenced by the Greeks both in literature and philosophy. Greek (Koine) was the common language of the day. It was spoken and understood almost everywhere and for this reason was the language in which the New Testament was written. Greek influences, the emphasis they had placed upon philosophy and learning, became factors with which Christianity had to deal. In Athens, Paul met the Stoics and Epicureans, and in many of the Epistles of the New Testament, Gnostic influences, very largely Grecian in origin, had to be dealt with because such teaching was contrary to the gospel of Christ.

Socrates emphasized the moral nature of man with a doctrine of "know thyself;" Plato added to this idea of the day the doctrine of "beauty;" Aristotle sought to cover all human knowledge. Epicurus and Zeno sought to make philosophy practical. Zeno taught pride and self control, but he also taught that suicide was allowable in case of failure. Epicurus was an athiest and urged that the main purpose of life was to "get pleasure." Human philosophy has never inspired morality (Rom. 1:18). In his own wisdom, man cannot rise above his own desires and appetites (Jer. 10:23). Widespread immorality was the outcome of human philosophy. Skepticism was the order of the day. There were many who worshipped the Emperor. Out of such human philosophy arose systems of heathen worship, such as existed at Corinth when Paul was there. Roman character crumbled before these influences. The pictures of life in Pompey preserved on walls of houses uncovered in that city, are too vile to look upon. Infanticide was so common that the empire was said to be crimson with the blood of infants.

4. Social Conditions. The elements of the Roman nature that had made them great as a nation had largely dissipated. The army officers

7

and their politicians had become extremely rich as a result of their military conquests. There were 85 million people in the empire. Seven million of them lived in Italy. There were six million slaves in the Roman empire. Freedmen constituted a very large class. They had either been given their freedom or had purchased it. The Plebeians were freeborn and regarded themselves above both freedmen and slaves. There was no middle class in Roman society. A few were extremely rich and the many were poor. The nobility were wildly extravagant. The masses were pauperized by the few who ground them to the earth. Small farms disappeared and great landed estates took their place. People crowded to the cities. Trade guilds were organized as protection against the capitalists. There were burial groups, all sorts of fraternal organizations, traveling craftsmen of various sorts. The race problem was acute. The Jews stood aloof from the Gentiles. The Greeks considered others as barbarians. There was no democracy, but a real caste system prevailed based on money and power.

5. Trade and Commerce. The door of commercial opportunity was open in the Roman world. Egypt grew the grain for the empire. Trade came from India, Spain, the Carpathian Mountains and even from Britain. Roman ships filled the seas. Wonderful highways like the Appian Way were far better than many modern highways. The freedom with which travel could be carried on was a great advantage to the spreading of the gospel in the New Testament day. The inns were often mere drinking houses and full of immorality. There was a great deal of travel for business, pleasure, knowledge and health.

Financial problems existed then also. In A.D. 33 there was a great panic caused by the failure of one of the banking houses in Rome, Maximus & Vibo, due to the failure of Seuthus & Son in Alexandria and Malchus & Company of Tyre.

Rome was easily the first city of the empire. Far east of Rome on the Euphrates, Babylon still existed, the center and symbol of oriental spendor and power. There were many Jews residing there. In Egypt there were the great cities of Memphis, Thebes and Alexandria, built by Alexander the Great, with its great university, library, and a tremendous amount of trade. It was the meeting place of east and west. Then there was Antioch of Syria, Tarsus of Cilicia, Ephesus in Asia, Pergamum, ancient capital of a great kingdom, Phillipi, the Roman colony in Macedonia, Thessalonica, the thriving commercial city existing today as Saloniki. There was also Athens with its temples and culture, and Corinth, once destroyed but now restored by Julius Caesar, and a great city of flourishing trade.

Due to the Assyrian and Babylonian captivity and then following that, Alexander's conquest, the Jews had been scattered throughout the empire. There were groups of Jews to be found in all of the chief Roman Cities and in many of the smaller ones. Those who had returned to Jerusalem under Cyrus' decree were but a small contingent compared to the rest. Under the Greek rulers kindness and special privileges had been extended to the Jews. They took to trade easily and became bankers and merchants. They flourished in Babylon where several millions remained. Special quarters were given to them in most cities. They were hated by the Gentiles because of their commercial rivalry, greed for money, and their religious and social exclusiveness. Representatives of all the twelve tribes still existed. There were no "lost tribes." They were scattered throughout the known world (Acts 2:6-11). They constituted a nucleus wherever the gospel went for they were already acquainted with the true God of Israel and with the Old Testament scriptures. Because of their prejudice, however, many times they rejected Christ and His gospel and became the chief persecutors of even their own nation who believed in and followed the Lord. Christianity was planted in the beginning between the great mountain of Jewish prejudice on the one hand and heathen philosophy on the other.

STUDENT WORK

1. The New Testament sets forth a system of _____, _____ , _____ ; it also reveals man's duty toward _____ , _____ , _____ .

2. What is the relationship between the two testaments? _____ _____

3. Can the two testaments be clearly understood separately? Why? _____

4. How old is the plan of human redemption? _____

5. Our way to salvation, though once a mystery, is now _____ .

6. The Old Testament reveals, particularly, what part of God? ____ _____

7. Some of the uses of the Old Testament today are:
   a._____   Passage:_____
   b._____   Passage:_____
   c._____   Passage:_____

8. Plainly revealed truths of the New Testament were incorporated in the Old Testament by what three methods? _____ , _____ , and _____ .

9. The Old Testament looks forward by those methods to the three offices that Jesus was to fill; those are:
   a. _____
   b. _____
   c. _____

10. How is the new "covenant" sanctified and ratified? _____ _____

11. Besides the New Testament itself, what else is needed to properly understand its teaching? Why? _____

_____

12. Which words best describe the religious background of Israel: constant, changeable, fixed, steady, flexible, upheaval, permanent, insecure. Be able to tell why.

13. Under the Romans, what group of men watched over Galilee?

    a. _____ Began in _____

    b. _____ Died in _____

    c. _____ _____ to _____ ruled over

    _____ and _____

    d. _____ _____ to _____ ruled over

    _____

    e. _____ _____ to _____

    f. _____ _____ to _____

14. Which of the following accurately describe the Sadducees? (politics, resurrection, wealth, power, religious leadership, angels, priests, larger number).

15. Which of the following are associated with the Roman Government? (Augustus, Black Sea, Pharisees, righteousness, Caesars, peace, wickedness, war, justice, morality, world empire).

16. What was it about the Jewish political situation that demanded two trials for Jesus? _____

17. The three main groups of Grecian philosophers were the _____ _____, _____, and _____. What were the natural results of their human philosophies?

    a. _____ d. _____

    b. _____ e. _____

    c. _____

18. Which of the following characterize the social conditions of the Roman empire? (virtue, small farms, dissipation, race problems, good dispersion of wealth, pauperization, democracy, social equality, extravagance, trade guilds).

19. How widespread was the dispersion of the Jews, and how did they come to live in so many distant places? _____

_____

_____

10

20. Did the trade and commerce of the day work to the advantage or disadvantage of the Jews? Illustrate. _____

_____

True or False

_____ 1. No one understood the plans for the redemption under the Old Testament.

_____ 2. God's redemptive plan is so revealed that we may study the two testaments independently of each other and still understand it.

_____ 3. All we need to properly understand the teachings of the New Testament is the book itself.

_____ 4. The primary message of the Old Testament is "the coming of Christ, our Savior."

_____ 5. Synagogue worship began in the days of Josiah.

_____ 6. Everywhere they went the Jews emphasized the Law and the worship of the one God.

_____ 7. The Roman emperors during the spread of the church were Nero and Claudius.

_____ 8. Aristotle taught that life's main purpose is to "know thyself."

_____ 9. There was a great deal of social mixing between the Jews and the Gentiles.

_____10. The church was planted between the most powerful of human philosophies and the most extreme religious prejudice.

The Synoptic Gospels - Matthew

A. The Four Gospels.

It is fortunate that the four gospels are placed first in our New Testament, though perhaps, they were not written first. They record for us the historic facts that form the very basis of faith in Christ, and are almost exclusive as a source of information and authority on this subject. They tell us all that we are really permitted to know in detail about the earthly life of the Son of God, in whom we believe. The word "gospel" seems to have acquired its usage from Wycliffe's translation and comes from "godspel" (which means to tell about God). There is not a single new, certain, or valuable fact about the life of Christ on earth that can be learned from the classical writers, Christian tradition, the Apocryphal Books, or the early Christian writers. Since the message of the "gospel" is the good news of the Messiah's coming and of the establishment of the Kingdom of God among men, it soon came to be used as a title for the books containing the history of these wonderful events. The usage of this word, however, in the New Testament scriptures, always denotes "the message preached."

The preparation made for the spread of the gospel was amazing. The way for the revelation of the Son of God and the establishment of His kingdom among men, as we have shown in Lesson 1 of this series, was prepared by three great events which preceded. Those events were the career of Alexander the Great, the rise of the Roman empire, and the dispersion of the Jews. The Grecian empire had given to the world a unity of language, making the communication of the gospel possible in every land. The Roman empire established among the nations a social order and a political unity which was favorable to the propagation and consolidation of this new religion. The scattering of the Jews further undermined heathen religion and influences and prepared the world for a higher system of moral ethics and for faith in the one true and living God. The gospel began in Jerusalem, the center of the Jewish religion; it was preached in the language of Greece; and it was scattered throughout the Roman world. The letters of Hebrew, Greek and Latin inscribed above the cross were the testimony of the world's three noblest languages to the undying claims of the Christ who suffered to unite all nations into the one great family of God.

An investigation of the four gospels reveals that Matthew, Mark and Luke are in many respects alike, and at the same time unlike the gospel of John. This similarity is the reason why the first three gospels are called the "synoptic" gospels. These three dwell mainly on Christ's ministry in Galilee, whereas John's gospel features His ministry in Judea. The first three tell us the story in detail of only one of our Lord's visit to Jerusalem, the one which ended in His crucifixion, while John records for us four visits to Jerusalem prior to that one. The first three deal primarily with His miracles, parables, and addresses to the multitudes that followed Him while John records for us the higher, deeper, and more individual of His discourses. The first three give emphasis to historical incidents in the life of Christ. The fourth emphasizes its spiritual meaning. The first three are more objective; the fourth more subjective. The first three are gospels of action, while the gospel of John is one of meditation and contemplation. The first three are more fragmentary than the fourth.

The similarities between the gospels of Matthew, Mark and Luke have created in the minds of some a question of whether or not they were written independently of each other. A number of suggestions will help to clarify this point. First, each writer had a distinctive purpose in view (Mt. 1:1; Mk. 1:1; Lk. 1:1-4; Jn. 30:31). Second, written gospel messages were preceded by the oral preaching of the messages. Factual material relating to the earthly life of our Lord was a permanent part of the preaching in the early church (Acts 2:22-36; 10:34-43; 1 Cor. 15:1-4). Third, each of these gospels was directed to a certain class of people. Matthew wrote primarily to the Jews. Mark wrote particularly from the Roman point of view. Luke addresses himself to the Greeks. John's gospel has been called the "universal" gospel. Fourth, written sources of information concerning the life of Christ and their usage would not be eliminated by the fact of Divine inspiration. Luke refers to such in his gospel (Lk. 1:1-4). Along with this source of written material the writers certainly were acquainted with each other. Fifth, the superintending and directory power of the Holy Spirit, which overruled and prevailed in the selection of the contents, is the most important factor (2 Pet. 1:20-21; Jn. 15:26). This does not mean simply a dictation method of inspiration, but rather, the use of human personalities, experience and abilities, with a Divine selection and guidance by the Holy Spirit. The gospels begin with the birth of Jesus and conclude with His ascension. They are, therefore, the history of the first advent of our Lord and together with the Book of Acts, which is the history of the Church in the Apostolic Age, constitute the five books which form the historical background of the entire New Testament.

B. The Gospel of Matthew.

1. The Author. The early Church almost universally ascribed the first gospel to Matthew as its author. Papias, Irenaeus and Origen, prominent among the early writers, attribute the gospel to Matthew as its author. Matthew was not conspicuous among the Apostles of our Lord, but was rather, obscure, and it would seem strange for tradition to assign the gospel to him in an early Age (100 - 150 A.D.). if indeed he had not written it. He was in every way well equipped for the task. He was a tax collector under Herod Antipas and had the standing of a civil servant. He would have known his native tongue (Hebrew or Aramaic) spoken by the Jews, and also Greek. The record of his calling reveals a ready acceptance, in-

13

dicating upon his part a cherished expectation of the Messiah's coming. Tradition tells us that for fifteen years he preached in Palestine and after that he went to such nations as Ethiopia, Macedonia, Syria, Persia and Parthia. His name was changed from Levi to Matthew, but he recalls his humble origin by referring to himself as "the publican." Some scholars claim that he was a first cousin of our Lord. He gave a farewell feast as he left his old occupation to follow Jesus. It was on a Jewish fast-day, with numerous guests, including Jesus (Mt. 9:10). Not one incident is recorded of him. He occupied a very humble and retiring position in the Apostolic group, and yet, by him was rendered a most memorable service.

2. *When Matthew's Gospel Was Written.* Many scholars tell us that Matthew's gospel was the first of the four. Among the early writers who so claim, again are Papias, Irenaeus, Origen, Eusebius, and others. It was natural that the Church would need such a history of the life of our Lord from the pen of an actual Apostle. How early the gospel was written, we do not know. It must have predated the destruction of Jerusalem, for while the gospel prophesies it (Mt. 24), it does not record its occurrence (70 A.D.). The date ordinarily assigned as probable is between A.D. 55 and 70.

3. *The Purpose of Matthew's Gospel.* While the writer of this gospel does not specifically mention his purpose and aim, yet, these can be ascertained easily and accurately by the general contents. This gospel serves as a link between the Old and the New Testaments. Its place at the beginning of our New Testament is very appropriate to the Jewish reader. It reflects the great themes of the Hebrew scriptures, the Law, the Messiah, the prophetic writings, and the Kingdom of Heaven. It was written from the very beginning (Mt. 1:1), to make an appeal to the Jew. It is a gospel of the Messiah, the "annointed One" (Ps. 2:2; Isa. 45:1), descended from David and Abraham. Only Matthew traces the genealogy to Abraham.

It appears to have a twofold purpose. First, to connect the message of the Old Testament with the gospel; second, to demonstrate the fulfillment of Old Testament prophecies in the coming of Jesus of Nazareth as the Messiah, the King.

In order that we might be able to see the twofold purpose mentioned above fully demonstrated in the contents of the gospel of Matthew, we call attention to the following:

a. It emphasizes that Jesus is the Messiah, the King. The word, "kingdom," appears 50 times, the words "kingdom of heaven," 33 times, and Jesus is repeatedly referred to as "the King" (Mt. 2:2; 21:5; 22:11; 25:34; 27:11, 37, 42). The "kingdom of God" is mentioned 5 times. The more common expression, "the kingdom of heaven," Matthew uses in deference to the Jewish disposition to hesitate to make a direct reference to Diety. The emphasis placed on this message that Jesus is the Messiah, would be found in these facts:

(1) Only Matthew traces the genealogy of Christ back to Abraham.

(2) Only in this gospel is the story of the visit of the Magi, who brought their gifts to the King.

(3) Only Matthew makes reference to Jesus being born "King of the Jews."

(4) Only Matthew cites the prophecy that a ruler would come out of Bethlehem to rule God's people.

(5) Matthew records John the Baptist's message of preparation in terms of "the kingdom of heaven is at hand." Matthew emphasizes that Jesus is the seed of David. In Matthew's gospel the kingship of Christ is asserted, confessed and proved by the fulfillment of prophecy.

(a) By the recognition of His person (16:13-18).

(b) By His pronouncement of His authority (28:18-20).

(c) By the claim that His teaching constituted law (7:24-29).

(d) By the contrast in chapter 1 between His human genealogy, verses 1 to 17, and His miraculous birth, verses 18 to 25.

(6) All who were in His earthly line of descendancy were transient, but Christ is eternal. They perished in death, to live no more until all men are raised, but He has already been raised. He lives! He speaks! He blesses! He reigns! He saves! (Heb. 7:23-25).

(7) In His human lineage they were all sinful, but He was without sin. Rahab, Bathsheba, the wife of Uriah, Tamar, Amon, Solomon and David were all listed.

(8) They were earthly, but He was heavenly. He came, was born that He might die. He was the second Adam come into the world to undo the ruin of the first.

(9) They were Jews, but He was the Son of God; conceived of the Holy Spirit; born of a virgin; a body was prepared for Him (Heb. 10:5). His pre-existence is affirmed (Jn. 1:1-11); He was God before He came into the world, with God, and on an equality with God (Phil. 2:5-11).

b. Matthew's gospel is the gospel of fulfillment. There are about forty proof passages cited in Matthew from the Old Testament. In chapter 1, the lineage of Jesus is traced back to Abraham, proving that Jesus was the seed (descendant) of Abraham to whom God made the promise that in His "seed" all of the nations of the earth were to be blessed (Gen. 12:3; Gal. 3:16). This lineage also proves that Jesus was the "seed" of David, to whom Samuel promised that His kingdom would be established forever, and that from his seed one would be "raised up" to sit upon his throne (2 Sam. 7). Some of the instances of prophetic fulfillment that Matthew cites are:

(1) Mic. 5:2 - His place of birth - Mt. 2:1
(2) Isa. 7:14 - Born of a virgin - Mt. 1:18-23
(3) Jer. 31:15 - The massacre of infants - Mt. 2:16
(4) Hos. 11:1 - The flight into Egypt - Mt. 2:14-15
(5) Isa. 9:1-2 - The Galilean ministry - Mt. 4:12-16
(6) Zech. 11:12 - Sold for thirty pieces of silver - Mt. 26:15
(7) Zech. 11:13 - Money returned by Judas - Mt. 27:3-10

(8) Ps. 27:12 - False witnesses accusing - Mt. 26:60-61
(9) Isa. 53:7 - He was silent when accused - Mt. 26:62-63
(10) Isa. 53:12 - Crucified with thieves - Mt. 27:38
(11) Ps. 22:6-8 - Mocked and insulted - Mt. 27:39-40
(12) Isa. 53:9 - Buried with the rich - Mt. 27:57-60
(13) Ps. 16:10 - Resurrected - Mt. 28:9

Since Matthew wrote for the benefit of the Jews and for the purpose of establishing faith in their hearts in Jesus as the promised Messiah, he constantly refers to Old Testament scriptures with which they were familiar, and the fact that Jesus fulfilled everything that had been prophesied about Him, to establish His identity. The most common expression found in the gospel of Matthew, you will note as you read it, is "that it might be fulfilled which was written in the prophets, saying."

c. Matthew contrasts Christianity and the righteousness of God revealed in the New Covenant with the Pharasaic concept of righteousness under the Law. The words "righteous" and "righteousness" occur more often in Matthew than all of the other three gospels combined. The spiritual principles of righteousness and the Kingdom of God were set forth in the Sermon on the Mount, more fully recorded by Matthew than any other gospel writer. This Sermon affirmed Jesus' regard for the Law (Mt. 5:17), but it demanded a standard of righteousness far above the outward ceremonially professed righteousness of the Pharisees. God is set forth as the perfect example of righteousness (Mt. 5:48). In this contrast in the Sermon on the Mount, Jesus emphasized that His authority was superior and took precedence over the authority of Moses and the Law. In this connection He points out the difference between the demands of the Law, which required outward conformity, and the criterion of righteousness set forth in the gospel, which requires conformity not with outward requirements alone, or with human expectations or standards, but consists in knowing Christ, hearing His sayings and doing them (Mt. 7:23-24; 5:17-20; 5:21-22; 5:27-28). In addition to this, Matthew selects those teachings of Christ and the facts from His life that emphasize His identity as the true Messiah, and the correct principles of citizenship in the Kingdom of God. Nowhere else is recorded the severe denunciation of the Pharisees and their hypocrisy from the lips of Jesus (9:11; 12:1; 15:1; 16:1; 23).

d. Matthew emphasizes the judgment of God against the Jewish nation and their impending destruction because of their unfaithfulness. Then he rounds out his message that God had fulfilled faithfully His promises (Rom. 15:4), and yet, because justice and righteousness is a part of God's very nature, His dealing with the Jewish nation for rejecting His grace and rebelling against His will was characterized by severity (Heb. 2:14; 10:26-30).

4. *The Contents and Character of the Gospel of Matthew.* The gospel of Matthew can be divided into the following sections:

a. Introduction (1:1-4:11)
  (1) The genealogy
  (2) The birth and the childhood of Jesus
  (3) The preparatory ministry of John
  (4) The baptism of Jesus
  (5) His temptation
b. The Ministry of Jesus (4:12-16:21)

  (1) Galilee, the beginning place (Isa. 9:1; Mt. 4:14-16)
  (2) The words and acts of Christ. This section is introduced by the expression "from that time forth began Jesus to preach," and sets forth the words and acts of Christ in four stages:

    (a) The first stage of this section consists of the Sermon on the Mount and ten miracles.

    (b) Beginning at chapter 10 a wider phase in the Words and Deeds is found in the great Sermon preached to the twelve, following their being called to the Apostleship. This is followed by the inquiry from prison of John the Baptist concerning the identity of the Jesus of whose work he was hearing so much, and the discourse of Jesus to the multitude concerning John. Then in the latter part of chapter 11, Jesus upbraids the cities wherein most of His. mighty works were done because of their unbelief. In chapter 12 the Pharisees are condemned by the Lord for their lack of understanding and their misapplication of the Law of God through Moses. In this instance, as in many, Jesus pointed out their inability to discern between human traditions and the Law of God. In this discussion with the Pharisees, the Lord evidenced that He spoke with authority, by healing many that followed Him, and in one miracle particularly, the healing of the man possessed with a demon, blind and dumb, was done on the Sabbath. This discussion with the Pharisees continued through chapter 12. In the last part of this chapter, Jesus emphasizes that spiritual relationships are more enduring and take priority over human relationships.

    (c) The third phase of the teaching of Christ is begun in chapter 13. In this chapter, we have seven consecutive parables, and the reason for His teaching in parables, as He himself expressed it, was "unto you" (His disciples), "it is given to know the mysteries of the Kingdom of Heaven, but to them" (the unbelievers, and particularly perhaps, the Pharisees), "it is not given" (Mt. 13:11). This section of Matthew's story ends with the miracles of feeding the five thousand and Jesus walking on the water.

    (d) A fourth stage of the sermons and miracles of Jesus opens in chapter 15. In this sermon, which offended the Pharisees, Jesus emphasized the fact that human traditions make void the word of God (Mt. 15:6). This section includes also the healing of the Syro-Phoenician girl, the healing of many who were sick, the feeding of the four thousand, the mocking unbelief of the Pharisees as they asked for a sign from Heaven, the warning against the teaching of the Pharisees and Sadducees, and the confession of Peter, "thou art the Christ the son of the living God."

c. In chapter 16:21, Matthew begins the second great section of his story in the life and ministry of our Lord with the expression once again, "from this time forth began Jesus." This period of the life of Christ is no longer primarily concerned with an appeal to the multitude, but rather, is devoted to the training of the disciples He is preparing, His struggle with the leaders of the people, His final rejection, His trial, and His death. From the time that He was confessed as the Christ by Peter and the other Apostles, He began to show His disciples (16:21), that He must go to Jerusalem and die and on the third day be raised. In chapter 17, we have the incident of the Transfiguration, in which Jesus, in glorified form, holds a conversation with Moses and Elijah concerning His death. He taught His disciples (Mt. 17:14-21), that only a lack of faith upon their part could keep them from doing what He had commissioned them and given them the power to do. He emphasized also in this connection the importance of their willingness to suffer, and again, the necessity of submission to the government under which they lived by paying their taxes.

The disciples were taught also not to allow their unselfish ambitions to interfere with their duty in the Kingdom of God, but to humble themselves that in God's sight they might be exalted. Jesus taught them also that they were not to allow their personal conduct or attitude to become an occasion of stumbling to a brother, and in the event of an offense arising between brethren, He gave them a formula for it's solution (Mt. 18:15-20). In this connection also, He emphasized in the latter part of chapter 18 that when a man will not forgive his brother he cannot expect God to forgive him.

d. The words "and it came to pass when Jesus had finished these words He departed from Galilee, and came into the borders of Judea beyond the Jordan," introduce the last phase of the life of our Lord in chapter 19. In this phase He is openly rejected by the leaders of the people that He had spent so much time trying to teach. When they tried to put Him in conflict with the Law of Moses and thus find some charge to make against Him, He unhesitatingly affirmed that His authority was to be given precedence over the Law of Moses (Mt. 19:9). He taught His disciples that humility and submissiveness such as characterize a little child must belong to those who would be citizens of the Kingdom of Heaven.

The interview with the rich young ruler (Mt. 19:16-22), brought the disciples to ask the question "What shall our reward be?," to which Jesus replied, "a hundredfold in this world and in the world to come, eternal life" (Mt. 19:29-30; Mk. 10:31).

Following the parable of the laborers in the vineyard, Jesus again foretold to the twelve His suffering and death as He was going up into Jerusalem. He taught them in response to the request of the mother of the sons of Zebedee for a place of prominence for her sons in His Kingdom, that if a man would be great in the Kingdom of God, he must become the servant of all (Mt. 20:26-28). Coming out from

Jericho, with a great multitude following Him, He healed the two blind men.

In chapter 21, His triumphant entry into Jerusalem is recorded. The people would have taken Him and proclaimed Him their king, but He refused to conform to their desires, for His Kingdom is not of this world (Jn. 18:36). Open conflict with the religious leaders of His day was emphasized by the Lord driving the money changers out of the temple and when they challenged His authority, He emphasized that they were not interested in authority, as evidenced by their rejection of the baptism of John, who was God's messenger.

In the parable of the wicked husbandman, He pointed out the unbelief and rebellion of the Jewish nation and foretold the coming of the judgment upon it in its destruction. In chapter 22, He pictured again their rejection of God's mercy and grace in their unbelief and rebellion by teaching the parable of the slighted invitation to the marriage feast.

The Pharisees sought to bring Him into conflict against Caesar and the Roman government, but Jesus taught "render unto Caesar the things that are Caesar's; and unto God the things that are God's." This last period of His life was characterized by:

(1) A discussion with the Sadducees concerning the resurection (Mt. 23:23-33).

(2) His discussion with the lawyer concerning the great commandments of the Law (Mt. 22:34-40).

(3) His challenge of their unbelief by the question, "What think ye of the Christ? Whose son is he?"

(4) His open and severe denunciation of the hypocrisy of the scribes and the Pharisees (Mt. 23).

(5) His discussion with His disciples concerning "the destruction of Jerusalem, the sign of His coming, and of the end of the world" (Mt. 24).

(6) The parables of the virgins and of the talents, bearing upon the immediate incidents in their context, are followed by a description of the coming of the King in the last judgment of all nations, seated upon the throne of His glory (Mt. 24:31-46).

(7) The plot to take His life, His betrayal by Judas, His prayer in the garden, and His arrest by the mob (Mt. 26).

e. Closing Events of His Life. Beginning with Matthew 26:57 and continuing through 27:26, the trial of Jesus in both the Jewish and Roman phases of that trial is recorded. The events connected with the death of Jesus are found in 27:27-56. His burial is recorded in verses 57-61. In chapter 28 the fulfillment of His promise "after three days I will rise again," in spite of all their precaution, is recorded in the story of His resurrection from the dead.

Following His resurrection, His appearance to the eleven Apostles on the mountain in Galilee was the occasion for the commission:

Go ye therefore, and teach all nations, baptizing them in the name of the Father, and of the Son, and of the Holy Ghost; teaching them to observe all things whatsoever I have commanded you; and lo, I am with you always, even unto the end of the world.

STUDENT WORK

1. Just how authoritative are the four gospels regarding Christ's life? _____

2. What is the main message of the gospels? _____
_____

3. What three events paved the way for the revelation of Christ, and what did each contribute?

   a. _____

   Contribution _____

   b. _____

   Contribution _____

   c. _____

   Contribution _____

4. Which of the following characteristics of John distinguish it from the "synoptics"? (Meditation, parables, Galilee, several visits to Jerusalem, historical incidents, Judea, individual discourses, objectiveness, spiritual meaning of Christ's life, subjectiveness, action, completeness)

5. Matthew's gospel, written to _____, has a twofold purpose:

   a. _____

   b. _____

6. Which of the following are NOT characteristics of Matthew? (a link between the two testaments, prophecies, Jewish appeal, Christ the Servant of man, the Law, Roman readers, the Messiah, the Kingdom, a descendant of Adam)

7. Locate the following prophecies and note the record of fulfillment.

   a. "The Lord . . . shall call his name Immanuel." _____

   Fulfilled: _____

   b. "If ye think good, give me my hire;" _____

   Fulfilled: _____

   c. " . . . he bore the sin of many and made intercession for the transgressor." _____

   Fulfilled: _____

20

d. "Thou wilt not leave my soul to Sheol." _____

    Fulfilled: _____

8. What is the difference between the demands of the Law and those of the righteousness of the gospel? _____

    _____

9. Locate the following passages, stating their location (chapters and verses).

    a. Baptism of Jesus: _____

    b. Sermon on the Mount: _____

    c. Group of seven parables: _____

    d. Walking on water: _____

    e. Parable of the marriage feast: _____

    f. The resurrection: _____

10. Beginning in Mt. 16:21, Jesus stresses virtues and characteristics that His disciples are to develop. Which of the following are *not specifically mentioned* in the lessons? (humility, faith, submission to government, contentedness, suffering, innocence of children, authority, temperance, forgiving, unselfish love)

True or False

_____ 1. Some new and interesting information about the life of Jesus was obtained in the Epistle of Barnabas, an "apocryphal" book.

_____ 2. The first three gospels are called "synoptic" because they are so much like the gospel of John.

_____ 3. Matthew's primary message is the Kingdom and Jesus as its King.

_____ 4. Matthew shows that Jesus is a descendant of David, Moses, and Abraham.

_____ 5. Matthew is the only gospel that records both the visit of the Magi, and the prophecy that a ruler would come out of Bethlehem.

_____ 6. Matthew records the most severe denunciation of the Pharisees of the gospels.

_____ 7. The second major section of the book begins in chapter 16 and is concerned with the training of the disciples and Jesus' coming rejection and death.

The Gospel of Mark

A. The Author.

The author of the second gospel is pretty certainly identified as "John," whose surname was "Mark" (Acts 12:12, 25; 15:37); also called "John" (Acts 13:5, 13), and "Marcus" or "Mark" (Acts 15:39; Col. 4:10; 2 Tim. 4:11). Although his name does not appear within the gospel, early Christian writers such as Papias, Eusebius, Irenaeus, Clement of Alexandria and Origen uniformly attribute it to him. All these witnesses agree on two facts, 1) that Mark was the companion of Peter and had a very special relationship with him, and 2) that he was the author of the gospel which bears his name.

John Mark lived in Jerusalem and was the son of Mary (Acts 12:12), whose home was the scene of the prayer meetings of the Jerusalem church. It was to her house that Peter went immediately upon his miraculous delivery from prison (Acts 12:12). Perhaps the intimacy of Peter with Mary's family brought about an early acquaintance between the Apostle and her son, John Mark, and established the close relationship between the Apostle Peter and John Mark in later life and work.

John Mark also had a very close connection with the Apostle Paul. It was interrupted by his turning back from Pamphylia on the first tour, but was renewed later on when he was restored to the Apostle Paul's confidence. This is manifest in Paul's references to him in Col. 4:10 and 2 Tim. 4:11. John Mark was a cousin to Barnabas (Col. 4:10), and this probably explains Barnabas' insisting on taking John Mark with him on the second journey, in spite of Paul's attitude (Acts 15:37-39).

The fact of his mother's home being a gathering place of the disciples in Jerusalem brought him into constant association with the leading men in the church.

B. When Mark's Gospel Was Written.

Tradition favors the idea that Mark wrote his gospel while he was in Rome. In regard to the date of its writing, there is a great deal of uncertainty among the early writers. It is very unlikely, however, that he wrote it prior to 50 A.D., and certainly not later than 70 A.D. We may probably place it between 64 and 70 A.D. It was written in Greek, according to the united voice of ancient writers.

C. The Purpose of Mark's Gospel.

The opening words of Matthew's gospel are: "The book of the generation of Jesus Christ, the son of David, the son of

22

Abraham," by which, as already pointed out in Lesson 2, he indicates his purpose to show that Jesus of Nazareth is the long promised Messiah of David's line and the seed of Abraham, in whom all nations are to be blessed. Mark, on the contrary, passes by the genealogy of Jesus and begins his gospel with the statement: "The beginning of the gospel of Jesus Christ, the Son of God;" Mark recognizes Him as the Son of David and the promised Messiah and the King of Israel (10:47-48; 11:10; 15:32). Since, however, he was writing among Gentiles and for Gentiles (the Romans particularly), the great fact which he is intent on setting forth in his gospel is the person and the character of Jesus Christ as the Son of God. Evidence that he had the Gentiles particularly in mind in this testimony is to be found:

1. In the explanation of Jewish customs (14:12; 15:42).

2. By his translation of Aramaic expressions, Boanerges, 3:17; Talitha cumi, 5:41; Corban, 7:11; Bartimaeus, 10:46; Abba, 14:36; Golgotha, 15:22.

3. The fact that the law of Moses is not mentioned by Mark and the Old Testament is quoted only one time in his narrative.

4. The Gentile sections of the gospel (chapters 6 through 8).

5. That it was the Romans whom Mark expressly had in mind is evidenced by:

a. The explanation of a Greek term in Latin (12:42).

b. The preponderance of the activity of Christ, emphasis upon His power, and the finality of His authority (2:10); also His patience and endurance (10:17).

c. Chapter 10:12 forbids the practice that was not Jewish, but Roman.

d. The most common expression in the gospel of Mark is the word, "straightway," or "immediately." This word is used 42 times. In 14 of these instances it is used of the personal activity of Jesus. Since the Roman people were a people of action and understood power and authority, Mark wrote his gospel in Rome, with an appeal particularly to the Romans.

D. The Contents and Character of the Gospel of Mark.

The gospel of Mark can be divided as follows:

1. Introductory events (1:1-13).

a. The coming of His herald (1:2-8).

b. His baptism by John in the Jordan (1:9).

c. His endowment with the Holy Spirit (1:10).

d. The Divine witness to His Sonship (1:11).

e. His conflict with Satan (1:12-13).

2. The early Galilean ministry (1:14; 7:23). Mark omits entirely the early Judean ministry (Jn. 2:13-3:42).

3. The tour to Tyre and Sidon (7:24-30).

4. His teaching and work in northern Galilee (7:31-9:50).

5. The closing ministry in Perea and the journey to Jerusalem (10:1-52).

6. The week of suffering, ending in His crucifixion, resurrection,

the commission to the Apostles, and His ascension into Heaven (chapters 11-16).

Mark's gospel is the shortest of the four. His style is vivid and picturesque. It opens with an immediate declaration of the Sonship of Jesus, His Divinity.

1. To emphasize this, Mark records 19 miracles of Jesus in his short record.

2. Mark's narrative concerns itself mainly with the work which the Lord did. With this, is interwoven His teaching, since it was the Lord's custom to use the opportunity afforded by surrounding circumstances to teach.

3. Mark records only four of the parables of Christ.

4. He takes notice of the beneficence of the works of Christ (1:23-3:27).

5. His writing is very graphic and realistic in the details that are given.

   a. The action and gestures of Jesus (7:33; 9:36; 10:16).

   b. The looks of inquiry (5:32), prayer (6:41; 7:34), approval (3:34), love (10:21), warning (10:23), anger (3:5), and judgment (11:11).

   c. His vivid description of details: hunger (11:12); seeking rest and seclusion (6:31); sleeps on a boat cushion (4:38); pities the multitude (6:34); wonders at their unbelief (6:6); sighs over their sorrows and blindness (7:24; 8:12); grieves at their hardness (3:5); rebukes with sadness the wrong thought of His mother and brothers, and in indignation, the mistaken zeal and selfish ambitions of His disciples (8:33; 10:14); concern for the disciples and multitudes (1:32; 3:10; 1:22; 2:12; 4:41; 10:32).

6. Mark's gospel is a narrative of the person of Christ. Mark introduces Him as the Son of God, the author of the gospel, and records Peter's confession of Him as the Christ, God's Son (8:29). He gives the evidence of this truth by recording His resurrection (chapter 16), yet Jesus is pictured by Mark as the servant of all (10:35); the disciples grasped at an early date the Kingdom of Christ, but it was not until after His death and resurrection that they came to an understanding that He had also been pictured in prophecy as the suffering Son of God, a sacrifice for sin, and the servant of mankind (Isa. 53). This aspect of His coming had been forgotten by them in their aspirations for the restoration of the old, earthly, national kingdom of fleshly Israel, which had caused them to fail to see the other side of the story, namely that in Him was to be blended power and submission; that He did achieve victory through apparent defeat. The Jews wanted the restoration of the national kingdom of fleshly Israel and an earthly king to sit upon the literal throne of David in Jerusalem. Jesus Christ did not fit into their plans and they rejected him (1 Cor. 1:23; 1 Pet. 2:6-8). The hope of their hearts should have been centered in the Sonship of Jesus Christ and the coming of a spiritual king and kingdom.

24

7. The closing passage of this gospel (16:9-20) has caused a great deal of discussion among the scholars. The discussion centers in the discussion of whether or not Mark actually wrote these verses and whether they belong to the conclusion of his gospel. While many do not accept them as written by Mark, there are many others, if not more, who do accept them. Those scholars, for the most part, who do not believe they belong to the end of Mark's gospel do not question their inspiration and most of them do not deny that the sustance of the passage is in harmony with the rest of the divine record.

Some, like A. T. Robertson (*Studies in Mark's Gospel*, pages 126-134), think that the ending of Mark's gospel was probably lost from the manuscripts and that some day it may be found. Many of the later manuscripts do contain it and many of the scholars agree that the passage was recognized as belonging to the Gospel of Mark from the second century onward.

It was known to and quoted by early writers in the second century. Tregelles said concerning it, "It is perfectly certain that from the second century and onward, these verses have been known as a part of this gospel (whoever was their author)" (*A New Introduction to the Study of the Bible,* Barrows, page 359).

It is certainly apparent that Mark's gospel was abruptly ended without it. This section contains important testimony: 1. The resurrection on the first day of the week, 2. the appearance of Christ to Mary Magdalene, 3. His appearance to the two disciples on the way to Emmaus, 4. His appearance to the eleven apostles and His rebuking of their lack of faith, 5. the record of the giving of the great commission to the apostles, 6. the ascension, and 7. the execution of the commission and the confirmation of the words preached by the signs that followed the preaching.

STUDENT WORK

1. Upon what evidence do we believe Mark wrote this gospel? ____

_____

2. The main purpose of Mark's book, written while he was in
   _____ , is to _____

3. How do the following passages show that *Mark* was written to the Gentile Romans? List the passage, then explain. _____

   a. "And when even was now come, because it was the Preparation, that is, the day before the Sabbath,"
   _____ ; _____

   b. "but ye say, If a man shall say to his father or his mother, That wherewith thou mightest have been profited by me is Corban, that is to say, Given to God;"
   _____ ; _____

25

c. "And there came a poor widow, and she cast in two mites, which make a farthing."

_____ ; _____

d. "and if she herself shall put away her husband, and marry another, she committeth adultery."

_____ ; _____

4. Matthew pictures Jesus as the Messiah; he is pictured by Mark as

_____

5. What hope did Mark want his readers to have in their hearts; why had they overlooked it? _____

_____

Matching: Put the letter of the correct answer in the blank beside the item it most correctly matches in the left column.

6. _____ Early Galilean ministry   a. Shortest
7. _____ Coming of John the baptist   b. 17
8. _____ Of the four gospels   c. Sighs
9. _____ Miracles   d. 1:14
10. _____ Gestures   e. 19
11. _____ Details   f. Looks of Chirst
12. _____ Realistic writing   g. 1:2-8

The Gospel of Luke

A. The Author.

The author of this gospel was also the author of the book of Acts of the Apostles (Lk. 1:1-4; Acts 1:1-5). Early writers are consistently agreed that the author of both books was Luke, a physician and close friend and associate of the Apostle Paul.

In Col. 4:14, Paul calls Luke the "beloved physician;" in Philemon 24, "a fellow worker;" and shortly before his death in Rome, the Apostle refers to the fact that "only Luke is with me" (2 Tim. 4:11). In the sections of the book of Acts of the Apostles, in which Luke uses the personal plural pronoun "we," it is evident that the writer of the third gospel and the book of Acts was a companion of Paul on many of his travels. Some of the early Christian writers say that Luke was a Gentile who had become a Jewish proselyte. Jerome says that he was a Syrian, born at Antioch. He is separated from the "circumcision" named by Paul, Aristarchus, Marcus, Barnabas and Justus, and is named with Epaphras and Demas to form the Gentile group (Col. 4:9-11).

The preface to his gospel has been pointed out by critics as pure classical Greek, indicating that he was a Gentile by birth and education, yet, he was intimately acquainted with Jewish rights, customs, opinions and prejudices, as well as with Jewish phraseology, indicating that he might have been a Jewish proselyte.

It is thought by many scholars that he was probably the "brother" mentioned in 2 Cor. 8:18, 12:18. He does not profess to be an eye-witness of what he recorded (Lk. 1:2). He wrote as a recorder or historian of the testimony gathered from eye-witnesses. His home is uncertain, but there is some indication that it may have been at Antioch. He shows a very definite interest in the City of Antioch (Acts 11:19-21; 13:1; 14:26; 15:22, 23, 30, 35; 18:22). He first meets Paul at Troas (Acts 16:1-12). He remained in Philippi when Paul and Silas left (Acts 16:40); and was at Philippi when Paul came back on his third tour (Acts 20:3-5). His later years were spent chiefly in the company of Paul (Acts 20:3; 28:31).

B. When Luke's Gospel Was Written.

The book of Acts, written by Luke, closed its history with Paul's two years of imprisonment in Rome, and therefore, could possibly be dated about 60 A.D. The gospel of Luke preceded the book of Acts and likely was written during the period of Paul's stay as a prisoner in Caesarea before going to Rome. This would place the writing of the gospel of Luke about 60 A.D.

C. To Whom Luke's Gospel Was Written.

Both the gospel of Luke and the book of Acts were

27

directed to an individual by the name of Theophilus. Luke refers to him (Lk. 1:3) as "most excellent." Of this man we know little. The honorary title used by Luke was an official designation (Acts 26:25), so that Theophilus may have been a Roman officer who had been introduced to the gospel message. Just as Matthew recorded his gospel for the benefit of the Jews, and as Mark wrote for the particular benefit of the Romans, it is indicated that Luke probably wrote for the particular benefit of the Greeks. He was eminently qualified to write to the Greeks and to tell them the gospel story in an attractive style. He was well educated and the Greeks emphasized culture and learning. He invited their attention in the beginning by writing his preface in their own classical tongue. He announced that it would be an orderly account of the life of Christ (Lk. 1:1). This would have been attractive to the Greeks.

He presents the origin of Christianity from the viewpoint of one outside of Judaism. His viewpoint is, therefore, not limited to a picture of the Messiah of promise and prophecy, but is that of a world-wide Savior, a Christ who lived upon the earth as the Son of Man as well as the Son of God. He traces His genealogy, in accommodating this viewpoint, from Adam as well as Abraham and David. It is, therefore, a gospel narrative adapted to meet the needs of the Gentiles as well as the Jews.

D. The Purpose of Luke's Gospel.

From the introduction of the gospel itself, a key to the book (Lk. 1:1-4), a number of inferences can be drawn that point out some of its distinctive characteristics, and at the same time the purpose of the writer.

1. A number of works were in existence which contained only a partial and possibly a somewhat garbled account of the life and work of Jesus. It was Luke's purpose to set forth the true account "to draw up a narrative" (1:1) of the available facts arranged systematically.

2. These facts were already known by the Christians of that day and were accepted. Luke says they have been "fulfilled among us" (1:1).

3. Counting himself as well informed and as capable of writing an accurate account of the life of Jesus of Nazareth, he chose to accept the responsibility ("it seemed good to me also," 1:3).

4. He had gathered his information from competent sources ("who from the beginning were eye-witnesses and ministers of the word," 1:2).

5. He was not only conversant with the facts, both by observation and inquiry, but he was also a contemporary of the main course of action, in the sense that he lived in the generation in which these things had occurred and of those who had witnessed them. The expression "having traced the course of all things accurately from the beginning" (1:3), does not imply that Luke was personally present at all of the history that he records, but it does indicate that he had first-hand knowledge and that he had verified the facts of which he

wrote by the testimony of those who were eye-witnesses of these affairs. His use of the expression, "from the very first," indicates his claim to contemporary knowledge which went back over a number of years of his life, during which he had associated with Apostles, eye-witnesses, and possibly with personal friends or even relatives of the Lord Jesus Christ, and that this knowledge had not been recently acquired.

6. Luke's knowledge covered all of the major facts, containing many things that do not appear in the other accounts and is the most generally representative life of Christ.

7. He not only professes in his introductory statement to write accurately but in logical order. He addressed this gospel and the book of Acts to Theophilus, which literally meant "lover of God," or "loved by God," who had been informed orally no doubt concerning Christ, but who needed further instruction to establish him in the faith, and Luke's obvious purpose was to convey a complete knowledge of the truth.

E. Contents and Character of the Gospel of Luke.

1. A brief outline of the contents of Luke's gospel may be presented in the following points:

    a. The introduction (1:4-13).

    b. The beginning of His public ministry in Galilee (4:14-9:50).

    c. The journey toward Jerusalem through Samaria and Perea, with the emphasis mainly on His ministry in Perea (9:51-19:28).

    d. The last days of the life of Jesus, including the crucifixion (19:29-23:55).

    e. The resurrection, the final commission to the Apostles, and the ascension (chapter 24).

2. The distinctive features:

    a. The opening events of the gospel are closely identified with the current history. Zechariah received the announcement of the birth of his son "in the days of Herod, king of Judea" (1:5). The time of the birth of Christ is linked with the days of Caesar Augustus (2:1), and the ministry of John begins "in the fifteenth year of the reign of Tiberius Caesar" (3:1). Luke as a historian points out that Christ came at a crucial time in human history and under unique circumstances. Augustus Caesar ruled in peace and prosperity. Great opportunities existed. People were religiously inclined. The conquered and oppressed Jewish nation longed for the coming of the Messiah and their liberation. It was indeed "in the fullness of time" (Gal. 4:4).

    b. Luke uses great detail in giving the account of the birth of Jesus. He tells of the annunciation, Mary's conception by the Holy Spirit, Jesus' birth and His early years, including the scene in the temple (2:41-52). He gives the account of the coming of John as the forerunner of the Messiah in fulfillment of Isaiah's prophecy (Isa. 40:3 ff.). Jesus is baptized by John, tempted by Satan, victorious by the power of the Holy Spirit (4:14), and begins His public ministry in Galilee.

c. The Galilean ministry dramatically begins with the announcement by Jesus in the synagogue that He was God's "annointed" (Messiah), that His coming fulfilled Isaiah's prophecy of the "acceptable year of the Lord" (Lk. 4:16-21). Following this, Luke records a number of the miracles designed to establish this claim to Divinity. After His night of prayer, He chose and instructed His twelve disciples, then after further miracles and teaching, His coming death at the hands of His enemies is foretold.

d. Luke 9:51 through 18:30 is peculiar to the third gospel. Jesus, in traveling from Galilee to Jerusalem (9:51), passes through Samaria and Perea before entering Judea. This section emphasizes His choice of the way to Jerusalem and the suffering which He did undergo there. He definitely defines the meaning of discipleship and dispatches the Seventy on a preaching tour. He had sent out the Twelve to preach the Kingdom of God and to heal (9:2). The larger group was commissioned to go two by two to heal and to preach the approaching Kingdom (10:9).

e. In this section Luke records a number of the parables of Christ: The good Samaritan (10:25-37), prayer in the story of the importunate friend (11:5-13), the grace of God in seeking the lost (Lk. 15), the rich man and Lazarus (16:19-31), and the meaning of true righteousness in the incident of the Pharisee and the Publican (18:9-14), are all included in the number.

f. The closing scenes of the life of Christ begin in Luke 18:31 with the bold announcement, "behold, we go up to Jerusalem." The record of the very steps of that journey are found in 18:31-34; 19:28; 19:37; 19:41; 19:45. In Luke 21:20-24, it is foretold that Jerusalem was marked for destruction.

g. In chapters 22 through 24, Luke records the last events of the life of Christ on earth in greater detail than either Matthew or Mark. He alone records the discussion between the disciples concerning who was the greatest (22:24-30), the penitent thief on the cross (23:39-43), and the full account of the appearance of Christ to the disciples from Emmaus (24:13-35). His gospel ends with the story of the ascension of Jesus into Heaven (24:50-53). It is interesting to note that he resumes his history in the book of Acts at this very point.

h. Luke's gospel is the gospel of the "Son of Man," emphasizing the human side of the life and work of Christ, but showing the compassion of Christ toward the poor, the lowly, the outcasts, and the distressed.

(1) Instances: The poor disciples (6:20); the sinful woman (7:37); Mary Magdalene (8:2); the Samaritans (10:33); Publicans and sinners (15:1); the deserted beggar (16:20-21); the lepers (17:12); and the dying thief (23:43).

i. Luke's gospel is the gospel of the universal grace of God (2:32; 3:6; 24:47).

j. The gospel of Luke contains three parables not found in

30

other gospels: The friend at midnight (11:5-8); the unjust judge (18:1-8); the Pharisee and the Publican (18:9-14).

k. Great emphasis in this gospel is given to prayer. Luke records seven prayers of Christ: At His baptism (3:21); in the wilderness (5:16); before choosing the disciples (9:29); the prayer given to His disciples (11:1); the prayer for Peter (22:32); in the garden of Gethsemane (22:44); and on the cross (23:46).

l. Luke emphasizes the recognition bestowed upon women: Mary, the mother of Jesus, Elizabeth, Mary and Martha, the daughters of Jerusalem (23:27), and several widows are mentioned (2:37; 4:26; 7:12; 8:3; 21:2).

m. There are six miracles and nineteen parables found only in Luke. The six miracles are: The draught of fishes (5:1-11); the widow's son raised (7:11-17); a woman with an infirmity healed (13:10-17); a man with dropsy healed (14:1-6); ten lepers cleansed (7:11-19); Malchus' ear healed (22:49-51).

n. Another distinctive character of Luke's gospel is the emphasis given to the Holy Spirit. In the book of Acts the Holy Spirit works through the Apostles, but in the gospel record, the Holy Spirit is active in the life of the Son of Man. Instances: Jesus conceived by the Spirit (1:35); attested by the Spirit (3:22); led into the wilderness by the Spirit (4:1); anointed by the Spirit (4:18); rejoicing in the Spirit (10:21). See also Acts 10:38.

o. To summarize:

(1) Luke portrays Jesus as the Son of Man, the Savior for all, with His genealogy traced to Adam, the father of the race, and therefore a universal Christ.

(2) Jesus, the friend of sinners, the unfortunate and downtrodden.

(3) Jesus, as the solution to life's problems. His teaching, full of grace and truth, is practical and offers the world a means of happiness here and hereafter.

STUDENT WORK

1. _____, the author of the third gospel, also wrote _____ , both of which are addressed to _____ .

2. The author is associated with which of the following? (Paul, Marcus uncircumcision, Greece, Barnabas, good education, Jewish knowledge, Pharisees, Sadducees, classical Greek).

3. Does it appear that Luke was an eye-witness of Jesus? _____ How did he get his information? _____

4. How does *Luke* differ from *Matthew* and *Mark* in regard to the persons addressed? _____

31

5. Give Luke's qualifications for writing to the Gentiles.

a. _____

b. _____

c. _____

6. Why is Luke able to give us a different slant on Christ and His work? _____

_____

7. This book was written for what basic reason? _____

_____

8. If we were to summarize the outline of Luke's contents, we would see that Luke presents Jesus from three basic viewpoints; i.e., he shows Jesus as:

a. _____

b. _____

c. _____

True or False

_____ 1. Luke was one of the more talented Jewish writers.

_____ 2. Luke was written before Acts.

_____ 3. Luke's is the most logically and systematically arranged of the first three gospels.

_____ 4. Though *Mark* is less orderly than *Luke, Mark* more generally represents the life of Jesus than either of the other gospels.

_____ 5. Luke pays special attention to tying the gospel narrative in with the current historical developments in the land.

_____ 6. Luke records the Lord's sending His disciples out to preach and heal on three different occasions.

_____ 7. Only Luke records Jesus' being crucified between the two thieves.

The Gospel of John

A. The Author.

John was one of the sons of Zebedee, and a brother of James (Mt. 4:21-22; Mk. 1:19-20). Zebedee, his father, was a fisherman of Galilee and John himself was a partner with his brother, and evidently with Andrew and Peter, in the fishing business. He was called to become a disciple of Jesus while he was mending his nets (Mt. 4:21-22). It is probable that Salome was his mother, who likely was a sister of Mary, the mother of Jesus (Mt. 27:56; Mk. 15:40; Jn. 19:25). His family had hired servants (Mk. 1:20), and ministered to the needs of Jesus and His disciples (Mt. 27:55-56).

He was a disciple of John the Baptist (Jn. 1:35), and one of the first six disciples called (Jn. 1:37-51). He had a home in Jerusalem (Jn. 19:26-27). He is named in the list of Apostles (Mt. 10:2), and is included in the innermost circle of disciples. He was present with Peter and James at the raising of Jairus' daughter (Mk. 5:37); Lk. 8:51). These three were also witnesses of the Transfiguration (Mt. 17; Mk. 9, Lk. 9). He refers to himself as "the disciple whom Jesus loved" (Jn. 13:23; 19:26; 20:2; 21:7, 20). He was closely associated with Peter in much of his work (Acts 3:1; 8:14; Gal. 2:9).

He is conceded by many scholars to be also the author of 1 John, 2 John, 3 John and Revelation, and is regarded, therefore, as having written five of the books of the New Testament. History indicates that he spent the latter part of his life in Asia Minor; residing probably at Ephesus. He was banished to the Isle of Patmos, a small island in the Aegean Sea, supposedly during the reign of Domitian. Traditionally, John is commonly thought to have been the only Apostle who did not suffer martyrdom; however, there are some indications that even he may have done so. He was the youngest of the Apostles and lived to the most advanced age of any.

He seemed to have possessed an unusually ardent temperament, and along with his brother James, was described by the Lord as "sons of thunder" (Mk. 3:17). His temperament is indicated in his readiness to rebuke the man casting out demons (Lk. 9:49), and in his desire to call down fire from Heaven upon the Samaritan villages that would not receive Jesus (Lk. 9:51-56). Both James and John requested their mother to petition Jesus to grant them seats of prominence in His Kingdom (Mt. 20:28). In all these instances, they were sharply rebuked by Jesus. At the Last Supper, John occupied a place of prominence and intimacy next to Jesus (Jn. 13:23). At the trial of Christ, because of his acquaintanceship with the high priest, he was allowed to accompany Jesus into the Court and stood by Him. He was a witness of the death of Jesus also, and to him, as He suffered upon the cross, Jesus committed the care of His mother (Jn. 19:26-27). He stayed with Peter during the time that Christ was in the tomb and with him was one of the first visitors to the empty tomb where, as he looked at the empty grave clothes, he saw and believed (Jn. 20:8).

As a disciple of Christ, his intense nature and ardent temperament was subdued and trained so that he became the Apostle of love, whose devotion to the Lord to the end of his life was not exceeded by any other character in New Testament history. John is the example of the man who had the disposition and temperament to become a great sinner, but who instead became a great witness for the Lord and a faithful saint.

B. When John's Gospel Was Written.

While the scholars have been divided in their opinions as to the date when this gospel was written, it seems to be pretty commonly believed, by the bulk of them, to have been written at Ephesus after his return from Patmos. This would place the date probably about 96 to 98 A.D. This fourth gospel was incorporated into Tatian's Diatessaron about the middle of the second century. A fragmentary manuscript of John 18:31-33, 37, 38, in the John Ryland Library, Manchester, England, provides evidence that John's gospel was in use during the first half of the second century. It was apparently written in Gentile surroundings and for universal usage, as John goes to some length to explain the feasts and customs of the Jews to those unfamiliar with them (Jn. 2:13; 4:9; 19:31).

C. To Whom John's Gospel Was Written.

Internal evidences indicate that John's gospel was not written for the benefit of the Jews especially. As has been suggested above, the author explains words and customs for which a Jew would have needed no explanation (Jn. 1:38, 41; 5:1-2; 7:2; 4:9). The simplicity and the manner in which the story is told by John, and the lack of any display of learning, gives to the gospel of John universal appeal. It is frequently called the universal gospel.

D. The Purpose of John's Gospel.

John states more clearly than any other gospel writer the exact purpose for writing the gospel in chapter 20:30-31:

And many other signs truly did Jesus in the presence of His disciples, which are not written in this book: But these are written, that ye might believe that Jesus is the Christ, the Son of God; and that believing ye might have life through His name.

Three words particularly stand out with significance in this passage: 1) *signs*, 2) *believe*, and 3) *life*. These words set forth the meaning and purpose of the miracles of Christ. John records a total of seven miracles: changing water into wine (2:1-11); healing the nobleman's son (4:46-54); healing the impotent man (5:1-18); feeding the five thousand (6:1-14); walking on the water (6:16-21); healing the

34

blind man (9:1-12); raising of Lazarus (11:1-46). These miracles, or "signs" are all for the purpose of evidencing the truth of John's affirmation that "Jesus is the Christ, the Son of God."

There are three great channels of testimony that run throughout the Gospel very prominently.

1. *The Divinity of Jesus.*
 a. The pre-existence of Christ (1:1-14).
 b. The testimony of John the Baptist (1:15-36).
 c. The miracles of Christ as listed above.
 d. The claims that Jesus made for Himself to qualities clearly supernatural in character. These claims are expressed in what has been called the "I am's":
  (1) The bread of life (6:36).
  (2) The Light of the world (8:12; 9:5).
  (3) The door (10:7).
  (4) The good shepherd (10:11-14).
  (5) The resurrection and the life (11:25).
  (6) The way, the truth and the life (14:6).
  (7) The true vine (15:1).

2. John's gospel was designed to emphasize *what faith in Christ means.* His answer to this question is not so much in any formal statement as by means of illustration. The noun "faith" or "belief" never appears in the Gospel, but always the visible form of the word is used. Ninety-eight times John uses this word to point out what the response to Jesus should be. As examples, note: "belief on his name" (1:12); "believe on him" (3:16); "believe on him that sent" Jesus (5:24).

Along with the word "belief," a number of synonymous words occur: "receive" (1:12); "drink" (4:14); "eat" (6:51); "come" (6:37); "enter" (10:9).

John very clearly pictures the personal interviews that Jesus had with people who came face to face with Him. There are 27 such interviews, some very brief, others in greater detail. Examples: Nicodemus (Jn. 3); the Samaritan woman (Jn. 4); the blind man (Jn. 9); Mary and Martha (Jn. 11).

3. John's gospel likewise emphasizes salvation or *eternal life as the objective of faith.* The hope of eternal life as the objective of faith in Christ is set forth by the writer of this gospel in the following passages: John 3:15-17; 3:36; 4:36; 5:24; 5:28-29; 5:39-40; 6:54, 68; 10:28; 12:25; 17:2-3; 20:30-31.

E. Contents and Character of John's Gospel.

A brief outline of this gospel can be set forth in five main points:

1. The prologue (1:1-18).
2. The public ministry of Jesus (1:19; 12:50).
3. The private ministry of the Son of God (13:1-17:26).
4. The suffering of the Son of God (18:1-20:31).

35

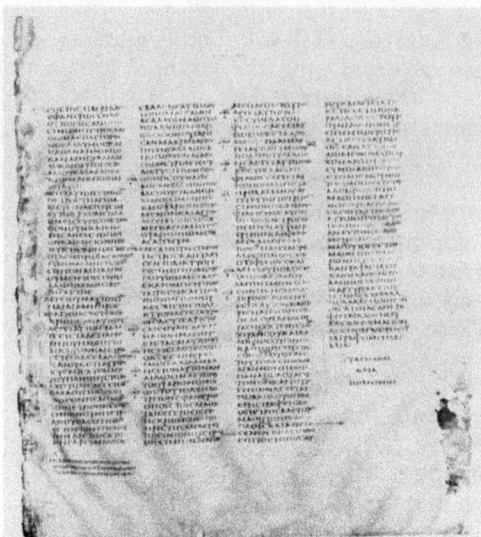

The end of the gospel of John from the Codex Sinaiticus. This manuscript of the New Testament dates from the fourth century and is now in the British Museum.

5. Postscript; the final appeal (21:1-25).

John's gospel is very different in style, character and plan from the other three gospels. Some of these differences may be noted in the following:

1. Apart from the week of the Lord's suffering in Jerusalem, there are only two points of obvious and undoubted contact between John's gospel and the "synoptic" gospels. They are:

    a. The feeding of the five thousand (6:1-14).

    b. The walk on the sea (6:6-21).

2. John gives in detail only a few incidents in the life of Jesus, embracing actually just a few days in His life. Seven chapters of John's gospel (13 through 19) are used in describing the night of the betrayal, the trial, and the crucifixion on the next day. In this is included the farewell discourse of Christ to His disciples and the details of the trial, but actually only a few hours were involved in these events. Perhaps no more than 20 days out of the 3½ years of our Lord's ministry are specifically described in John's gospel.

3. John, more than any other gospel writer, tells his story from a personal point of view. He begins his narrative in this fashion (1:14), "*we* beheld his glory."

    a. Includes himself among the disciples and their failure to comprehend at first some of the things which Jesus said (2:22; 12:16).

    b. It is sometimes difficult to know when Jesus ceased speaking and John began his reflection (3:23-26).

    c. He emphasizes the importance of being an eye-witness and, therefore, competent to testify. He was present in the scenes so vividly described by him, such as the night of the betrayal, the trial in the hall of the high priest, and the crucifixion and death of Jesus.

    d. John recalls the scenes described by him in their entirety and even in intimate detail.

36

(1) The six disciples at the beginning of His ministry (chapter 1).

(2) The six water pots at Cana (2:16).

(3) The boy with the five loaves and two fishes (6:9).

(4) The appearance of Lazarus when he came forth from the grave (11:44).

(5) The kinds and weights of the spices brought by Nicodemus to embalm the body of Jesus (9:38-40).

(6) The careful folding of the linen cloths (20:4-8).

4. John gives a great deal of emphasis to the fact of the Fatherhood of God. He makes reference to this over 100 times in his gospel. Examples: 4:23; 5:21; 7:16; 10:29; 14:10; 14:23; 17:5, 17:11.

STUDENT WORK

1. Which of the following characterize or relate to the author of John: (fishing, Andrew's brother, cousin of Jesus, Ephesus, Bethany, high temper, Jericho, Sanhedrin, old age, intimacy with Jesus, doubter, priestly father, exile).

2. John, who wrote the following books: _____ _____ , _____ , _____ , and _____ ; is described as the example of the man who had _____ _____ but who instead _____ .

3. When, from where, and to whom was *John* written?
   a) _____   b) _____
   c) _____

4. The purpose of the book, stated in _____ is what? _____

5. How does John attempt to prove his point; what method does he use? _____

6. Three significant words describing the purpose of *John* are: _____ , _____ , and _____ .

7. There are three main areas of testimony in *John:* a) _____
   b) _____   c) _____
   To which of these three areas do the following passages relate?
   _____ a. "He that heareth my word, and believeth Him that sent me, hath eternal life." _____ (passage)

37

_____ b. "For of his fulness we all received, and grace for grace." _____ (passage)

_____ c. "When I am in the world, I am the light of the world." _____ (passage)

_____ d. Interview with Nicodemus _____ (passage)

_____ e. "He that eateth my flesh and drinketh my blood hath eternal life; and I will raise him up at the last day." _____ (passage)

_____ f. "This is life eternal, that they should know thee. . . ." _____ (passage)

8. Indicate whether the following items in *John* are a) similar to, or b) different from, the other three gospels.

_____ a. Style.

_____ b. Walking on the sea.

_____ c. The week of suffering in Jerusalem.

_____ d. Writing from a personal viewpoint.

_____ e. Covers no more than 20 days.

_____ f. Claims to be an eye-witness.

_____ g. Feeding the five thousand.

_____ h. Character of the book.

9. The following passages in *John* emphasize what fact? _____

a. ". . . the true worshippers shall worship the Father in spirit and truth:" _____ (passage)

b. "My Father who hath given them unto me is greater than all:" _____ (passage)

c. "Believest thou not that I am the Father, and the Father in me?" _____ (passage)

38

The Book of Acts

A. The Author.
There are no serious doubts as to the authorship of the book of Acts of the Apostles. Luke is assigned as its author. As early as the last part of the 2nd century, Irenaeus cites passages so frequently from the Acts of the Apostles that it is certain that he had constant access to the book. He gives emphasis to the internal evidence of its authorship. Tertullian also ascribes the book to Luke, as does Clement of Alexandria.

1. The Preface of the Book. The writer addresses Theophilus (Lk. 1:3), who is the same individual to whom the gospel of Luke was also directed, and makes reference to a "former treatise" which dealt with "all that Jesus began to do and to teach until the day he was received up" (1:1-2). This is very evidently a reference to the third gospel.

2. The book of Acts and the gospel of Luke are identical in style, as a number of scholars have pointed out and demonstrated.

3. The book of Acts comes as an historical sequel to the gospel of Luke, taking up with the very events, and at the point where the gospel of Luke concludes, namely the resurrection, the appearances following the resurrection, and the commissioning of the Apostles to the task for which they had been selected and trained by the Lord, and the ascension of Jesus.

4. Several portions of the book of Acts are written in the first person plural, called the "we" sections of the book, signifying that the writer was an eye-witness of what he wrote and the companion of Paul (16:10-17; 20:5-15; 21:1-18; 27:1; 28:16).

5. Both the gospel of Luke and Acts of the Apostles frequently use medical terminology, which seems sufficient to indicate the profession of Luke, "the beloved physician" (Col. 4:14).

B. When the Book of Acts Was Written.
The time of the writing of the Book of Acts seems to coincide reasonably with the close of its historical account. Paul is in prison, still alive in Rome. Evidently, the history recorded in Acts would not have so abruptly ended, if Paul's death had taken place and it is unlikely that such an event as the destruction of Jerusalem would not have even been mentioned in such an historical account, if it had already occurred. We, therefore, place the date of the writing of Acts of the Apostles as prior to 70 A.D. and after Paul reached Rome, probably in 63 A.D., or thereabout.

C. To Whom the Book of Acts Was Written.
Although the record of Acts is addressed personally to

Theophilus, as was the gospel of Luke, it was intended surely for a much wider reading. The origin of Christianity among the Jews, as a prepared people, is prominently noticed in the facts of the beginning (Acts 2). It is also emphasized that the unfailing practice was to preach the gospel first always to the Jews.

However, much of the book is concerned with the history of the transfer of the center of interest in the spread of Christianity from Jerusalem to Antioch, and from the Jewish phase of gospel preaching to the concentrated effort to spread the gospel to the whole Gentile world. This is portrayed as the Lord's own plan (Acts 1:8, "you shall be my witnesses both in Jerusalem, and in all Judea and Samaria and to the uttermost part of the earth"). Luke does not turn away from his purpose in the gospel written by him, namely to present the origin and history of Christianity from the viewpoint of one outside of Judaism.

The book of Acts, therefore, is an historical account adapted to meet the need of the Gentiles as well as the Jews. This reflects Luke's association with Paul and becomes the basis of what is often thought to be Pauline influence on the record.

D. The Purpose of the Book of Acts.

The common purpose of both the Gospel of Luke and Acts of the Apostles is expressed in Luke 1:4. We find a number of specific aims, in addition.

1. An *Historical* Motive. A comparison of Luke 1:1-4 and Acts 1:5, shows a continuation in the historical motive. The subject of the gospel of Luke is "the things that Jesus began to do and teach." The book of Acts gives the history of the continuation of the work that Jesus had begun as the Holy Spirit carried on His Purpose and that work in the lives of the Apostles. This continuation was outlined in the purpose expressed by the Lord in Acts 1:8, just before His ascension.

2. The *Defense* Motive. In addressing himself to the Roman world, Luke constantly calls attention to the fact that the gospel enjoyed an interested hearing at the hands of government officials. In every contact with government officials recorded in Acts, Christianity either received a favorable hearing or was ignored, but never opposed. In Chapter 13, Sergius Paulus, the proconsul of Cyprus, believed the message of Paul; the officials at Philippi apologized for the rough treatment of Paul and Silas which had been provoked by soothsayers (16:35-39); Gallio, at Corinth, simply ignored the preachers (18:17); the officials at Ephesus (19:31) were sympathetic and the "townclerk" came to the rescue of the Christians during the riot. Felix, Festus and Agrippa (24-26), all sympathetic, heard Paul's message and declared that He had "done nothing worthy of death." Luke, no doubt, gave emphasis to these favorable attitudes upon the part of the officials for the purpose of contrast in the face of increasing hostility toward Christianity.

3. The *Biographical* Motive. While Luke's record is primarily devoted to the revelation of the gospel and its being preached throughout the world, the beginning, growth and spread of the church of the Lord as a consequence, and to the work of the Holy Spirit in the revelation of Divine truth and its confirmation; yet, in a very pronounced way, he divides the historical record of Acts into two different sections biographical in nature by recording in the first section (1 through 12) the history of Peter's work, and in 13 through 28 a record of the work of the Apostle to the Gentiles, Paul.

Luke's story is a vivid picture of the use and employment of humanity in the persons of Peter and Paul, Stephen, Philip, Barnabas, Timothy and Titus, in the fulfillment of the purposes which had brought Jesus Christ into the world and of God's purpose from eternity in the accomplishment of human redemption through the preaching of the gospel.

E. Contents and Character of the Book of Acts.

There are five lines of historical reference distinct and continuing that can be definitely traced throughout the Book of Acts. Just as the gospels give us the history of the coming of the Messiah and His life upon the earth, so the book of Acts of the Apostles records for us the history of the beginning, growth and spread of Christianity for at least the first 30 years, from the ascension of Jesus to the imprisonment of Paul.

It has been suggested that the book of Acts furnishes the historical setting for the most of the New Testament epistles, especially those of Paul, and that these epistles can be placed like jewels in the setting of its history. An interesting study of such an arrangement can be found in *The Life and Epistles of Paul*, by Coneybeare & Howson. As an analysis of the book and its historical data, we suggest five lines of historical reference:

1. The Apostolic Office and Work. The book derives its name from the work of the Apostles of our Lord and from this record of their work we are able to learn of the Apostolic office in operation and the work that Jesus selected and trained the Apostles to do, as well as the place they fill in the church through the work which they did.

a. They were witnesses for Christ (1:8; 1:21-22).

(1) In order to be qualified to testify for Christ they had to be eye and ear witnesses of that concerning which they bore testimony (1:22; 26:16-18; 2 Pet. 1:16-21; 1 Jn. 1:1-4).

(2) The second qualification for competent witnesses is that they must be able to accurately remember what they have seen and heard. Jesus provided the Apostles with the Holy Spirit to guide them in refreshing their memories and guaranteeing its accuracy (Jn. 14:25-26).

(3) A competent witness must also be able to clearly and definitely express in accurate form the testimony which he gives. This

also was guaranteed upon the part of the Apostles as the witnesses of Christ by the Holy Spirit's power to overrule and guide them in the selection of even the words which expressed their testimony (1 Cor. 2:12-13).

b. The Apostles were also the ambassadors of the Lord (2 Cor. 5:20; Acts 4:18-20; 5:28-32). They were authorized to speak for Him and to make known His Divine decrees unto all the Nations of the earth. This testimony which they bore is binding both in Heaven and on earth upon all men forever (Mt. 18:18).

c. The Apostles also sat upon thrones with authority to rule over the church of our Lord (Mt. 19:28; Acts 2:42; 15; Gal. 2:1-9; 1 Jn. 4:6).

d. They were also "earthen vessels," expendable in the purpose of Christ to reveal the will of God (2 Cor. 4:7). This passage points out that the "light of the knowledge of the glory of God" which was first revealed in the "face of Jesus Christ" is now shed abroad in the hearts of men in the "light of the gospel of the glory of Christ" revealed by the Apostles through the power of the Holy Spirit.

2. The book of Acts, however, could have as well been called the "Work of the Holy Spirit" in the scheme of redemption.

a. The Spirit began His mission which was promised by Christ (Jn. 14:16-17, 25-26; Jn. 16:7-15; Acts 1:8) on the day of Pentecost (2:33; 2:15-21; 2:1-4). The mission of the Holy Spirit as recorded in the book of Acts can be set forth in the following four points:

(1) The revelation of the Gospel (2:4; 1 Cor. 2:10-13; Eph. 3:3-5).

(2) The confirmation of the word revealed by the miracles and signs which followed (Mk. 16:15-20; Acts 6:6-8; 8:6-13; 19:6; Heb. 2:1-4).

(3) The conviction and conversion of sinners was also a part of the mission of the Holy Spirit as promised by Jesus in John 16:8-11. This mission was accomplished through the power and influence of Divine truth as the Spirit enabled the Apostles to preach it.

(4) The Holy Spirit likewise continued to guide, direct, and edify early Christians through gifts bestowed of an extraordinary nature and through the revelation of the will of God concerning their lives and the accomplishment of His purposes (5:32; 4:31; 9:31; Rom. 8:14).

3. A third line of historical reference prominent in the book of Acts is the story of the preaching of the gospel. In this record of gospel preaching given through a variety of expressions, the message preached can be identified; and in addition to what they preached, we can learn much of how they preached it under different circumstances. As a study of this history in the book of Acts, we suggest the following points among many to be considered:

a. "Continued stedfastly in the Apostles doctrine" (2:42).

b. "Spoke the word of God," "preach the word," "the word of the Lord" (4:31; 13:44; 18:11; 14:25; 15:35-36; 16:32).

c. "Teach and preach Jesus Christ" (5:42; 8:5; 8:35; 9:20; 11:20).

d. "Preaching the things of the Kingdom of God" and the "name of Jesus Christ" (8:12; 19:8; 20:25; 28:23; 28:31).

e. "Preach the gospel" (14:7-21; 16:10).

f. "The decrees for to keep, that were ordained of the apostles and elders which were at Jerusalem" (16:4).

g. "The way of salvation," "the way of God more accurately" (16:17; 18:26).

h. "Reason with them from the scriptures" (17:2).

i. "Shrank not from declaring unto you anything that was profitable," "the gospel of the grace of God," "the whole counsel of God" (20:20, 24, 27).

j. "Concerning the faith in Jesus Christ . . . righteousness, temperance, and judgment to come" (14:24-25).

4. A fourth line of historical study in the book of Acts is that of conversion. In the history of Acts, several conversions are related which do not bear testimony concerning human experiences, but which passed under the observance of the Holy Spirit twice: 1) When they occurred the preacher was guided by the Holy Spirit; 2) when they were recorded the Holy Spirit recorded them. In these records of conversion there are several things common to them all.

a. In each case of conversion the gospel was preached. There is not a single record of anybody being converted by some miraculous experience separate from the power and influence of Divine truth.

b. When men were saved by the power of the gospel, it was always because they believed the truth that was preached.

c. Faith in the gospel which they heard always produced the works of obedience to the will of God which that gospel commanded them to perform (2:38-41; 8:12; 18:8; 16:32-34; 6:7; 9:35; 11:21; 17:4; 19:17-18; 19:5; 16:14; 9:18; 8:35-38).

5. Another very prominent thread of historical evidence which can easily be traced all the way through the book of Acts is the story of the church, what it was, of whom it consisted, its organization, its mission and work, its worship and its growth and development. From all of this history, we can learn what the church was in the beginning under Apostolic guidance, as God designed it and as Christ built it, and therefore, what it must be today.

a. The church in the book of Acts was made up of those who believed, obeyed the gospel demands, and were added together to make up the body of the saved (2:41; 4:4; 5:14; 6:7; 9:42; 11:24; 13:12; 13:48; 14:1; 17:4; 12:12; 17:34; 28:24; 2:47). All of these expressions tell the same story, that is, what men did in obedience to the gospel and how they were added together to constitute the church. The "believers" referred to in many of the above passages were always baptized or obedient, therefore saved believers.

b. The identity of the church and its singularity are distinguishable in this historical record at a number of points.

(1) The vital activity in which the early church continued stedfastly (2:42-44).

(2) The organization of the early church (14:23), "elders in every church" (Phil. 1:1).

(3) The worship of the church (11:25-26) on the Lord's day (20:7).

(4) The purity of the church in character seen in the fact that sin was not tolerated (5:11).

(5) The work in which the early church engaged.

(a) Evangelism on 1) the personal level (11:19-20), and 2) congregational level (11:22). The church which supported the preacher always sent directly to the preacher (Phil. 1:5; 2:25; 4:14-16; 2 Cor. 11:7-9). In no case is there any record of any church sending a contribution to another church to help the receiving church support a preacher.

(b) Benevolent work: 1) The church providing in Jerusalem for its own needy (Acts 2, 4, 6); 2) congregational co-operation in benevolence by one church contributing to another church which was unable to care for its own (11:29-31; 1 Cor. 16:1-4; 2 Cor. 8, 9).

The pattern of this benevolence was as follows: 1) The contributing church raised its own funds from its own members "according to their ability" (11:27-30; 1 Cor. 16:1-4); 2) the contributing church selected its own messengers by which to forward its contribution to the church in need; 3) the receiving church was always a church in need because of being unable to provide for its own destitute; 4) the contribution made to assist the needy church was delivered into the hands of the elders of the church in need to be distributed to those destitute under their supervision (11:27-30; 1 Cor. 16:1-4; 2 Cor. 8, 9).

In no case did any contributing church send through or by the agency of another church, and there was no centralized oversight of more than one church exercised by any eldership. It is also worthy of note that there is no authority for the organizing of a benevolent society in addition to the church to do its benevolent work.

(6) The church met the problem of false doctrine by an appeal to Apostolic authority (15:1, 5, 22, 40).

(7) The church was edified under its own elders through its own program of teaching, and by the exhortation and encouragement of gospel preachers (11:22; 13:1-3; 16:40; 20:1).

(8) Those who constituted the church wore a new name given by the mouth of the Lord (Isa. 62:2; Acts 9:15; 11:26).

STUDENT WORK

1. Who wrote the Book of Acts of the Apostles? _____ What other book did this same author write? _____

2. To whom did the writer address this book? _____
3. The book of Acts is primarily: biographical, doctrinal, historical. (circle the correct answer)
4. What is inferred by the sections of the book in which the writer uses the first person plural pronoun "we"? _____
5. How do the events recorded in the book of Acts indicate the date of its writing? _____
6. How would you divide the book generally as to preaching the Gospel among the Jews and Gentiles? _____ As to the work of Peter and Paul? _____
7. Name some of the historical accounts where Christians in their work came into contact with governmental officials: _____
   _____
8. The notives apparent in the writing of Acts are apparently:
   a) _____ , b)_____ , c) _____ ,
9. Name some of the prominent characters who had a part in the spread of Christianity in the record of Acts: _____ ,
   _____ , _____ , _____ , _____ , _____ ,
   _____ , _____ , _____ , _____ .
10. Name five lines of historical record that can be traced through the book of Acts: a) _____ , b) _____ ,
    c) _____ , d) _____ , e) _____ .
    Suggestion: A good study project of the book of Acts would be to read the book searching out and marking in some distinctive manner the passages that record the history of each one of these five historical records.
11. The Apostolic Office included the function as: a) _____ ,
    b) _____ , c) _____ , d) _____ .
12. The work of the Holy Spirit in the book of Acts can be sum-marized in four functions: a) _____ , b) _____ ,
    c) _____ , d) _____ ,
13. Some of the descriptions setting forth what was preached in the Gospel in the beginning are: a) _____ ,
    b) _____ , _____ , _____ ,
    c) _____ , d) _____ ,
    e) _____ , f) _____ ,
    g) _____ , h) _____ ,
    i) _____ , j) _____

45

(Cite the passages from Acts in which you find these descriptions of the Gospel).

14. What assurance do we have that the cases of conversion recorded in Acts contain no error? a) _____ , b) _____ ,

15. What factors are always present in every one of these cases of conversion? a) _____ , b) _____ , c) _____ .

16. Who made up the church wherever it was planted? _____ How did people become a part of the church? _____

17. What passage in the very beginning of the church sets forth its vital activities? _____

18. Give the passages in Acts that set forth its pattern of church government or organization: _____
Give another passage cited from the Philippian letter: _____

19. What passage in Acts specifies in apostolic example the day of assembly to break bread? _____

20. Name the passage and characters that exemplify that God will not tolerate sin in the church: _____ , _____ .

21. Name the two levels in the history of Acts of how the evangelistic work was carried on and cite the passages that demonstrate them. Discuss.
a) _____ , _____ , _____ .
b) _____ , _____ .

22. What scriptures in Acts set forth the pattern for the benevolent work of the church? _____ , _____ , _____ . Cite some additional passages from the New Testament on this point.
What are the steps in the pattern for one church sending a benevolent contribution to relieve another church that is in need?
a) _____
b) _____
c) _____
d) _____

23. What standard settled all doctrinal differences in the New Testament church? _____ Cite the example: _____

46

The Epistle to the Romans

A. The Author.

That Paul is the author of the epistle to the Romans is so generally accepted that the few who have questioned it are not seriously regarded. The Apostle to the Gentiles was peculiarly equipped to write such an epistle to the Roman church for many reasons. In the first place he was born and educated in Tarsus, the capital of Cilicia. This city was renowned for its educational advantages. Here, among other things, he learned the trade of tent making with which he partially supported himself in later years while he preached the gospel. In Tarsus they manufactured a rough cloth from the hair of goats which was widely used in the making of tents. The influence of a Grecian education is manifest in Paul's writings. He uses the logical method of presenting truth. His method of linking together his arguments and driving relentlessly toward the ultimate conclusion or principle to be established was not characteristic of Jewish writers in general.

His later education was Jewish, at the feet of Gamaliel. He was, therefore, thoroughly acquainted with the attitudes, doctrines, and modes of reasoning used by the Jews who were the early adversaries of the gospel. It is evident in the Scriptures that the Holy Spirit in employing men as instruments in revealing truth did not change their mental habits, discard their vocabularies, and force all into the same mold, but used each man's capabilities and training; yet, selecting and choosing out of each that which expressed in God's own words the truth to be revealed. This is certainly demonstrated in the preaching and writing of Paul, the apostle.

B. Date of Writing.

In the Epistle itself we learn that Paul was about to go to Jerusalem with the collection by churches of Macedonia and Achaia "for the poor among the saints" (15:25-27). He frequently stressed this collection in the earlier letters to Corinth (1 Cor. 16:1-4; 2 Cor. 8, 9), evidencing that these letters were written about the same time. Romans, however, must have been written later than 2 Corinthians, for he was on the verge of departing for Jerusalem. 2 Corinthians was written from Macedonia; from Macedonia he went to Greece. He refers to Cenchreae (16:1), which is the seaport of Corinth. He is entertained by Gaius (16:23), whom he had baptized at Corinth (1 Cor. 1:14). Erastus seems to have lived at Corinth (16:23; 2 Tim. 4:20). He hoped that after he had gone to Jerusalem with the messengers selected by the churches to deliver their contribution to the Jerusalem church that he would then be free to journey to Spain through Rome. He speaks of this hope. The time of the writing of the Roman letter then was likely in the spring of 57 or 58 A.D.

C. To Whom Addressed.

Paul had been sent out as a special apostle of Christ to the Gentile nations of the world. He had borne much fruit among many of them, but though it had often been his desire and purpose to go to Rome, he had been hindered from doing so (1:13). Rome was the center of the world's life. Paul was vitally interested in preaching the gospel throughout the whole Roman empire. While still further delayed by the necessity of taking the contribution for the poor saints to Jerusalem, he writes to the Roman Christians, preparing the way for his intended visit to them.

1. *The Origin of the Church in Rome.* The origin of the church in Rome is unknown. The tradition that the church in Rome was founded by the apostle Peter is inconsistent with the facts and without any supporting evidence. There is no indication in the word of God and no established fact of history that Peter was ever in Rome. Most of the learned writers deny it. We suggest a number of facts pertinent to a proper consideration of this point.

a. Peter's own epistles were neither addressed to nor written from Rome.

b. In Paul's letter to the church at Rome he makes no mention of Peter.

c. In epistles written from Rome by Paul while he was in prison there the apostle Peter was not mentioned.

d. No mention is made of Rome in the writings of Peter and no inspired writer mentions Rome or Peter in connection with Rome.

The probability is, either some of those present on the day of Pentecost (Acts 2:10 — sojourners from Rome) returned to plant the religion of Christ in that city, or in the dispersion of Jewish Christians from Jerusalem (Acts 8) some journeyed as far as Rome and preached the gospel there. There is evidence that many Jews lived in Rome. Probably they had made many proselytes to the Jewish religion from among the heathen. Jews had been introduced into Rome in large numbers by Pompeius the Great (63 B.C.). Augustus, influenced by friendship for the first Herod, had improved their condition and assigned them the section of Rome beyond the Tiber, which Josephus says they had occupied through the years. Claudius, when quarrels arose between them and the Christians, passed a decree for their banishment (Acts 18:1-2), but they were too strongly established for the decree to be entirely effective. In the Neronian persecution (A.D. 64), Tacitus states that Christian martyrs formed a great multitude. At the time the letter was written the church at Rome does not appear to have been very large since nothing is mentioned about the church as a whole or about any appearance of an organization of the church; neither bishops nor deacons are mentioned.

The church at Rome was composed of both Jewish and Gentile elements. Paul addresses both in the letter. In chapter 11:13, he writes, "I speak unto you Gentiles," and yet in chapter 7:1, he says, "I speak to them that know the law."

2. *The Condition of the Church at Rome.* It was but natural that a church made up of both Jews and Gentiles would experience some strife. Many of the problems dealt with in the Roman letter were due to the fact that complete reconcilliation to being on an absolute equality in Christ was difficult for both Jew and Gentile. It was either because of such difficulty already being evident among those who composed the church at Rome, or in order to prepare them against the trouble that would eventually arise when Judaizing teachers came their way, that he wrote this letter as he did.

D. Purpose and Message.
The purpose and message of the book can readily be seen from a number of things that are emphasized pointedly in the epistle. They are as follows:

1. The depravity to which sin leads, and the fact that when man abandons God to follow its course that God will "give them up," is illustrated in the Gentile nations rejecting God to walk in the vanity of their own minds after knowing Him (1:18-32). Three times in these last verses of the first chapter, as he describes the moral destitution of these Gentile nations, Paul says, "God gave them up."

2. God does not respect the person of any man enough to wink at his sin. Sin was just as sinful upon the part of the Jew as upon the part of the Gentile (chapter 2).

3. There is a universal need for salvation because "all men have sinned" (3:23).

4. God's grace alone was able to provide this salvation and this provision was made by the blood of Christ and offered unto men in the gospel of Christ (3:26).

5. Justification was not by the works of the law or else it would have been a Jewish affair, since the law was given only to the Jews. This would have made God a respecter of persons in providing justification for the Jew without the Gentile.

6. The law of Moses was not given to reveal God's plan for making man righteous, but it was given to reveal sin and through the knowledge of it, to make the whole world conscious of the fact that they stood condemned before God and therefore needed a Savior (3:19-20).

7. Paul points out that justification is not to be attained by the works of the Law, but rather through a system of faith which he calls "faith of Christ" (3:22), in which system the righteousness of God, or God's plan for making men righteous, is revealed (1:17). This revelation of God's righteousness in the gospel is the reason why he affirms that the gospel is God's power unto salvation unto "all them that believe."

8. The Jews had failed to attain unto God's righteousness because they "sought it not by faith" (9:32). They refused to let the Law serve the purpose that God had intended, of preparing them for the reception of Christ (Gal. 3:24). They had developed a system of

49

righteousness of their own, based upon their human traditions, and hence, had rejected the righteousness of God. For this reason they had been rejected by God as a nation and the judgment of God poured out upon them.

9. This national rejection did not mean that the Jew, as an individual, could not be saved through the "faith of Jesus Christ," for Paul affirms "so all Israel shall be saved" (11:26); that is, in this manner or through "the faith of Christ."

10. Christianity, as Paul so well emphasized in this letter, should blot out all national enmity and bring them in Christ to love one another as brethren and to enjoy the fullness of Christian fellowship. Spiritual, rather than fleshly relationships, are to be considered.

E. Contents and Character of the Book.

A very practical and helpful approach to a proper analysis of the book of Romans and its message can be made from the viewpoint of Romans 2:11, as the general theme of the whole letter, "for there is no respect of persons with God." This theme rests upon and is developed by three major arguments:

1. God's condemnation rests upon all men alike without respect of persons because of their sins (1:18-3:23).

2. God's way of making men righteous through Jesus Christ, offered in the gospel and appropriated by man's faith, is available to all men alike without respect of persons (3:19-5:21).

The Roman Forum was the hub of Roman life. Most of the religious, political, economic and social events of importance took place here. The Forum is a favorite attraction of tourists to Rome.

3. God's grace, offering righteousness unto all men upon the same conditions or requirements, makes God no respecter of persons (5:22-8:30).

Chapters 9 through 11 call attention to the sad plight of fleshly Israel. Paul expresses his great love and sympathy for Israel, but he points out that God's promises are fulfilled in spiritual Israel as the children of promise through Isaac (9:13). It was the will of God that the Gentiles should also be offered God's grace and mercy (9:24-26). The Gentiles' acceptance had caused a "hardening" upon the part of fleshly Israel, creating bitterness, resentment, rebellion, and evidencing their unbelief. Fleshly Israel had made the sad mistake of trusting in their works of the Law and had rejected God's offer of righteousness through the system of faith. Only a remnant would therefore be saved (9:27-33). They trusted their own righteousness instead of God's. They rejected Christ who fulfilled the Law and they were still looking for the "descent" and "ascent" of the Lord while the "word of faith" reveals that it had already been accomplished (10:1-8). God required the same conditions of salvation upon the part of both Jew and Gentile (Rom. 10-12). The prophets had prophesied that the gospel would be taken to the Gentiles that they might be saved, but the Jews had not believed the prophets (10:13-21). God had not rejected all Israel, but only those who were unbelievers and were disobedient, and who had hardened their hearts, thus rejecting God's grace (11:1-10). While Israel's rejection had worked out to the advantage of the Gentile by causing the gospel to be more completely propagated among them, they were not to gloat over the rejection of the Jew but to realize that if the Jew had been cut off because of unbelief, they also could suffer a similar fate (11:11-23). The Jew could claim again the mercy of God individually, by turning from his unbelief and disobedience (11:26-32).

In chapter 12 we find a great chapter on sanctification, which comes as the fruit of justification. Those who have been dead in trespasses and sin, by having been made free from sin, are alive unto God and are to give themselves in complete dedication as "living sacrifices."

In chapter 13:1-7, Paul emphasizes to these Roman Christians the importance of being subject to civil authorities. He calls attention to God's moral law based upon the principle of "love thy neighbor as thyself," and exhorts them to be aware of the consideration and duty they owed one to another (13:8-15:13).

In chapter 16, his final greetings and farewell is found. Phoebe is commended and personal greetings were extended to the brethren in Rome with a final benediction.

STUDENT WORK

1. Where was Paul reared? _____ What occupation did he learn in his early life? _____

2. What evidence of a Grecian influence are apparent in Paul's writings?

    a) _____, b) _____,

    c) _____

3. From 15:25-27 we learn that Paul was about to set out on what mission? _____

    _____

    About what year was the Roman letter written? _____

    Was it written before or after the Corinthian letters? _____

4. What had been the desire of Paul concerning the Church at Rome which he had been prevented from fulfilling? _____

    _____

    Cite the passage: _____

5. True or False:

    _____ a. Paul established the church in Rome.

    _____ b. Peter wrote some epistles to the Romans also.

    _____ c. Paul's letter to the Roman Christians made no mention of Peter.

    _____ d. In Paul's letters written from Rome at a later date,

    _____ e. Peter was mentioned as being in Rome.

6. What is the probable way the church in Rome came into existence? _____

    _____

7. There was considerable population in the city of Rome. How did that affect the church in Rome? _____

    _____

8. Cite the passages dealing with the following:

    a. The depravity and spiritual destitution to which sin leads.

    _____

    b. Sin is just as sinful for the Jew as for the Gentile.

    _____

    c. All men have sinned and need salvation.

    _____

    d. God's way of making men righteous is by the blood of Christ, through the "faith of Christ" and can be appropriated by man's faith. _____

    _____

e. Justification was impossible by the "works of the law of Moses." _____

_____

f. The purpose of the law was to make known sin and bring the Jew as well as the Gentile under condemnation. _____

_____

g. God's way of making men just or righteous was not manifested in the law but apart from it through the Gospel of Christ.

_____

h. The Jews had not attained unto the righteousness of God because they sought it not after due order, that is, by faith.

_____

i. While the nation of the Jews was rejected because of rebellious unbelief, all Jews could be saved individually through faith.

_____

9. What key verse states the primary theme of the Roman letter? _____ What is that theme? _____

10. Upon what three principal arguments does Paul base this theme?
   a. _____
   b. _____
   c. _____

11. What theme does Paul discuss in Romans chapters 9 through 11?

_____

12. What is the primary theme of chapter 12? _____

_____

13. What does Paul teach to be the Christian's obligation toward the government in chapter 13? _____

14. What is the principle of righteousness upon which moral duty is based? _____

First Letter to the Corinthians

A. The Author.

The question of authorship of the letters to the Corinthian church has been definitely settled from the earliest times. The external evidence of the fact that Paul is the author has been maintained and even the most radical critics have conceded that they were the core of the apostle's writings. Internal evidence substantially establishes the fact that they were written by Paul. They bear his name, were written in his style, and carried his familiar greetings (1:3; 16:21-24; 2 Cor. 1:1-2; 10:1).

B. The Date.

In order to understand when the Letter was written, it is necessary to gather a few essential facts.

1. There was a letter which preceded 1 Corinthians, which has not been preserved for us. Paul mentions it in 1 Cor. 5:9. Some have thought that this first letter to which he refers is probably incorporated in 2 Corinthians, in chapter 6:14 through 7:1. Since the letters were not divided into chapters and verses when they were written, this could easily be possible, but about it we cannot be certain. We can be certain, however, that if the letter to which Paul referred was lost without trace, it contained no additional truth that is pertinent to our knowledge of God's will.

2. It was likely while Paul was in Ephesus in the year A.D. 55, that he learned that the Corinthian church was involved in several very serious problems. News came from those who were at the household of Chloe of the divisions that existed among the brethren at Corinth (1:11). Stephanas, Fortunatus and Achaicus came to Ephesus bringing news of the conditions at Corinth (16:17). Then we learn also in 1 Corinthians 7:1, that the Corinthian church had sent a letter to Paul in which they had raised a number of questions with which Paul deals in the letter we know as 1 Corinthians. This letter was evidently dispatched to Corinth by Timothy (4:17).

3. This letter stirred the Corinthian church rather deeply, and although we have no record of it directly, it seems likely that Paul must have paid a personal visit to Corinth following the first letter. He mentions in 2 Corinthians 12:14 and 13:1-2 that he is coming to them for the "third time." The only other visit of which we have a record is in Acts 18:1-17, when the church was established at Corinth.

4. Evidently the visit and the letter did not correct the situation and some scholars think that Paul wrote still another letter much more severe in tone, which has also been lost. It is thought by some that 2 Corinthains 2:4 and 7:8 are references to what the scholars have called the "severe letter."

5. Paul was very much concerned about the effect of this letter. He was waiting for Titus to come from Corinth with an answer, and when Titus was delayed, Paul set out to meet him in Macedonia (2 Cor. 2:13; 7:5, 13). When Titus brought the news that all was well, Paul then wrote 2 Corinthians, which is sometimes called "the letter of reconciliation."

C. The City.

Corinth was situated geographically at the center of the Grecian peninsula. It was built upon an isthmus and was strategically important in the conquest and defense of the Grecian peninsula. It was the only line of march for an invading or retreating army. The ancient city was fortified by a wall, some traces of which still remain.

There was a citadel rising abruptly 2,000 feet above sea level, flat, and with extensive space on its summit. Because of its steep sides it could be guarded by a few soldiers. The view from the summit to the sea, both from the east and from the west, is magnificent.

The city itself was built upon a small tableland, with no great elevation connected with the northern base of the citadel of Corinth. At the edge of the lower level lies the harbors which made Corinth the city of trade both from the east and west. Cenchreae furnished a splendid harbor on the east and Lechaeum on the west. The isthmus at the narrowest point is about three miles wide. Nearer Corinth, it was six miles in width. Toward the west was the Adriatic and toward the east the Aegean Sea.

The city had been destroyed by Mummius about 146 B.C. After it had lain in ruins for about 100 years, Julius Caesar, recognizing the strategic importance of the isthmus, established a Roman colony there, made up largely of freedmen (former galley slaves for the most part), in 46 B.C. The new city grew and attracted both Jews and Greeks, until they were more numerous than the Romans. It probably exceeded, in Paul's day, a population of 400,000 people. It has the Constitution of a colony and was the metropolis of a province given the name of Achaia. Gallio was the proconsul in Paul's day.

The character of the people of the city was reflected in the problems which the church experienced. They were characterized by dishonesty, suspicion, speculation, egotism, and a voluptuous disposition. Profligacy and vice ruled the city. The temple built to the goddess Venus (Aphrodite) supported 1,000 religious prostitutes. Surely, no place offered less opportunity for the gospel, seemingly, than Corinth, yet providence sent him there and caused Paul to stay a year and six months for God "had much people in that city."

D. The Church.

Paul established the church at Corinth (Acts 18:8), and after about three months, Silas and Timothy joined him. He found there Priscilla an Aquila.

After Paul left, Apollos went to Corinth and met with unusual success in preaching the gospel. Division arose in the church because some were glorying in men and following after them rather than after Christ.

The licentious character of the people (6:11) became evident in the sins committed by some who had great difficulty in living the Christian life. Even their worship degenerated and became so disorderly that Paul charged them with eating and drinking damnation to themselves in the observance of the Lord's Supper (11:30).

This church had also been disturbed by Judaizing teachers who undertook to exalt themselves by destroying the confidence which the Corinthian brethren had in Paul.

Probably no letter written in the New Testament more clearly reveals the character and problems of the people to whom it was addressed than the Corinthian letters. Figuratively, Paul removed the roof and allowed us to have a view into these internal problems and the character of this congregation.

E. The 1 Corinthian Letter.

The address of this letter is in itself significant. Paul wrote unto the "church of God which is at Corinth, even them which are sanctified in Christ Jesus, called to be saints," and then he enlarged the scope of the letter to include "all that call upon the name of the Lord Jesus Christ in every place."

1. In the first four chapters of 1 Corinthians, Paul deals with the division. In doing so, he pointed out several major reasons for it: a. Their trusting in human wisdom; b. their glorying in men rather than

The Temple of Apollo at Corinth. Paul warned the saints about the meat offered in the "idol's temple" (1 Cor. 8:10).

in Christ; c. their carnality of mind which made spiritual understanding and reception of truth impossible; d. their failure to distinguish between things that were Holy and things profane, and consequently, their defilement of the Temple of God.

2. The remedy for this division prescribed by Paul is found in 1 Corinthians 1:10: a. "That ye speak the same thing"; b. "that there be no divisions among you"; c. "that you be perfected together in the same mind and in the same judgment."

3. In chapter 5 Paul deals with the corrupt influence of heathen morality which had caused the church at Corinth to harbor a man who flagrantly disregarded common decency and righteousness by living in open adultery with his father's wife, his own stepmother. Paul's instruction concerning the correction of this grievous wrong was that they publicly withdraw from him (4:5), and that they individually enforce this withdrawal by "having no company with him" (5:9).

4. Many of these Corinthian Christians were evidently engaged in the commerce and industry for which the city was famous and became sometimes involved, even with each other, in financial disputes and other disagreements, and they were disposed to settle their differences in courts before heathen judges. This, Paul condemns and instructs them how they should be settled (6:1-11).

5. Their moral laxity made it difficult for them to honor marriage as they should and one whole chapter was devoted to answering questions about this relationship (chapter 7). The rules peculiar to this chapter were laid down, not as general rules to govern in all circumstances, but were to be limited in their application to the special circumstances which Paul had in mind, and which he describes as the "present distress" (7:26-32).

6. The practice of eating for food the remnants of the bodies of animals which had been offered in heathen sacrifice had been called in question by Jewish brethren. Paul taught that this was a matter of personal liberty, if it did not violate their own consciences, but that they were not to exercise such personal liberty, if it meant the destruction of brethren in Christ (chapters 8 and 10).

7. In 1 Corinthians 9, Paul discusses the obligation of the church to support and sustain those who give their time to the teaching and preaching of the gospel of Christ.

8. The eleventh chapter of 1 Corinthians deals with abuses in the assembly for worship. Verses 1 through 16 emphasize God's order of authority and point out that certain women were violating it by publicly praying and prophesying in the assembly and further disrespecting their obligations to be in subjection to man, by refusing to wear the veil, which in the "East" and among the Greeks was a customary token of a woman's recognition of the authority of man over her.

9. Their practice of having a feast in the assembly before they observed the Lord's Supper, and glutting themselves with food and

wine so that they could not spiritually discern the meaning of the Lord's Supper, Paul condemns (11:19-34). He instructs them that when they come together it ought to be for worship and that they ought to do their eating and drinking in their own houses.

10. Due to their exaltation of selfish ambitions and fleshly values, they had fallen into serious dispute and strife about which of the spiritual gifts with which they had been endowed should be given priority. In chapters 12, 13 and 14, Paul deals with this matter, discussing the nature of these gifts, their utility and duration, the indispensability of each member in his personal capacity to serve, and emphasizes the necessity of love as a motive in all of it.

11. There were evidently some among them who were questioning the resurrection from the dead (15:12). Paul declares: a. Christ has risen (15:1-11); b. the meaning of the resurrection (15:12-57); c. the universality of the resurrection because Christ has been raised (15:20-22); and d. the Christian is to have a new body in the resurrection (15:42-49) and shall "inherit the kingdom of God" (15:50).

12. The final problem with which Paul deals in the letter is the question of how the collection for the poor among the saints in Jerusalem was to be raised. First Corinthians 16:2 shows the only Divine plan that God has ever given for financing the work of the church.

In this matter of benevolence the church was to raise its own contribution by the giving of its own members on the first day of the week (16:2). The principle of what should be done with this money is made evident by the fact that the church was to select its own messengers to entrust with the delivery of this contribution (16:3-4). Finally, it is apparent that the contribution was to be delivered for distribution to the church that was in need, namely, Jerusalem, and the pattern in Acts 11:27-30 shows that it was put in the hands of the elders of the local church who had the oversight of its distribution.

The 1 Corinthian letter closes with personal exhortations and salutations.

STUDENT WORK

1. What are the evidences that Paul was the author of the two letters to the Corinthians? a. _____
   b. _____, c. _____
2. From whom did Paul learn while he was at Ephesus about the condition of the Corinthian Church? _____, Passage
   _____.
3. How do we know that Paul had written a previous letter to Corinth? Passage _____
4. Cite the passage that tells us that the Corinthians had written Paul asking some questions about various problems: _____

58

5. What passage gives us the history of the establishment of the Corinthian Church on his first visit there? _____
6. What passages indicate that Paul had visited Corinth a second time? a. _____, b. _____
7. Where was Corinth located? _____
   What was the character of its citizens? _____
   What were they religiously? _____
8. What was one of the basic causes of so many problems in the Corinthian Church? Give passages: _____
9. What problem in this church did Paul deal with in the first four chapters? _____ How did this condition misrepresent Christ? _____
   Give passage: _____
10. Give two reasons that Paul assigns for wearing the name of Christ?
    a. _____, passage _____
    b. _____, passage _____
11. What three remedies did Paul give the Corinthians for this division that existed?
    a. _____
    b. _____
    c. _____
    Give passage: _____
12. What serious problem did Paul discuss in chapter 5? _____
    What did he command them to do in order to solve it? _____
13. What chapter deals with the problem of how to settle their personal difficulties and differences? _____
14. What does Paul discuss in chapter 7? _____
    What verse in that chapter gives the reason for his instructions on this subject? _____ What was it? _____
15. What rules did Paul lay down to guide Christians in matters of "personal liberty"?
    a. _____ passage _____
    b. _____ passage _____
16. Name some of the arguments Paul made in chapter 9 to prove that "they which preach the Gospel should live of the Gospel."
    _____
    _____

59

17. What example on apostasy does Paul use to warn of its danger in chapter 10? _____

18. What abuses were being practiced in the assembly of the Corinthians? (chapter 11)
   a. _____ , b. _____

19. What is the subject matter of chapters 12, 13, and 14? _____
   _____

20. What two principles does Paul prescribe to regulate activity in the assembly?
   a. _____
   b. _____

21. What are the consequences of disbelieving the resurrection of Christ pointed out in chapter 15? a. _____ ,
   b. _____ ,   c. _____ ,
   d. _____ ,   e. _____ .

22. What pattern did Paul give both to the Corinthians by which to raise the resources to fulfill the obligation they had toward relieving the poor saints? _____
   Passage _____
   How were they to send this contribution to the Jerusalem church?
   _____ Passage _____

Second Letter to the Corinthians

A. The Author.

Both the external and internal evidence points unquestionably to the fact that 2 Corinthians was also written to the Corinthian church by Paul. The second letter evidently did not become circulated as early as the first and hence, we do not find it quoted by writers as early as was the first. Certain early writers, however, did quote from it, such as Polycarp, Athenagoras, Theophilus of Antioch, Tertullian, and Clement of Alexandria. From the year 175 on, there is an abundance of evidence that 2 Corinthians was recognized as an epistle of Paul.

The internal evidence also is very strong. The writer twice refers to himself as Paul (1:1; 10:1). The style of the letter in its naturalness and vividness, as well as the character of its details, give strong proof of Paul's being its author.

In addition to this, its close relationship with the first Corinthian letter, which unquestionably was written by Paul, is likewise an indication that Paul was the author of this one also.

B. The Date.

Paul left Ephesus shortly after writing the first epistle to Corinth. From 2 Corinthians 12:14 and 13:1, since Paul writes of coming to them a "third time," it is possible that he made a brief trip across the Aegean Sea to Corinth, after the first letter had been written. Acts 20 tells us that he went to Macedonia to meet Titus, having failed to find him at Troas, and having found Titus, he received from him news concerning the situation in the church at Corinth. It was from Macedonia, probably Philippi, that Paul wrote the second epistle (7:5-16). It must have, therefore, followed the other letter to the Corinthian church after only a few months and was likely written somewhere around 56 or 57 A.D.

C. The Purpose of the Letter.

The second letter to the Corinthians is autobiographical in nature. It is intimately personal, made up of explanation, defense, protest, appeal, reproach, warnings, and is characterized by the most subtle irony.

In spite of Paul's denunciation of factions in 1 Corinthians, the party spirit was not corrected. It seems likely that the group of Judaizing teachers that had opposed and undermined the work of Paul almost everywhere he had gone, had come to Corinth also, and through their encouragement and leadership the Jewish party had gained in strength and encouraged them to challenge the authority of Paul. They had evidently represented themselves as purely "Christ's"

(10:7) and as "Apostles of Christ" (11:13). This party had made false attacks against Paul and had insulted and opposed him in every possible way. They were thus seeking to destroy Paul's influence that they might the better offset his teaching and establish themselves in the confidence of the Corinthian brethren.

These circumstances made it necessary for Paul to engage in a defense of himself rather extensively in this letter. This defense was not in the interest of self vindication in any sense, but rather for the purpose of preserving his influence and protecting the Corinthians against these false teachers. In the first seven chapters of the letter, Paul repeatedly defends his ministry in preaching the gospel to the Gentiles. In chapters 10 through 13, he presents a powerful defense of his apostolic office and authority. In chapters 8 and 9, in the very midst of the letter, he digresses from both lines of thought to stir up the Corinthians in an exhortation that they carry out their intention and promise to make up a contribution for the poor among the saints in Jerusalem.

D. Contents and Character.

1. In defense of his ministry, Paul denies that he had shown any fickleness, or instability of character, or integrity in his failure to come to them personally as he had promised (1:15-20). In these verses he calls their attention to the fact that his plans were always dependent upon the providential will of Almighty God. In the first part of chapter one, he points out that in the great trial which he endured in Asia (Acts 18), in which his life had been seriously endangered, that God had comforted him and delivered him that he might comfort them.

2. He had been accused of being severe and austere in his letters, but weak in his personal presence (19:9-11). He promised in answer to this that if it became necessary for him to do so, he would be just as severe with them personally when he came as he had been in the letters that he had written. In 2 Corinthians 2, he refers to the fact that he had written them severely, with anguish of heart and many tears; not, however, for the purpose of grieving them. He calls also to their attention the fact that the sinful man with which he had dealt in 1 Corinthians 5 should be completely forgiven and reinstated in their fellowship, and their love confirmed toward him, since he had repented. In chapter 3, he calls to their attention that they themselves are the evidence of the effectiveness of his ministry (3:1-3). In this same chapter he draws a contrast between the Law of Moses and the gospel of Christ that is very impressive. He points out that the Law of Moses was: a. Written and engraven on tables of stone, while the gospel of Christ is written in the heart by the Spirit (3:3); b. he designates the Law of Moses as the "ministration of condemnation," and designates the New Covenant, or the gospel, as the "ministration of righteousness" (3:9); c. the Law of Moses is referred to as the "ministration of death," while the gospel of Christ is called the

"ministration of the Spirit" (3:6-7); d. he refers to the Law of Moses as "that which is done away" and to the gospel of Christ as "that which remaineth" (3:11). This was his answer to the Judaizers, showing that the New Covenant is more glorious than the Old.

3. In chapter 4, Paul emphasizes that in his ministry as an "earthen vessel" God's purpose was to cause "light to shine out of darkness" and to shed abroad in the hearts of men "the light of the knowledge of the glory of God," which was first revealed in the person of Christ, but is now revealed in the gospel which Paul and others who spoke by inspiration revealed and preached (4:1-7). In the latter part of chapter 4, he points out the persecutions that he had endured for the sake of fulfilling his ministry and affirms his willingness to undergo such suffering for their sakes (4:8-12).

4. No finer description of the proper perspective or outlook one can have in life can be found in the entire scriptures than Paul's statement from chapter 4:13 and 5:11. In this entire section, the "Spirit of faith" is to believe and speak as it is written. In evaluating the factors that enter our outlook on life, Paul bases his statement on: 1. The eternal nature of the spirit that dwells within a man; b. things which we can see are temporal and will not last, while things which are spiritual are eternal; c. we will one day put off that which is mortal and be clothed with immortality through the experiences of death and the resurrection, this world is not our home; d. since we are creatures of ability, we are responsible unto God and must give an account before the judgment seat of Christ.

5. In 5:12-21, Paul points out that a man commending himself or glorying in appearance is entirely vain. We ought to be sober minded enough to know that Christ died for us and that it is only in Christ that the old man can be crucified, we can be new creatures, and reconciled unto God. In this connection he affirms that in his ministry as an apostle he was an "ambassador for Christ" (v. 20), and that to him had been committed the "word of reconciliation."

6. He besought them not to receive the grace of God in vain and not to blame any offense upon his ministry for God, but recalled to them that his ministry had been wrought among them in much patience, afflictions, necessities, distresses, etc. (6:1-13).

7. In chapter 6:14-18, Paul admonishes them to compromise in no way or undertake to have any fellowship with the idolatry that characterized the heathen people of that city, but to keep themselves "separate" and to "cleanse ourselves from all filthiness of the flesh and spirit, perfecting holiness in the fear of God" (6:17-7:1).

8. In the last part of chapter 7 (v. 2-16), he assures them of his continued love for them, that he glories in them and will continue to be concerned about them. He had been comforted by the coming of Titus who assured him that his letter concerning their problems, and the case of the adulterous man (1 Cor. 5), had accomplished the result and had brought about repentance and a correction of the wrong. He contrasts Godly sorrow that works repentance unto life

with worldly sorrow that may be full of regret for various reasons but does not bring genuine repentance and, therefore, results in death. He expresses confidence in them in all things.

9. Chapters 8 and 9 of the second letter are given over to a discussion of and an exhortation concerning the contribution which they had promised more than a year before for the relief of "the poor among the saints in Jerusalem." He uses the brethren of Macedonia, who in the deepness of their poverty, had abounded in liberality and given beyond their ability for this same cause, as an example, and exhorts the Corinthians to exercise themselves in the fulfillment of that which they had obligated themselves to do in the grace of Christian liberality and as a demonstration of the sincerity of their love. He suggests that their abundance be the means of supplying the lack upon the part of these Jerusalem saints, in order that there might be an equality, and points out the gathering of the manna in the wilderness as an example (Ex. 16:18).

From these two chapters we are able to deduce easily the Lord's "pattern" for one church helping another, as follows: a. The church receiving was a church unable to provide for its own, therefore, in need of help; b. the church contributing raised its own money by the giving of its own members in the assembly on the first day of the week (1 Cor. 16:1-4); c. the contributing church sent its money through an individual messenger which was chosen by them (1 Cor. 16:3-4; 2 Cor. 8:19); d. from another example we learn that this contribution was to be delivered to the elders of the church in need (Acts 11:27-30).

10. In chapter 9, Paul gives the wonderful assurance that when a Christian gives as he "has purposed in his heart," cheerfully, "God is able to make all grace abound . . . that ye always having all sufficiency in all things, may abound to every good work." He further assures them that their giving will enrich "in everything to all bountifulness which causeth through us thanksgiving to God."

11. In chapters 10, 11 and 12, Paul makes a direct defense of his apostleship: a. By affirming his authority as an apostle; b. by the fact that his labors and their fruits gave evidence of the Lord's commendation and made it unnecessary for him to commend himself; c. by calling to their attention the fact that he had begotten them in Christ through the gospel and had, as he expresses it in chapter 11 "espoused them as a chaste virgin to Christ;" d. he affirms that he was not a whit behind the chiefest apostle and that he had been abased only in the fact that he had preached the gospel to them without receiving or accepting anything from them but was supported by other churches (this was evidently providential guidance that he might "cut off occasion from them which desire occasion; that wherein they glory, they may be found even as we"); e. he brands the false teachers as false apostles in their claims and suggests that they have been "transformed into ministers of righteousness" by Satan, and that their end will be according to their works; f. in 11:18-22, he

points out he had more reason to glory in the flesh than any of them; g. in 11:23-33, he points out that he had truly wrought the "signs of an apostle," which is evidently a reference to his miraculous endowments; h. he refers to an experience which coincides with his being stoned at Lystra and dragged out of the city and left for dead (Acts 14:19), and affirms that he had been "caught up into Paradise and heard unspeakable words which is not lawful for man to utter;" i. he referred to a thorn in the flesh which had been of great trouble to him and that he had prayed for the Lord to remove it but had been only given the assurance "my grace is sufficient for thee for my strength is made perfect in weakness."

12. The last part of chapters 12 and 13 are given over to specific exhortations that they might "walk in the same spirit," be united among themselves, and "examine yourselves, whether ye be in the faith." He bids them farewell with the exhortation "be perfect, be of good comfort, be of one mind, live in peace; and the God of love and peace shall be with you" (13:11).

STUDENT WORK

1. 2 Corinthians was written from what place and at what time?

   _____

2. Who had disturbed the Corinthian church and tried to destroy their confidence in Paul? _____

   How had they represented themselves? _____

3. Paul made an extended defense of himself in 2 Corinthians and related much of his own personal history. Why? _____

   _____

4. What does he defend in chapters 1-7? _____

   In chapters 10-13? _____

5. To what does he devote chapters 8 and 9? _____

6. List some of the charges against which Paul defends himself?

   a. _____ ,   b. _____ ,

   c. _____ ,   d. _____ ,

   e. _____

7. What did Paul instruct them to do about the sinful man who had repented?

   _____

8. What are the four points of contrast between the law of Moses and the gospel of Christ given in chapter 3?

LAW OF MOSES	GOSPEL OF CHRIST
_____	_____
_____	_____
_____	_____
_____	_____

9. What procedure did God use in shedding forth into the hearts of men "the light of the glorious Gospel of Christ"? (chapter 4:1-7)

_____

_____

10. What does Paul say the perspective (viewpoint) of the Christian life would be? (chapters 4:8-5:10) What is the basis of this point of view? Discuss. _____

_____

11. Define "the spirit of faith" (4:13): _____

_____

12. In what official capacity did Paul affirm that he served in the Kingdom of Christ? _____

13. What does he give in chapter 6:1-13 as evidence of his faithfulness in his ministry? _____

14. What exhortation is given in chapter 6:14-7:1? _____

_____

15. What is dealt with in chapters 8 and 9? What are the essential points in the divine pattern Paul gives for one church helping another church that is in need?
   a. _____
   b. _____
   c. _____
   d. _____

16. Name some of the defenses he makes of his apostleship? (chapters 10, 11, 12)
   a. _____ ,   b. _____ ,
   c. _____ ,   d. _____ ,
   e. _____ ,   f. _____

17. Describe the suffering Paul had experienced for the sake of Christ (11:23-28).

_____

18. What was his final exhortation (13:11)? _____

_____

Letter to the Galations

A. The Author.

There is no book in the Bible, the authorship of which is more certain that the epistle Paul wrote to the churches in Galatia. It is so certain from the internal evidence that Paul is its author that it cannot be called in question. In the salutation it is addressed from "Paul, an Apostle, (not of men, neither by man, but by Jesus Christ, and God the Father, who raised him from the dead;) And all the brethren which are with me, Unto the churches of Galatia."

The first two chapters of the letter constitute a rather detailed autobiography of Paul's life from the time of his conversion to the writing of the letter. He tells us in chapter 2 of his return to Jerusalem with Barnabas and Titus "after 14 years." This means that there were 14 years from the time of his first visit to Jerusalem after his conversion recorded in Acts 9, at which time he spent only 15 days. Prior to this first visit the Divine record tells us that he had spent three years after his conversion preaching in Arabia and that he had returned to Jerusalem through Damascus.

He had spent some time preaching in the regions of Syria and

The Street called Straight in the modern city of Damascus. Even though this street is several feet above the level of the city in which Paul obeyed the Gospel and began his work for Christ it is still a vivid reminder of the ancient city street.

Cilicia during this 14 years, which included his work in Antioch as recorded in Acts 11. So, the letter to the Galatians was undoubtedly written by the Apostle Paul.

B. The Date of Its Writing.

We do not know the precise year of Paul's conversion, but it must have occurred somewhere between A.D. 31 and 36. The 17 years intervening between the time of his conversion and the visit to Jerusalem, which he identifies as "after 14 years" (2:1), would bring the writing of the letter to a time subsequent to the meeting in Jerusalem to settle the matter of circumcision (Acts 15). The letter was also written following the visit of Peter to Antioch after the Jerusalem meeting (2:11-14). This would at least place the date of its writing after A.D. 49, for this is approximately the year when the Jerusalem meeting concerning circumcision was held. It was likely written after 1 Thessalonians, which can be dated about A.D. 50 to 51.

Many of the scholars think Galatians fits in between 2 Corinthians and Romans as to date, and that it was, therefore, probably written between 55 and 57 A.D.

C. To Whom It Was Written.

Galatia was originally an area in the northeastern part of Asia Minor. It is the Greek form of the word corresponding with the Roman "Gallia," or Gaul. It was one of the original provinces of Asia Minor and received its name from the circumstance of its being inhabited by the Gauls. They had overrun Rome in the 4th Century B.C. and had invaded Asia Minor and northern Greece in the 3rd Century B.C. A part of them had remained in Galatia, which had a mixed population of Greek, Roman and Jewish people also. They were reputed to be quick tempered, impulsive, and yet, fickle. They were impressed readily and easily influenced, and quick to give up. They received Paul with enthusiastic joy and then suddenly turned from him (4:13-16). Two visits of Paul to Galatia are recorded in Acts; the first during his second missionary journey (Acts 16:6), and the second at the beginning of his third journey (Acts 18:23). Galatians 4:13-16 indicates that the letter was written after his second visit.

When the Romans subjugated the land of Asia Minor in 25 B.C., they reorganized the territory to include an area to the south of the original Gaulic region and designated the whole new province, Galatia. There has been some controversy about whether or not Paul addressed his letter to the Roman Province of Galatia or to the original Province of Galatia. Luke uses the name in both senses in the record of Acts of the Apostles. Paul preached in south Galatia on his first tour. South Galatia included the churches in Pisidia, Lycaonia and Phrygia, but the second visit recorded in Acts 16:6 evidently refers to his going into north Galatia. The natural conclusion would be that Paul addressed the letter to all of the churches in the entire Roman Province of Galatia.

D. The Purpose of the Epistle.
1. The reason for the writing of this letter is evident from the contents, as is its authorship. The Galatian churches had begun well (5:7), but soon after Paul's departure, Judaizing teachers had drawn them away to the form of error mentioned in Acts of the Apostles (15:1), that is, "except ye be circumcised after the manner of Moses, ye cannot be saved." They sought to impose on all the Gentile converts fleshly circumcision, as practiced by the Jews, as essential to salvation. Thus, they bound redemption in Christ to the Law of Moses and taught justification as dependent upon the works of the Law, even though it had been provided by Christ and His sacrifice. This, of course, was not only false, but it was fundamental error. The main section of Galatians was directed against it by Paul with unsparing severity, while at the same time manifesting a wonderful tenderness of spirit.

2. His argument in Galatians that "by the works of the Law can no flesh be justified" parallels his argument on that point in the Roman letter and the two should be studied together concerning this matter. Paul's argument against this false doctrine in Galatians is certainly controversial in its form and yet, is expressed with warmth and vehemence, and becomes a Divine model by which we learn how fundamental error should be treated.

3. These Judaizing teachers, as they usually did, had attacked the apostleship of Paul. They worked upon the theory that if they could destroy confidence in him as an Apostle of Christ, they could more easily influence the people who had been converted by him and establish their false doctrine. One of the sections of the letter deals particularly with this matter, as did 2 Corinthians.

E. Contents and Character.
The epistle naturally falls into three divisions:
1. The first is mainly historic (chapters 1 and 2). The false teachers had charged that Paul was not one of the twelve original Apostles and that he was not, therefore, an Apostle at all, and that what he knew about Christ and His gospel he had learned from men. They sought to array Paul against Peter and the other Apostles in the matter of circumcision and the Law of Moses. This false charge explains why Paul gives in the first two chapters in some detail an autobiography of his life as a Christian and his service to the Lord.

a. He affirms that his Apostleship is "not of men, neither by man, but by Jesus Christ and God the Father" (1:1).

b. He also affirms that the gospel which he preaches was not received of man, nor taught by man, but that it came to him by the revelation of Jesus Christ (1:11-12).

c. That upon his conversion he went not up to Jerusalem to

receive instruction from the Apostles, but into Arabia where he spent three years (1:15-17), and that after three years he made a brief visit of 15 days to Jerusalem where he saw Peter and James only (1:20-24).

d. He calls attention also to the fact that 14 years after this first visit he went up to Jerusalem not just because the brethren wanted him to go, but "by revelation;" not to be instructed by the Apostles, but to confer with them concerning preaching the gospel to the Gentiles, which task had been committed to him by the Lord, and that he was accorded full recognition by "James, Cephas and John who were reckoned as pillars" (2:1-10).

e. He points out also to sustain his Apostolic authority and to disprove the charge of dependence upon other Apostles, that when Peter came to Antioch, he withstood him to the face on the question of circumcision, because he had been guilty of hypocrisy through fear of Jewish brethren. In giving us this account, he points out the substance of the rebuke administered by him to Peter which contains an argument (drawn in part from Peter's own practice) against compelling the Gentiles to live as the Jews (2:11-21).

2. The second part of the letter unfolds the great argument that God's way of making men just or righteous is by faith in Christ rather than by the works of the Law of Moses.

a. Abraham was justified by faith before the Law, as an example (3:6-9, 18).

b. The Law cannot justify sinners but only condemns (3:10-12).

c. Christ redeems men from the curse of the Law and makes all the children of Abraham, and heirs to all the promises which God made to him, through faith in the gospel (3:13-15).

d. The Abrahamic covenant based upon faith preceded the Mosaic Law and could not be annulled by it (3:15-17).

e. The purpose of the Law was not to justify but to prepare men to accept Christ, in whom all distinction between Jew and Gentile is abolished (3:19-29).

f. Before Christ, the people of God were like a child who has not received his inheritance, but is kept under tutors and governors (like the Law safeguarded the Jews), but who, in Christ, arrives at full age and is given possession of the inheritance (4:1-7).

3. The Apostle adds (4:8-5:12) various arguments and illustrations, making pointed reference to the false teachers who were subverting the simplicity of the faith in Christ. He solemnly warns the Galatian Christians that when they receive circumcision in the flesh, they bind themselves to keep the whole Law as ground of their justification. This means that they had "fallen from grace" (5:4), so that "Christ is become of no effect."

4. The third part of the Galatian letter is of practical character. The Apostle, with much affection, exhorts the Galatians to use their Christian liberty in a worthy manner and to put to death their fleshly lusts. He points out their obligation to restore brethren who have

been overtaken in sin, to bear one another's burdens and to be diligent in every good work. The first part of chapter 6 very pointedly emphasizes their duty to one another as brethren in the Lord (6:1-10). In the last part Paul contrasts the vainglory and hypocrisy of the Judaizing false teachers with his own stedfast purpose to "glory only in the Cross of Christ" in whom "neither circumcision availeth anything nor uncircumcision, but a new creature" (6:12-16).

5. In addition to the above detailed analysis of the contents of Galatians, it should be kept in mind as one reads and studies the letter, that the most common exhortation which occurs in it is the exhortation to hold stedfastly to the "liberty" that is in Christ and not be bound again to the Law of Moses or brought again in subjection to fleshly lusts, but rather to walk after the Spirit and not after the flesh (5:1-26). To study the letter and miss this message would mean to fail to see the basic exhortation underneath all of it: "Stand fast in the liberty wherewith Christ hath made us free, and be not entangled again with the yoke of bondage" (5:1). It is this exhortation that has caused the Galatian Epistle commonly to be called the "Magna Carta of Christian Liberty."

STUDENT WORK

1. What are the evidences of Paul's authorship of Galatians?

   a. _____ ,   b. _____

2. Was Galatians written before or after the meeting about circumcision in Jerusalem in Acts 15? _____

3. Was Galatians written to an individual ( ), a local church ( ), or to several churches ( )? (Check the correct answer)

4. Galatia had been settled by the _____ and took its name from them.

5. Where was Galatia and by whom was the province ruled?_____
   _____

6. What passage indicates Paul had visited Galatia twice before he wrote the letter? _____

7. Who had "hindered" the Galatians and what false doctrine did they teach? _____
   _____

8. What argument in Galatians is parallel to Romans? _____
   _____

9. How does Galatians set a pattern for dealing with error?_____
   _____

10. What attack did these Judaizing teachers make upon Paul?_____
    _____

11. What defenses did Paul offer against this attack?

a. _____, b. _____,

c. _____, d. _____,

e. _____

12. What great theme does the second section of Galatians (chapters 3. 3 and 4) deal with? _____

_____

13. State the arguments made in the following passages:

3:6-9, 18 _____

3:10-12 _____

3:15-17 _____

3:19-29 _____

4:1-7 _____

14. What did Paul warn the Galatians would be the consequence of binding fleshly circumcision?

_____

15. What does Paul contrast in Galatians 5? _____

16. What are some of the duties Christians owe to each other pointed out by Paul in chapter 6?

a. _____

b. _____

c. _____

d. _____

e. _____

f. _____

Letter to the Ephesians

A. The City of Ephesus.

Ephesus was the capitol of Pro-consular Asia. It was about a mile from the seacoast and was the great religious, commerical and political center of Asia. There were two buildings that gave it prominence. First, a Great Theatre was there which is said to have had a seating capacity of 50,000 people, and second, the Temple of Diana which was one of the Seven Wonders of the World. The temple was 342 feet long and 164 feet wide, built of finest marble. It was supported by a mass of columns 56 feet high. It took 220 years to build it. It was the center of the worship of the goddess, Diana, which Luke mentioned (Acts 19:23-41). It was, perhaps, next to Rome, the most important city that Paul visited.

We read of the establishing of the church in Ephesus on the second missionary tour (Acts 18:18-21). Priscilla and Aquila evidently remained there when Paul left. While he was on his third journey, he spent three years preaching there (Acts 20:31). During this period he aroused, by his preaching against heathen worship, enough opposition to cause a riot, endanger his life, and make it necessary for him to leave and go into Macedonia (Acts 20:1). On his third journey he stopped at Miletus, 30 miles away, and sent for the elders of the Ephesian church, to whom he delivered his farewell address before going to Jerusalem (Acts 20:16-38). The church in this city, not only is prominent in the book of Acts and the history of Paul's work, but also because of the letter that he directed to it, and in addition, for the fact that it was one of the "seven churches of Asia" to which Jesus himself also wrote a letter by John.

Very evidently, while Paul was in Asia, much evangelism was carried on throughout the area of Asia Minor and many other churches were established. Luke records "that all they which dwelt in Asia heard the word of the Lord Jesus, both Jews and Greeks" (Acts 19:10).

B. Date of Writing.

While there has been a great deal of discussion among the scholars concerning the question of whether the Ephesian letter was written while Paul was in prison in Caesarea, Rome, or Ephesus, for he was in prison at all three places; yet, the weight of the evidence clearly and conclusively points to the fact that the Ephesian letter was one of the "prison epistles" written from Rome, and the date must have been 62 or 63 A.D.

C. The Purpose of the Letter.

From the information gathered in the speech that Paul made to the Ephesian elders recorded in Acts 20, the Ephesian letter

73

itself, the letters that Paul directed to Timothy while he was preaching in Ephesus, and from the letter that Jesus wrote by John to this church, it is easy to learn that apostasy was impending and that the chief purpose of Paul in writing the letter, as well as in his address to the elders and his letters to Timothy, was the prevention of apostasy on the part of the church. The church was apparently being threatened by false doctrines. These false doctrines took the form of Judaism and Gnosticism, which were characteristic of the whole of Asia Minor, and the contents of the letter evidence very clearly that Paul was addressing himself to these false doctrines along with the danger of their reverting to the seductive and licentious heathen religion from which they had turned away.

The epistle was probably intended to be a general epistle to be circulated and read for the instruction of the churches throughout Asia Minor. The words, "in Ephesus," are lacking in some ancient manuscripts, although they are present in others. Some have supposed that since this address is lacking in some manuscripts, that it was to be an epistle not only for Ephesus, but for the other churches as well. In connection with this, it has also been suggested that it is the Laodicean epistle referred to in Colossians 4:16. The remarks of Paul in such passages as 1:15 ff. and 6:22, seem to indicate, however, that while it may have been intended as a letter for general circulation, the writer also had in mind a definite group.

D. Contents and Character.

This epistle falls naturally into two divisions of about equal length, the first argumentative and the second practical. In the argumentative section Paul sets forth:

1. The plan of God from eternity for human redemption through Jesus Christ and in the church (1:3-23; 3:8-12).

2. This redemptive plan for all humanity, formed in the mind of God before the world began, has been fulfilled in the coming of Christ as a Savior and the establishment of the church, the body of Christ, in which all the fullness of God's grace can be enjoyed. It is offered unto men through and in the gospel revealed through the Apostles and prophets by the Holy Spirit (1:9-14; 3:1-7).

3. The scheme of redemption for all humanity provides for no distinction between the Jew and the Gentile in the body of Christ, but of the two Christ has made, by the cross, "one new man, so making peace," and broken down the middle wall of partition that existed between them, having abolished by his death, the Law of Commandments contained in ordinances (2:11-16).

4. God's plan for human redemption is characterized by a complete unity in both principle and arrangement, the essential elements of which are outlined in Ephesians 4:1-6.

5. Paul emphasizes in the Ephesian letter that the redemption provided in God's plan is, in its fullness, to be enjoyed only in the church, the body of Christ, who is its head (1:20-23; 2:13-16, 19-22; 3:13-21).

6. Paul emphasizes further to these Ephesian Christians the necessity of having "no fellowship with the unfruitful works of darkness" (5:7-13), in order to offset the Gnostic teaching that purity of life in the flesh was of no importance if sanctification of the spirit was achieved. This was an important part of the whole Gnostic system of religion. It was a system made up of a combination of human philosophy and religion. It was necessary, therefore, for Paul to emphasize the absolute essentiality of the proper relationship with Christ as the head from whom the needs of all the body might be supplied (4:16). He gave emphasis also to the fact in connection with this point, that while they had been "dead in trespasses and sin," they had been redeemed by the grace of God through their faith, and it was essential in order to continue to enjoy this redemption, that they should continue to walk in the good works which God had ordained (2:1-10; 4:17-5:13).

7. He admonishes them that they not be careless and indifferent, but diligent in doing the will of the Lord in all of the individual relationships in life (5:14-6:9).

8. He closes the letter with an exhortation that they might "put on the whole armor of God" that they might stand against the "wiles of the devil" in the evil day and with an exhortation that they should pray always not only for him, but for all the saints (6:10-24).

E. Distinctive Themes.

Several distinctive themes run all the way through the Ephesian letter:

1. It is the great epistle of the entire New Testament on the church. Its general theme could well be said to be Christ and the church. In it the church is set forth as: a. The Body of Christ (1:23); b. the Temple of God, "God's habitation in the Spirit" (2:19-22); c. the Family of God (2:19; 3:14-15); d. the Bride of Christ (5:22-32); e. "the fulness of him that filleth all in all" (1:23).

In the letter to the Colossian church, Paul emphasizes the fundamental truth that "Christ is the fulness of God." In the Ephesian letter, he defines "the church as the fulness of Christ." These two expressions are comparable. Christ, as the "fulness of God," means that in Christ all that God means to a human soul and all that His grace has provided for our redemption can be found and only in Christ (1:3). The church, as the "fulness of Christ," means that all which Christ can mean to a human soul can be enjoyed in His body which is the church, and in it only. It further means that all of the provisions of God's grace through Jesus Christ can be enjoyed only in the church.

2. In the Ephesian letter, the expression, "in Christ," is the most common expression to be found. It occurs quite a number of times. For example, in Ephesians (1:3, 4, 7, 9, 10, 20; 2:10, 13, 21, 22; 3:6, 11, 12, 21; 4:21, 32). Through parallel passages, we learn in 2:13 and 2:16, that the expression "in Christ," as it is commonly used, denotes

relationship and means to be in the spiritual body of Christ, which is the church.

3. Since it has been pointed out that "Christ and the Church" is the main theme of the Ephesian letter, or the church "as the fulness of Christ," it is well to suggest to the student that there are three main arguments on this theme developed in the Ephesian letter and that a climax in the discussion of this theme is reached in 5:22-32. They are: a. The attitude of Christ toward the church, namely His love for it; b. the sacrifice Christ made for the church ("Christ also loved the church and also gave Himself up for it," 5:25); c. the very vital relationship which Christ sustains to the church as pointed out in subdivision 5 of paragraph D.

4. Paul gives emphasis to the fact that the plan of salvation, as it is revealed in the gospel, was formulated in the "eternal purpose" of God before the world began and has been fulfilled: a. In Christ as a savior; b. in the revelation of the mystery of God in the gospel; c. in the church as the fulness of Christ (3:1-12; 1:3-14).

5. "Walk," denoting a course of conduct or way of life, is used seven times in this letter: a. "In time past ye walked according to the course of this world" (2:2); b. "created in Christ Jesus unto good works, which God hath before ordained that we should walk in them" (2:10); c. "walk worthy of the vocation wherewith you were called" (4:1); d. "walk not as other Gentiles walk, in the vanity of their mind" (4:17); e. "walk in love" (5:21); f. "walk as children of light" (5:8); g. "walk . . . as wise" (5:15).

6. UNITY

a. The distinction and enmity destroyed between Jew and Gentile by the death of Christ, "one new man so making peace" (2:15).

b. "Reconcile both unto God in one body by the cross" (2:16).

c. "Through Him we both have access by one Spirit unto the Father" (2:18).

d. "Endeavoring to keep the unity of the Spirit in the bond of peace (4:3 ff.).

(1) One God — Unity in worship.

(2) One Lord — Unity in authority

(3) One Spirit — Unity in life.

(4) One Faith — Unity in message.

(5) One Baptism — Unity in obedience.

(6) One Body — Unity in organization and fellowship.

(7) One Hope — Unity in desire and expectation.

STUDENT WORK

1. Where was Ephesus located? _____

What goddess was worshipped in a great temple built there?

_____

76

2. When was the church established there? _____
   Give the passage recording it: _____
   How long did Paul labor there? _____
3. Why did Paul leave Ephesus? _____
4. What was the occasion of Paul's farewell to the elders of this
   church and where is the record of it? _____
   _____
5. How widespread was Christianity in Asia? _____
6. When was the letter written?_____
7. Why was the letter written? _____
8. Into what two divisions can the contents of Ephesians be divided?
   a. _____ ,   b. _____
9. The purpose of God from eternity is summed up in two passages
   in Ephesians. What are they?
   a. _____ ,   b. _____
10. What events have fulfilled this purpose of God in human redemp-
    tion?
    a. _____ ,   b. _____ ,
    c. _____ .
11. What effect on Jew and Gentile did the death of Christ bring
    about? _____
    _____
12. What are the essential elements in the unity of the peace?_____
    _____
13. In what relationship can one enjoy the fulness of the redemption
    provided in Christ? _____
14. How did Paul meet the false doctrine of the Gnostics that the
    purity of life in the flesh was not essential if sanctification of the
    spirit was achieved? _____
    _____
15. Specify the passage that teaches diligence in doing the will of the
    Lord in all individual relationships: _____
16. Name five figures that set forth the nature of the church:
    a. _____ ,   b. _____ ,
    c. _____ ,   d. _____ ,
    e. _____

17. "Christ is the fulness of God" is the theme of the _____
letter; and the "Church is the fulness of Christ" is the theme
of the _____ letter.

18. What is the most common expression in the Ephesian letter?

_____

How many times can you cite its occurrence? _____

19. What are the three arguments on the theme of "Christ and the
Church" in Ephesians?

    a. _____

    b. _____

    c. _____

20. What is the Christian to walk in? _____

Ruins of the marble street at Ephesus. Paul spent three years at Ephesus (Acts 20:31). This street was probably built a short time after Paul was there. It is lined with shops and public buildings.

Letter to the Philippians

A. The City of Philippi.

Philippi received its name from its founder, Philip of Macedonia. In Acts 16:12, Luke refers to it as the leading city of Macedonia, and also mentions its status as a Roman Colony. This status was a distinction in which the citizens of such a city took a great deal of pride, and this attitude is indicated by the complaint against Paul and his associates for seeking to introduce customs and practices contrary to the Roman pattern (Acts 16:21-26). The city originally belonged to Thrace. In 358 B.C., it was seized by Philip, King of Macedonia and the father of Alexander the Great. It was the place where Marcus Antonius and Octavius defeated Brutus and Cassius (42 B.C.), which defeat overthrew the Roman Oligarchy and Augustus (Octavius) became Emperor. There are many ruins of the old city, but of its destruction, we have no information. The site has never been excavated and it is at present uninhabited. It was on a great highway through which all the traders from east and west had to pass. It was, as customarily was true, for Paul a strategic center for evangelizing Europe. It was well watered, in the midst of a very fertile territory, and close to it were some very rich gold mines.

B. The Church at Philippi.

The church at Philippi was established by Paul on his second journey, about 52 A.D. He had set out from Antioch and had traveled by land to revisit the churches which had been planted on his first journey. Luke records in Acts 16 that Timothy joined him at Lystra, and having gone through "the region of Phrygia and Galatia having been forbidden by the Holy Spirit to speak the word in Asia; and when they were come to Mysia, they assayed to go into Bithynia; but the Holy Spirit suffered them not; and they passing by Mysia came down to Troas. And a vision appeared to Paul in the night; there was a man of Macedonia standing beseeching him, and saying, come over into Macedonia and help us; and when he had seen the vision straightway we sought to go further into Macedonia, concluding that God had called us to preach the gospel unto them" (Acts 16:6-10). The "we" at verse 10 indicates that Luke joined the company at Troas.

They sailed from Troas, and evidently, with a favorable wind, crossed the Aegean Sea in two days to Neapolis, a journey that would ordinarily have taken five days. From Neapolis they went up to Philippi. These circumstances: God's intervention preventing Paul from speaking the word in Asia, Mysia and Bithynia; the vision at Troas; a ship being immediately available; and a favorable wind on his journey; indicate that God was guiding Paul to the city of Philippi.

79

The city of Philippi did not have enough Jewish citizens to have a synagogue. There was a meeting place for prayer just outside the city, where Paul found Lydia and a group of women on the Sabbath engaged in worship. To them he preached the first gospel sermon that was ever preached on the continent of Europe (Acts 16:13). Lydia and her household became the first converts in Philippi, and later, the jailor and his household were converted. Thus, the church in Philippi began.

The church at Philippi was very little troubled, evidently, by Judaizing teachers, in contrast with many of the other places where Paul labored. It must have been pretty largely Gentile. From the fact that Luke, the historian, in Acts ceases to use the plural "we," it is to be presumed that when Paul left Philippi, Luke remained there to further aid in building up the church. Silas visited Philippi (Acts 18:5); Paul himself revisited the city upon at least two occasions (2 Cor. 2:13; Acts 20:6), so that there remained a very close contact between Paul and the Philippian brethren.

C. The Date.

It is very clear from internal evidence in the letter that it is one of the prison epistles, that it was written during Paul's imprisonment in Rome, probably in about 62 A.D.

D. The Character and Purpose.

Paul found occasion for writing the letter in the return of Epaphroditus from Rome to Philippi. The church at Philippi had sent Epaphroditus as their messenger to bring aid to Paul while he was in prison at Rome. He fell ill while in Rome and was "sick nigh unto death." Paul attributed his life being spared to the mercy of God, both toward Epaphroditus and Paul himself, and to the power of prayer (2:25-30). It is rather significant that in a number of such instances in the New Testament, the Apostles, who could have miraculously healed, did not do so in such cases, and these instances emphasize that the Divine powers which God had given them to confirm the gospel never were used for personal, private or selfish reasons.

Upon his recovery, Epaphroditus longed to return home. Paul was sympathetic to this desire and also knew of the concern of the Philippians for him, since they had heard that he was sick. Accordingly, the Philippian letter was prompted, along with other reasons, that Paul might express his gratitude both to Epaphroditus, their messenger, and the church in Philippi, for the aid which they had sent by this "messenger" to minister to Paul's need.

The Philippian letter has as one of its dominant themes the sincere gratitude that Paul had for the constant support that Philippi had given him in preaching the gospel "from the first day until now" (1:3-5).

E. Contents of the Letter.

1. Fellowship in Evangelism. From Philippians 1:3-5; 2:25; 4:14-18, we learn that the Philippian church from the beginning of its existence had been partners (had fellowship) with Paul by contributing to his necessities wherever he went. This furnishes us an "Apostolic example" of how a New Testament church selected a preacher in whom they had confidence and supported him in his work of preaching the gospel wherever he chose to labor over a period of more than ten years. From 2 Corinthians 11:7-9, we gain the additional information that they "cooperated" with other "churches" in supporting Paul at Corinth. The pattern for church support for a gospel preacher is definite and clear: a. Each church raised its own funds by the contribution of its own members; b. each church chose the preacher whom it would support; c. each church sent its contribution by its own "messenger" directly to the preacher; d. there was no "sponsoring church" arrangement, but it was a direct relationship between the supporting church and the preacher supported; e. it is significant that in 2 Cor. 11, we learn the money was not sent from the church at Philippi to the church at Corinth that they might support Paul, but that it was sent directly to Paul by the church at Philippi.

He affirms in 2 Cor. 11:7-9 that he received nothing from the Corinthian church, but that he "took wages" from other churches that he might preach the gospel unto them and he specified the brethren who came from Macedonia. It is no wonder that Paul could say "every time I think of you, I thank God for you" (1:3) when the Philippian church had been so faithful through all of the years in helping him do the great work he did for the Lord.

2. One of the major characteristics of the Philippian letter is its vibrant undertone of spiritual joy. It could be said that the sum of the whole letter is "I rejoice—you rejoice." The words, joy and rejoice, are the most common words in the letter. They were, perhaps, upon Paul's part, the result of the peace and contentment that he speaks of in the statement:

> But I rejoice in the Lord greatly . . . for I have learned in whatsoever state I am, therein to be content. I know how to be abased and I know also how to abound: in everything and all things have I learned the secret both to be filled and hungry, both to abound and to be in want. I can do all things in him that strengtheneth me (4:10-13).

When Paul and Silas were imprisoned in Philippi, bleeding from the stripes that were placed upon their backs and fast in stocks and bonds, they were able to sing songs of praises to God in the night. We see him in the Philippian letter a patient prisoner for the sake of Christ, feeble in frame, suffering from severity of circumstances, deserted by some who had professed to be his friends, literally in hunger and want, suffering from the vile schemes of bitter opponents, and with the sentence of execution by the chopping block hanging by a thread over him, but he could still rejoice in the Lord always. This was indeed "the peace that passeth understanding" and a wonderful example of the fact when that peace and joy is generally established in our hearts, it not only shines forth, but is unquenched even in time of storm. Paul could be glad in adversity, rich in poverty and calmly comforted in the face of death. He had reasons for rejoicing which he pointed out to the Philippians: a. His bonds and imprisonment had "fallen out rather unto the progress of the gospel" (1:12); b. he could rejoice that Christ was preached even though by some in envy and in strife (1:15); c. he could rejoice, though he was being sacrificed, because of the fruit that such sacrifice had borne in the faithfulness of such disciples as the Philippians (2:16-18); d. he could rejoice in the calm confidence of a faith that gave him the assurance "the Lord is at hand" (4:5); e. he could rejoice in the strength and satisfaction which the fellowship of the Philippians had brought to him in the preaching of the gospel (4:14-17).

3. Self sacrifice is another very dominant chord in this letter of joy and thanksgiving: a. He uses the Lord as the primary example "who, existing in the form of God, counted not the being on an equality with God a thing to be grasped, but emptied himself" (2:5-6); b. this sacrifice of self not only had been supremely exemplified by the Lord, but it had been emulated by Paul who, though he might have had "confidence in the flesh," had surrendered all advantage of that sort and "counted loss for Christ what things were gain to me" (3:3-7); c. Paul's selflessness is further asserted and demonstrated by his statement "for me to live is Christ, and to die is gain" (1:21); d. this theme of self sacrifice is also emphasized in his commendation of Timothy "for I have no man like minded, who will care truly for your state. For they all seek their own, not the things of Jesus Christ" (2:19-20); e. these same Philippians Paul uses as an example in stirring up the Corinthians to "prove their love by their liberality" (2 Cor. 8:7-8). He calls attention to the extreme sacrifice which the Macedonians (Philippians) had made: "How that in much proof of affliction the abundance of their joy and their deep poverty abounded unto the riches of their liberality, for according to their power, I bear witness, yea and beyond their power, they gave of their own accord" (2 Cor. 8:1-3).

4. The Philippian letter is likewise characterized by some very strong exhortations expressed in love, but in terms of the plainest meaning: a. He exhorts them to unity particularly as to a personal disturbance between two women, Euodia and Syntyche, whom he exhorts to be "of the same mind in the Lord" (4:2); b. he exhorts them to Christian maturity through diligence, constancy in their work, and faithful obedience (2:12-18); c. he warns the Philippians of the Judaizers who had created trouble in so many other churches through their ruthless selfishness and who might undertake to do so in Philippi (3:1-3); d. he exhorts them to keep their confidence in the Lord, their

minds pure, and to continue to follow that which they "both learned and received and heard and saw" in Paul (4:4-9).

STUDENT WORK

1. What do you know about the city of Philippi? _____

_____

2. What guided Paul to Philippi? _____

3. Who were the first converts in Philippi? _____

4. How do we know who joined the company at Troas? _____

_____

5. When Paul departed from Philippi, who of the company remained behind? _____ How do we know? _____

6. Where did Paul write from and when? _____

7. Whom had Philippi sent to Rome to "minister to Paul's wants"?

_____ What happened to him? _____

Paul sent the letter back by him to? _____

8. What made Paul so grateful for the Philippian church? _____

_____

9. How did Paul's fellowship with the Philippian church set for the church today a pattern in evangelism?

_____

Name the elements in this scriptural pattern for a church supporting a preacher:

a. _____ ,   b. _____

c. _____ ,   d. _____

e. _____

10. What is the dominant theme in Philippians? _____

_____

11. How could Paul rejoice while suffering in prison? What were his reasons?

_____

_____

12. What three examples did Paul give of self sacrifice?

a. _____

b. _____

c. _____

13. What example had the Philippians themselves set for others?

_____

_____

Letter to the Colossians

A. The City of Colosse.

The city of Colosse was located about 100 miles east of Ephesus, in the valley of the River Lycus. It was situated about 12 miles up the river from Hierapolis and Laodicea. The city of Colosse had once been a large city and an important one, but it had diminished considerably, and in the New Testament age it was considered neither as large nor important as its neighboring cities. Paul must have been in close proximity to the city and may have passed through it on his travels, but there is no indication that he had ever preached there or that he was responsible for the establishment of the church in that place. He learned of the faith of the Colossians by report (1:1). He was unknown by face to them (2:1).

Since Colosse was located in the Province of Asia, it is very likely that the evangelizing of the city took place during Paul's stay at Ephesus, for we are told in the book of Acts that during this period, people throughout Asia heard the word (Acts 19:10). Epaphras was a native of the city of Colosse, but very evidently heard Paul at Ephesus and returned to his home city to preach. He was responsible for the planting of the gospel in this community (1:7). He labored hard in the ministry (4:13), and continued to pray fervently for the saints there (4:12). He was called by Paul "a faithful minister of Christ on their behalf" (1:7).

B. The Church at Colosse.

Apparently, the church at Colosse was made up largely of Gentiles (1:27; 2:13). Paul uses the phrase in the letter, "aliens and enemies in your mind" (1:21). In 1:27 he speaks of making known the ministry of Christ among the Gentiles, referring evidently to the Colossians themselves. In 3:5-7 he gives a list of their sins before they became Christians and these sins were such as were characteristic of the Gentiles.

Despite the lack of personal contact, Paul assumed that the church was interested in his affairs. Evidently, he felt a responsibility toward the church in this community. Although he had not established it in person, it had been accomplished by a fellow worker.

The church was situated in a very wealty area. The area was famous for two closely aligned trades. There were great flocks of sheep on its fertile pastures, and it was one of the greatest centers of the wool industry. Connected with this industry was the production of garments which was centered in Laodicea. An allied trade was that of dyeing. There was a quality in the chalky waters of the Lycus River especially suitable for dyeing cloth. There was a certain dye named after the city, so that evidently the cities of this valley were very prosperous. In Rev. 3:17, Jesus said of Laodicea that in her own eyes she was rich and had need of nothing.

C. Date of Writing.

On this third preaching tour, Paul spent a long period at Ephesus. Upon his return from the third journey he was arrested in Jerusalem (Acts 21:30-36). He was taken to Caesarea and then to Rome. While he was in prison at Rome, Epaphras came to see him from Colosse and reported the condition of the church (Acts 28:30-31; Col. 1:8; 2:4 ff.). The imprisonment at Rome is dated about A.D. 60-62. This letter was written some time during that period. It was probably sent to Colosse along with the letter to Philemon, by Tychicus and Onesimus (4:7-9).

D. The Purpose and Character of the Letter.

Paul not only wrote the Colossians to express his interest in their spiritual welfare and to assure them of his prayers in their behalf (1:9 ff.), but there had arisen a serious threat to the church through the teaching of false doctrine, sometimes called "the Colossian heresy."

It is evident that Paul wrote primarily out of his desire to save the church from this heresy, for the heart of the epistle deals with it. The false doctrine very evidently denied the pre-eminence of Christ and His all sufficiency. If not in outright controversy of this fundamental Bible truth, at least in effect. Paul offsets this doctrine in the Colossian letter by setting forth what Christ is and what Christ has done in God's plan for human redemption. This is affirmed in the following points:

1. Christ is the image of the invisible God (1:15).

2. He is the firstborn of all creation (1:15). This expression does not, as sometimes is supposed, teach that Christ was created in the sense that God created the heavens and the earth and all things in them, but it refers to the fact that in God's plan from eternity, Christ was to be recognized as the "firstborn" and would, therefore, exercise the right to succeed the Father as the head of the household, and in the exercise of all authority.

3. That all things "were created, both in the heavens and on earth, visible and invisible, whether thrones or authorities, all things have been created through Him and for Him" (1:16).

4. Christ is "before all things and in Him all things hold together" (1:17).

5. He is also "head of the body, the church; he is the beginning, the firstborn from the dead; so that in all things he might have the preeminence" (1:18)..

6. It was God's plan that "in him should all the fulness dwell; and through him to reconcile all things unto himself" (1:19).

7. In Him are had all the treasures of wisdom and knowledge (2:2).

8. In Him dwells all the fulness of the Godhead in bodily form (2:9).

9. Christ is our life (3:4).

No greater claims of the pre-eminence of Christ and His all sufficiency have ever been made than Paul affirms in this letter concerning Him. He reaches the climax in the affirmation that "Christ is all and in all" (3:11). This presentation of what Christ is, and that the fulness of God's grace can be found in Him and in Him alone, completely destroyed the false doctrine of the heretics that Christ was simply a heavenly messenger and that His ministry needs to be augmented by the ministry of other "angels" or "heavenly messengers," which the Gnostics claimed.

10. It is significant in view of the false doctrine which Paul is controverting that while affirming the all sufficiency and pre-eminence of Christ in his agency in God's plan for human redemption, Paul at the same time emphasizes emphatically the humanity of Christ, his flesh and blood existence. It was in his fleshly body that he did his redeeming work (1:22). All of the attributes of Divine power, wisdom, and grace were demonstrated by Him in bodily form (2:9). This was to offset the Gnostic doctrine that all flesh and things belonging to this material earth are evil.

Mixed in with this "Colossian heresy" was some Judaistic influence. Quite a colony of Jews, consisting of about 2,000 from Babylon and Mesopotamia had been brought many years before by Antiochus the Great into the regions of Lydia and Phrygia and had prospered there. More of their fellow countrymen had come to share this prosperity. So Jewish influence made its effort to bind upon the Colossian Christians some of the external principles that were a part of Judaism. Paul deals with this by pointing out that by His death upon the cross, Jesus had taken the law (which excluded Gentiles) out of the way, nailing it to the cross, and that no Christian was to be judged or condemned for not keeping any of its ceremonies (2:13-17). Paul emphasizes, because of this Jewish influence, that circumcision is no longer a circumcision of the flesh, but rather is, in Christianity, a circumcising of the heart by the cutting off of our guilt of sin by Christ when we are buried with Him by baptism and raised up from death to sin, with Him, into newness of life through faith (2:11-12).

There had been mixed in with the other false aspects of this false teaching a philosophical element to which Paul refers in Colossians 2:6-11. Concerning this human philosophy, he admonishes that they are not to allow such to make spoil of them "through philosophy and vain deceit, after the tradition of men, after the rudiments of the world, and not after Christ." In the last part of this chapter, verses 22-23, Paul points out that all of the rules of self-inflicted punishment, extreme denial and privation, prescribed by human authority in the precepts and doctrines of men, were not to be observed for two reasons: a. Christians have died with Christ from the rudiments of the world and should no longer subject themselves to human authority or teaching as though living in the world, but should live in subjection to Christ; b. all of the precepts and doctrines of men perish with the using or observance of them and are of no spiritual value.

Another phase of this Gnostic heresy was that spirit is good and all fleshly things are bad. Since the Gnostics taught that all flesh is bad anyway and cannot do anything but evil, giving full satisfaction to fleshly desires would not corrupt or condemn the spirit of man which had been sanctified through faith in Christ, so their idea was fill your cup of pleasure full, gratify and fulfill all of your earthly desire, and you will be no worse off. Paul offsets this teaching in chapter 3 by emphasizing: a. We have died and our lives as Christians are hid with Christ in God, our affections, therefore, should be set upon things above (3:1-3); b. our members which are upon the earth (fleshly appetites and earthly desires) are to be put off or "put to death," and we are to "put on therefore as God's elect" the characteristics of righteousness that evidence the rule of Christ in our hearts; c. Paul further points out from chapter 3:18 through 4:6 that this necessity of submitting one's self in daily living to the will of Christ extends to all of the personal relationships in life. Whether in the family, in business, or any other, the Christian's obligation is to conduct himself always so completely in harmony with the will of Christ that we may "in word or deed do all in the name of the Lord Jesus, giving thanks to God the Father through Him" (3:17).

STUDENT WORK

1. Where was Colosse? _____
   Had Paul ever been there? _____
2. Was the church at Colosse mostly made up of Jews or Gentiles?

   _____

3. Was the church wealthy or poor? _____
4. Who brought to Paul in Rome news of the condition of the church in Colosse? _____

   _____

5. What was the date of writing? _____
6. What was the doctrine which the false teachers were denying?

   _____

7. In the following list of passages what does Paul affirm about this doctrine?
   a. 1:15 _____
   b. 1:15 _____
   c. 1:16 _____

    d. 1:17 _____

    e. 1:18 _____

    f. 1:19 _____

    g. 2:2 _____

    h. 2:9 _____

    i. 3:4 _____

    j. 3:11 _____

8. By what points did Paul also emphasize the humanity of Jesus?

    a. _____,   b. _____

9. What did Paul teach about Judaism? _____

_____

_____

10. What does Paul teach about human philosophy in religion?

_____

The New Testament:
Book By Book

Part 2

First Thessalonians

A. The City of Thessalonica.

On the second journey Paul made from Antioch he traveled by land, visiting the Churches which he had established on his first journey to Troas, where he had received the "Macedonian call" and with Silas, Timothy and Luke had crossed the Aegean Sea to the continent of Europe, where he planted the first church at Philippi. He stayed at Philippi for only a limited time and left Luke to further teach the church there. With the rest of his company, he traveled westward along a famous Roman Road known as the Egnatian Way that stretched westward across Macedonia from Philippi to the Adriatic Sea. He made short stops at Amphipolis and Apollonia and then journeyed on to Thessalonica, which was an important city at the head of the Thermaic Gulf.

Thessalonica was named for the step-sister of Alexander the Great. It probably had as many as 200,000 people in it when Paul ⊽isited it. It's modern name is Salonika. When Macedonia was made a Roman province in 146 B.C., Thessalonica was made the seat of government. It was a strategic location for a church, as later history concerning it's work shows (1 Thess. 1:8).

As a commercial city it had attracted a large community of Jews and they had a synagogue (Acts 17:1). Paul was given an opportunity to speak in the synagogue for three Sabbath days and "reasoned with them from the scriptures," showing that Jesus of Nazareth came in fulfillment of Old Testament prophesies and promises (Acts 17:2-3). While some of the Jews believed, there was a greater number of God-fearing Greeks and a number of the leading women (Acts 17:4). The Jews, becoming jealous, gathered up some wicked men from the market place and formed a mob. They attacked the house of Jason and took some of the brethren before the city authorities and accused them of harboring men "who have upset the world and have come here also" (Acts 17:5-8). Paul and Silas left by night and went down to Berea. The period of Paul's stay in Thessalonica may have been a little longer than Luke's account and Acts indicates. Three factors would seem to evidence this: (1) that there were a large number of Gentile converts (1 Thess. 1:9); (2) Paul engaged in some manual labor during this period (2 Thess. 3:8); (3) in Phil. 4:16 he indicates that from the Philippian church he had received aid more than once.

B. The Church at Thessalonica.

The church at Thessalonica had been a very faithful and active church up to the time of this first letter. Paul speaks of their "work of faith, and labor of love, and stedfastness of hope in our Lord Jesus Christ" (1 Thess. 1:3). He also states that they had set an example for all the believers in Macedonia and Achaia, particularly in the fact that from them "the word of the Lord has sounded forth, not only in Macedonia and Achaia, but also in every place your faith toward God has gone forth" (1 Thess. 1:8). Resentment over the Apostle's success in persuading the Thessalonians to accept his message and the evident change in their way of life, brought upon them severe persecution by the Jews. Paul was anxious to know of their state, so he sent Timothy from Athens to Thessalonica to get this information (1 Thess. 3:1-5; 2:17). Timothy brought back the news that the love of the Thessalonians for Paul continued and that they were standing fast in the faith (1 Thess. 2:14; 3:4-6; 4:9-10).

C. Date of Writing.
Some of the scholars put the date of the Thessalonian letter as early as 50 or 51, and it probably was written from Corinth.

D. The Author.
First Thessalonians contains the name of the author (1:1; 2:18); also, frequent references to Paul's journey to Thessalonica and beyond (1:5; 2:1-2; 5-11, 13, 3:1-6). The internal evidence unquestionably identifies the Epistle as one written by Paul. Historical evidence shows that it was recognized and quoted by several of the writers in the early part of the second century.

E. Contents and Character.
The First Thessalonian letter begins much the same way that the Philippian letter begins. After his salutation, he expresses very warmly his thanksgiving to God "always for all of you." The basis of such thanksgiving was their stedfastness in their faith, hope and love; the fact that they had readily received the Gospel even in the face of much tribulation; and their zeal and diligence in spreading the Gospel throughout that part of the world.

Thessalonica was a city filled with idolators, as were many others, but "they had turned to God from idols to serve a living and true God" (1 Thess. 1:9).

In the first part of the second chapter of the letter (2:1-12), Paul emphasizes the characteristics of his work among them by pointing out: (1) They had preached with boldness the Gospel in the face of much opposition (2:2); (2) Their preaching and their exhortation had been free from error, impurity or deceit, and they had spoken so as to please God because of having been entrusted by Him with the Gospel (2:3-4); (3) They had not used flattery as a pretext for greed (2:5); (4) They did not seek glory from men nor use their authority just because they were Apostles (2:6); (5) They had dealt tenderly with the Thessalonians, as a mother with her children (2:7); (6) They had preached the Gospel in love, both for the truth and for the Thessalonians (2:8); (7) They had worked with their hands in order that this might not be a burden to the brethren (2:9; 2 Thess. 3:8); (8) Their conduct while there had been devout, upright and blameless

The Vardar Gate inscription from Thessalonica. In Acts 17:6,9 the city officials of Thessalonica are designated "politarchs" in the Greek. This stone inscription names six rulers who are so designated. The stone is now in the British Museum.

(2:10); (9) They had encouraged and plead with them as a father would his own children (2:11).

This paragraph constitutes one of the finest statements in the entire New Testament concerning the attitude of those who preach and teach the Word of God.

In this same chapter (2:13), Paul makes a wonderful statement concerning the attitude with which they had received the Gospel: "You accepted it not as the word of men, but as it is in truth, the Word of God" (2:13). He commends them for following the example of the churches of Judea in faithfully suffering the persecution that came upon them after their conversion, even at the hand of their own countrymen (2:14-16). Paul states his desire to see them and his purpose "more than once" to come, and states that Satan had hindered (2:17-18). He refers to them as his "joy or crown of exultation" and "our glory and joy" (2:19-20).

He explains that when his anxiety in their behalf could be endured no longer Timothy had been sent to strengthen and encourage them (3:1-2). He reminds that he had warned them concerning the persecution that would come upon them (2:3-4). He greatly rejoices in Timothy's report of their love for him and their faithfulness in all their affliction, and assures them that he had prayed for them night and day and even now his prayer was that God might direct his way to them (3:6-11).

In chapter 4 we find a section emphasizing the necessity of holiness in life (4:1-8); an exhortation to brotherly love (4:9-10); and a plea for orderly conduct "to lead a quiet life and attend to your own business and work with your hands," for this is what he had commanded them to do. Such behavior was not only that they might supply their own needs, but in order to set the proper example before outsiders (4:11).

93

Beginning with verse 13 in chapter 4, he instructs them concerning the fact that they would not at the coming of the Lord be caught up in the air to meet the Lord, until the dead had first been raised, and exhorts them "to comfort one another with these words."

Chapter 5 emphasizes the need of watchfulness and sobriety in view of the Lord's coming (5:1-11). After a number of brief exhortations (5:12-22), Paul concludes the epistle with a prayer (5:23-24), some personal requests (5:25-27), and his blessings upon them (5:28).

Underlying this entire first epistle to the Thessalonian brethren, as a basis for: (1) exhortation to faithfulness in the face of persecution; (2) godliness in life and character, and (3) a motive for seeking to excel both in their devotion and service to God, is the doctrine of the second coming of Christ. Paul concludes each chapter in this Epistle with a reference to this hope (1:10; 2:19; 3:13; 4:16-17; 5:23).

STUDENT WORK

1. Where did Paul come from when he went to Thessalonica? _____

   _____

2. What famous road did he travel? _____

3. What size was Thessalonica and of what province was it the seat of government?   _____

4. What advantages did it have as a location for the church? _____

   _____

5. Discribe the population of Thessalonica as to the nationality of its people and cite the passages proving your description. _____

   _____

   _____

6. Where in Thessalonica did Paul first preach? _____

   _____

7. What did he preach? With what results? _____

   _____

8. How active was the church at Thessalonica and how well known did it become? Give passage. _____

9. What great motives did Paul commend them for and what did they produce? Give passage. _____

10. Did Paul have any opposition in this city? _____ Passages:

    _____ , _____ , _____ ,

    _____ .

11. What religion did most of those converted have before their conversion? _____

_____

12. What ended Paul's stay in Thessalonica? _____

_____

13. How was he supported while there? _____

14. Whom did Paul send to bring him news of the church at Thessalonica? _____

15. What news did Timothy bring concerning them? _____

_____

16. Name and cite the verse that tells Paul's attitude in preaching the Gospel in that city. _____

_____

17. What was the attitude of the Thessalonians in receiving what Paul preached? Give the verse. _____

18. Why did not Paul return to visit them as he had desired? _____

_____

19. What had he prayed for night and day concerning them? _____

_____

20. Cite a section of the epistle emphasizing the necessity of leading a holy life. _____ Brotherly love. _____ A quiet and orderly life. _____

_____

21. What great underlying hope did Paul cite as a reason for their faithfulness, enduring persecution, excellence of duration and service to God? _____

_____

_____

22. With what does he conclude each chapter of the letter? _____

_____

Second Thessalonians

A. The Author.

This epistle, like the first, is written in the name of "Paul and Silvanus, and Timotheus," and seems to have been sent from Corinth not many months after the first. Both epistles are ordinarily assigned a date somewhere between 50 and 53 A.D.

B. The Purpose of the Second Letter.

Paul's main design in the Second letter is evident. It was to correct a very serious error respecting the second coming of our Lord. It does not appear that either Paul or any of his helpers had visited Thessalonica since the sending of the first letter. Their misconception concerning the time of the Lord's coming seems to have arisen from either a complete misunderstanding of the first letter, or in some imaginary revelation which someone claimed to have received, or from a forged letter purporting to come from Paul (Coneybeare & Howson).

Some asserted that Paul had said Jesus was going to come right away or that His coming was eminent, or bound to occur shortly. They had used this misconception as an excuse for idleness and fanaticism. Paul wrote to correct this wrong impression and to restore them to their normal manner of life and remind them of their daily duties in serving the Lord.

He also wrote to express his joy and gratitude over their faithfulness in the midst of even more severe persecution and affliction. He, likewise, expressed his joy in the fact that he enjoyed their full confidence.

C. Contents and Character.

The outstanding features of the second letter to the Thessalonians are:

1. To further comfort and strengthen the Thessalonians in their persecution. He points out that this is a plain indication of God's approval and that the fact that they were allowed to suffer evidenced their worthiness of the Kingdom of God (1:4-5).

2. He assures them that it will be God's pleasure "to recompense them that afflict you with affliction and you that are afflicted with rest." He identifies this retribution as taking place when the Lord shall be revealed "from Heaven with His mighty angels and flaming fire" (1:6-7). This retribution, he suggests, will be two-fold in its nature: (1) The penalty of eternal destruction from the presence of the Lord and from the glory of His power will be the lot for those who "do not obey the gospel of our Lord Jesus;" (2) and that when he comes it will be "to be glorified in his saints and to be marveled at among all who have believed" (1:8-10).

96

3. He specifically instructs them that there were some events that would take place before the "coming of our Lord Jesus Christ and our gathering together to him" (2:1-2). Because of these events that were to precede the coming of the Lord, he instructs them that they are not to be disturbed or quickly shaken from their composure by any message, no matter from what source it purported to have been (2:1-2). These events that must transpire before the Lord could come, as Paul sets them forth, were: (1) There must be a falling away or an apostasy (2:3); (2) As the result of this falling away or apostasy, there would be revealed "the man of sin, the son of perdition who opposes and exalts himself above every so-called God or object of worship so that he takes his seat in the Temple of God, setting himself forth as God" (2:3-4). He reminds them that he had told them these things while he was with them the first time; (3) He points out that the revelation of this "man of sin" in the apostasy that was to come would be restrained. This restraint very evidently was Divine revelation which was in process but had not been completed (2:5-7); (4) He calls to their attention that the influence of evil had already begun its work (2:7); (5) He affirms that the lawless one to be revealed would endure until the coming of the Lord and would be destroyed by the "breath of his mouth" (2:8); (6) He identifies the lawless one by pointing out that he would come with all of the power, signs and false wonders of Satan and with all of the deception and deluding that would lead men astray who "receive not the love of the truth" (2:8-11); (7) He points out that the only protection from being deluded and believing a lie is the love of the truth (2:10-12).

4. In the second chapter, beginning with verse 13, and continuing through verse 17, Paul gave thanks to God that these Thessalonian brethren had been chosen "unto sanctification of the spirit and belief of the truth," and that they had been called into this "through the gospel." He further exhorts them to "stand firm and hold to the teaching which they had received from him, whether by word or letter."

5. In chapter 3, he requests the prayers of the brethren for him that the word of the Lord might spread rapidly and be glorified as had been true in their case (3:1). He also requests that they pray that he might be delivered from perverse and evil men (3:2). He expresses his confidence that the Lord will protect them and that they will continue to be obedient (3:3-5). He urges upon them that they refuse to fellowship all who lead an ungodly life and who refuse to walk according to the teaching which they had received from him (3:6). He reminds them that he led a disciplined life while among them and earned his own bread by his labor that he might not be a burden to any (3:7-9). He lays down further the restriction, "if any will not work neither let him eat," and exhorts that "each shall work with quietness, and eat their own bread," and attend to their own affairs (3:11-12). He urges further that they be "not weary in well doing" (3:13). He enjoins them that if any man abide not by the instruction of this letter that they were "to have no company with him to the end that

he may be ashamed" (3:14-15), and urges yet, that they count him not as an enemy but admonish him as a brother. He signs the letter with his own hand so that they may know that it is genuine, and gives them a final salutation, "the grace of our Lord Jesus Christ be with you all."

STUDENT WORK

1. About when did Paul write the two epistles to Thessalonians and how close together in time? _____

2. What was the purpose of the second letter? _____
_____

3. In this letter in addition to correcting their misunderstanding and quieting their misapprehension, what further did he exhort them to do? (1:4-5) _____

4. What outstanding passage in this letter assures the Christian of the rendering of divine justice unto both the righteous and the wicked? Give the passage. _____

5. What will be the reward of those who are righteous and faithful? Cite the passage. _____
What will the wicked suffer? Cite the passage. _____

6. What events did Paul assure them would precede the coming of Christ from heaven?

   (1) _____ ,   Verse _____

   (2) _____ ,   Verse _____

   (3) _____ ,   Verse _____

7. What power was restraining the impending apostasy? (2:5-7) ____
_____

8. When did this apostasy begin? (2:7) _____

9. How long would this "man of sin" continue and what would destroy him? (2:8) _____

10. What characteristics would this lawless one possess? _____
_____ Verse. _____

11. Who would be led astray by him? _____

12. What interest does Paul ask in their prayers? _____

13. How were the Thessalonian brethren called and unto what? _____
_____

14. How does Paul describe his own conduct while among them preaching? _____
_____

15. Whom does he tell them they are not to feed? _____

_____

16. Whom does he tell them not to fellowship? _____

_____

17. What is his final exhortation and benediction? _____

_____

_____

First Timothy

A. Introduction.

In addition to all of the letters that Paul wrote to various churches, there are four letters in the New Testament written by him to individuals. Two of these were written to Timothy, one to Titus, and one to Philemon. First and Second Timothy and Titus are often referred to by denominational scholars as the Pastoral letters. This designation, however, is due to the common misconception of what a Pastor is. The denominational concept is that a Pastor is the preacher "in charge of the affairs of the local church." The New Testament does not so teach. In Acts 20:17-28, we learn that *bishops, elders* and *pastors* are three different terms referring to the same group of men in the local church doing the same work. The preacher is not the pastor or shepherd of the flock, but the bishops and elders are. In New Testament days there was no distinction between bishops, elders, and pastors.

Timothy and Titus, however, were fellow-laborers with Paul in the work of preaching, and in these letters he writes to them, when he was ripe in years and Christian experience and about to finish his earthly sojourn, in order that he might give to these two young men who had been closely associated with him for a number of years, further encouragement, instruction, and strength for the work that they would need to continue to do when Paul had ended his earthly journey.

This letter was written after the close of the recorded history of the work of Paul in the Book of Acts. Luke closes the record of Acts with Paul still in prison at Rome, but leaves quite uncertain what happened to Paul in Rome. He tells us that Paul lived there two whole years in a state of semi-captivity, preaching the gospel without hindrance (Acts 28:30-31), but Luke does not record how that captivity ended, whether in Paul's release or in his execution.

It is generally presumed that this imprisonment in Rome ended in his death. However, there is a great deal of evidence, both in historical references in these epistles that do not fit into the record of Acts, and in tradition also, that the first imprisonment in Rome ended in his release, and that he enjoyed his liberty for two or three years before being reimprisoned and finally executed, probably about 66 or 67 A.D.

Some of the history which forms the background for such a conclusion is seen in several facts: First, Paul, while in prison in Rome, did not regard release as impossible. It actually appears that he expected it. In the letter to the Philippians, while in prison, he expressed trust in the Lord that he might shortly visit the Philippians (Phil. 2:24). When he sent the run-away slave, Onesimus, back to Philemon, he requested that lodging be prepared for him and that Philemon pray that he might be allowed to return to see him.

Second, Paul had planned for some time to visit the Church at Rome and to go on to Spain (Rom. 15:24-28). Clement of Rome, when he wrote his epistle to the Church at Corinth, about A.D. 90 from Rome, indicated that Paul had preached farther to the west.

Third, we know that Paul left Titus in Crete (Tit. 1:5) on his journey east. Paul expected to send Artemas or Tychicus so that Titus could come on to Nicopolis.

Fourth, the weight of the evidence indicates that First Timothy was written from Macedonia and Second Timothy from Rome. He indicates in this first letter that he had revisited Ephesus and had left Timothy there to carry on the work of the Lord, as he had left Titus in Crete (1 Tim. 1:3). He had sent Tychicus to Ephesus (2 Tim. 4:12). Trophimus had been left at Miletus sick (2 Tim. 4:20), and Erastus at Corinth. He had also visited with Carpus at Troas (2 Tim. 4:13). When Timothy was left in Ephesus, Paul was going to Macedonia (1 Tim. 1:3). His plan was to spend the winter at Nicopolis on the west coast of Achaia (Tit. 3:12).

These facts, gathered from the epistles to Titus and Timothy and nowhere mentioned in the Book of Acts, indicate very strongly, it seems, that Paul's first imprisonment at Rome was followed by a release, and that he made a trip east, probably because of his concern for the spreading of the doctrine of the Gnostics and other erroneous teachings that threatened the very existence of some of the churches in which he was so vitally interested. Following his trip in which these events occurred, he was either arrested again in Nicopolis, or when he crossed over to Italy, where conditions had changed and persecution under Nero against Christians, upon whom Nero laid the blame for the burning of the city, had become much more severe.

This time he was not allowed any liberty but was imprisoned, according to tradition, in the Mamertine dungeon. He spent a winter of loneliness and suffered from the cold. He missed the cloak which he left with Carpus at Troas (2 Tim. 4:13), and he dreaded the prospect of another winter without it (2 Tim. 4:13). His friends were imperiled when they sought to visit him. Some were ashamed of his bonds and afraid to come to see him; Onesiphorus, however, sought him out in Rome (2 Tim. 1:16). Some forsook him, as in the case of Demas, who went to Thessalonica (2 Tim. 4:10), and even Titus had gone to Dalmatia. Only Luke was his constant companion (2 Tim. 4:11), and he longed for his books, especially the parchments (2 Tim. 4:13). The Second Letter to Timothy was written evidently, according to all of this information, during his second imprisonment in Rome and shortly before his death. Timothy had also been made a prisoner and Paul refers in Hebrews 13:23 to him being set free. These facts constitute the historical background of these three letters.

B. Timothy, the Preacher.

Timothy himself is an interesting study. He was born in Lystra of a Greek father and a Jewish mother. He was reared in the

Jewish faith and was taught the Scriptures by his mother and grandmother from early childhood (2 Tim. 3:15; 2 Tim. 1:5). Paul discovered him at Lystra (Acts 16:1-3). At this point Timothy joined Paul in his labors and shared in them throughout the rest of his life. He was with Paul in prison in Rome during the first imprisonment, for his name appears in the heading of Colossians (1:1) and Philemon (1). After the release he evidently traveled with Paul as far as Ephesus and was left there to administer unto the needs of the Church. At the end of Paul's life he joined him again in Rome (2 Tim. 4:11-21). He was evidently a trustworthy, if not a forceful character. He gave the impression of immaturity, although he must have been about 30 years of age when Paul left him at Ephesus. The indication is that he was timid (2 Tim. 1:6-7), and that he had some difficulty with his health (1 Tim. 5:23).

C. The Letter.

1. The *occasion* for writing this letter is clearly stated in First Timothy 3:14-15, "that thou mayest know how thou oughtest to behave thyself in the house of God." We need to remember that Timothy was at Ephesus; that the whole of Asia Minor was threatened with the various false doctrines of Gnosticism; that because of this, apostasy was impending, as Paul had warned the elders themselves at Ephesus in his farewell speech at Miletus (Acts 20:18-32). It is understandable, therefore, that Timothy, the young preacher who had been left under the responsibility of meeting this false doctrine and saving the Church from apostasy, needed further specific instruction and encouragement in order to accomplish his task. This is Paul's reason for writing this Letter, which we are studying. The letter touches upon many things, all of which have to do with the manner in which "men are to conduct themselves in the house of God."

2. *Contents and Character.* The underlying theme of the entire First Letter to Timothy is a warning against the failure of faith. These warnings are found in a number of passages:

(a). The charge that Timothy was to instruct certain men not to teach strange doctrines (1:3).

(b). The warning against engaging in speculative instruction concerning myths and endless genealogies that would not further God's purposes (1:4).

(c). The goal to be reached was, rather, "love out of a pure heart and of a good conscience, and of faith unfeigned" (1:5).

(d). The danger of those who wanted to teach in spite of their ignorance (1:7).

(e). The imporance of "holding faith, and a good conscience: which some having put away, concerning faith have made shipwreck: of whom is Hymeneus and Alexander; whom I have delivered unto Satan" (1:18-20).

(f). The prophecy by the Spirit that "in latter times some shall depart from the faith, giving heed to seducing spirits, and doctrines of devils" (4:1).

(g). The warning that young widows would "wax wanton against Christ" — and would "have damnation because they cast off their first faith" (5:11).

(h). The danger of a failure to meet one's responsibility toward his household and becoming thus guilty of "denying the faith" (5:8).

(i). "If any man teach otherwise, and consent not to wholesome words, even the words of our Lord Jesus Christ, and to the doctrine which is according to godliness; he is proud knowing nothing . . . from such withdraw thyself" (6:3-5).

(j). "For the love of money is the root of all evil: which while some coveted after, they have erred from the faith" (6:10, 21).

The second underlying thought pervading the First Letter to Timothy concerns the Church (the house of God — 3:15), and how men ought to conduct themselves in its work. A number of references point up and emphasize some of these duties:

(a). To congregational prayer and worship (2:1-8).

(b). Specific instruction as to the obligation of women to "adorn themselves in modest apparel, with shamefacedness and sobriety; not with braided hair, or gold, or pearls, or costly array; but (which becometh women professing godliness)" (2:9-10).

(c). The obligation of Christian women to conduct themselves always in subjection to man, "I suffer not a woman to teach, nor to usurp authority over the man, but to be in silence" (2:11-15).

(d). The pattern of church organization is set forth in chapter 3, where Paul gives the qualifications of bishops and deacons (3:1-13). Among the qualifications emphasized for bishops or elders, Paul points out they must be "apt to teach" and able to exercise proper control over the affairs of God as a Christian father does over his family.

(e). The brethren are to be reminded of their duty, "nourished up in the words of faith and of good doctrine" (4:6).

(f). They are to be warned concerning the impending apostasy and some of the false ideas that would characterize it (4:1-5).

(g). The obligation of the church toward "widows indeed" is clearly defined, and Paul also clearly defines the qualifications of a "widow indeed" for whom the church can accept responsibility, but he also limits the right of the church to assume the obligation of regular care (enrollment) to those who are widows indeed, and specifically, that the church is not to be charged with the care of those who are not widows indeed (5:3-16).

(h). The church is charged with the obligation of assistance to elders who give their time to the work of the Lord and who labor in the work of teaching in order that they might carry on their work (5:17-18).

(i). Consideration is not to be given to indiscriminate accusations against elders. These accusations must be "at the mouth of two or three witnesses." However, when elders are guilty of sin they are to be reproved before all (5:19-20).

(j) Brethren are warned "that the love of money is the root of all evil" (6:10). Paul warns against elevating the desire for material goods above spiritual needs, and warns that a Christian's hope is not to be "set on the uncertainty of riches," but rather on "God, who giveth us richly all things to enjoy" (6:17).

A third general theme of the book especially applicable to all who preach the Gospel is found in First Timothy 3:16: "Take heed to thyself and to thy teaching."

(a). Paul exhorts Timothy concerning his attitude toward his work and those about him, and his personal example (4:6-16); 5:1 ff.; 6:11 ff.) This instruction related to dealing with false doctrine and teachers; older brethren, younger brethren, both older and younger women; and as a young man, the obligation to "exercise thyself unto Godliness;" give heed "to reading, to exhortation, to doctrine" (4:13); "neglect not the gift that is in thee . . . Meditate upon these things; give thyself wholly to them."

(b). Timothy was charged also to "rebuke them that sin . . . observe these things without preferring one before another, doing nothing by partiality. Lay hands suddenly on no man, neither be partaker of other men's sins: keep thyself pure" (5:20-22).

(c). He was to flee from any desire to be rich or to love money, by which many were caused to err from the faith (6:6-11); he was charged to follow after or seek "righteousness, godliness, faith, love, patience, meekness. Fight the good fight of faith . . . . keep this commandment without spot, unrebukable, until the appearing of our Lord Jesus Christ" (6:11-16).

(d). Paul closes the personal instruction to Timothy by charging him to "keep that which is committed to thy trust, avoiding profane and vain babblings, and oppositions of science falsely so called" (6:20).

STUDENT WORK

1. How many letters did Paul write to individuals and what are they?

_____

2. Why is it unscriptural to refer to a preacher working with a local

church as a pastor? _____

3. Why was Paul particularly interested in Timothy and Titus and wish to strengthen and encourage them? _____

4. How do we know that this letter was written subsequent to the period of New Testament history covered by the Book of Acts?

_____

_____

5. Was Paul in prison in Rome one time or twice? _____
State the facts that so indicate. Cite the passages: _____

_____

_____

_____

_____

6 Why was Paul interested in making a journey back to the east from Rome? _____

_____

7. What differences were there in the treatment of Paul during his first and second imprisonments? _____

_____

8. List some of the facts disclosed in the scriptures about Timothy (citing the passages). _____

_____

_____

9. What reason does Paul specifically assign for writing this first letter to Timothy? _____

_____

10. What are the underlying themes of this first letter? _____

_____

_____

11. What are some of the duties pointed out by Paul on the matter of "how men ought to behave themselves in the house of God"?

_____

_____

_____

_____

_____

12. What does Paul charge Timothy to do concerning his own conduct
    (1 Tim. 3:16), and what obligations did this involve? (Cite passages)

_____

_____

_____

_____

_____

Second Timothy

A. Background of the Letter.

The second letter to Timothy was, no doubt the last of Paul's Epistles. The last words of any great man challenge the attention and the hearts of those who have known him. Second Timothy contains the last utterances of one of the greatest soldiers of the Cross that has ever lived.

Paul found himself under very severe. circumstances. His first imprisonment had been entirely restrictive and yet, he had been able to look forward to his release. The second imprisonment, however, had been in the dungeon of the Mamertine prison, where it seems that only Luke, his faithful physician, was allowed to minister unto him (4:11); and. he felt sure that this imprisonment would end his earthly ministry (4:6). Paul longed for a last visit with his "son in the gospel," Timothy, and writes him requesting him to come and bring Mark with him, as well as the cloak that he had left at Troas, and his books, "especially the parchments" (4:11-13). The Letter, therefore, is to a great extent a personal letter of the great Apostle's farewell.

At the same time, he wished to encourage Timothy because of the heavy burden that he bore in the work at Ephesus. He also wished to exhort and encourage him that he might endure faithfully in bearing that burden in fulfilling his obligations.

The Letter is usually dated shortly before Paul's execution by Nero in Rome, perhaps between 66 and 68 A.D.

B. Contents and Character.

Intermingled with the feelings of a personal nature that find expression often in the Letter, and a very deep concern for Timothy as well, are his feelings for the Church and its future and faithful adherance to the Gospel. There are three main lines of thought that repeatedly occur. They are:

1. The increasing tendency toward heresy and the danger of apostasy that must be guarded against. Some of the references to this theme can be found in 1:15; 2:16-18; 2:23; 3:1-9; 4:3-4.

2. In view of the need of averting apostasy, Paul repeatedly emphasizes the necessity for strict adherance to the faith and encourages Timothy not only to do so, but to provoke such upon the part of the brethren as well. Such exhortations abound in many passages: (1) He reminds Timothy of the sincere faith which had been planted in his own heart by the teaching of his grandmother and his mother (1:5); (2) He reminds him of his obligation "to stir up," (fan into flame), the Divine endowment that had been bestowed upon him by the laying on of hands (1:6); (3) He encourages him to a spirit of fearlessness, power, love and soberness (1:7); (4) He urges that he be not ashamed of the testimony of the Lord, those who were prisoners

107

Daily study of the Bible is necessary if one wishes to know and do the will of God. Paul admonished Timothy to "study to show thyself approved unto God, a workman that needeth not to be ashamed, rightly dividing the word of truth" (2 Tim. 2:15).

for His sake, or to suffer hardship in the holy calling of God's own purpose and grace (1:8-9); (5) He recalls to Timothy the fact that by His appearance, Jesus Christ, our Savior, had abolished death and "brought life and immortality to light through the gospel" (1:10); (6) He points out that because he had been made a preacher, an Apostle, and a teacher, he had been caused to suffer many things for the sake of the Gospel and yet, was not ashamed. The reason he assigns: "I know whom I have believed, and am persuaded that he is able to keep that which I have committed unto him against that day" (1:12); (7) He exhorts Timothy, therefore, to "hold the pattern of sound words, which thou has heard of me, in faith and love which is in Jesus Christ" (1:13); (8) He urges further that he carefully guard or preserve that which had been committed unto him, (deposited with him), by the Holy Spirit (1:14); (9) He urges that he be strengthened in the faith that is Christ Jesus (2:1); (10) He reminds him of his obligation to "commit thou to faithful men the things which thou hast heard of me from many witnesses," that they may be able to teach others also (2:2); (11) He urges that he be strong enough to suffer hardship "as a good soldier of Christ Jesus" and reminds him that a soldier on service does not "entangle himself in the affairs of this life" (2:4); (12) He reminds him of the necessity, if he is to be crowned, of "contending lawfully" (2:5); (13) He exhorts: "Remember that Jesus Christ of the seed of David was raised from the dead, according to my gospel," and that the word of God is not bound (2:8-9); (14) He gives assurance that the saying is faithful: "For if we be dead with him, we shall also live with him: if we suffer, we shall also reign with him: if we deny him, he also will deny us" (2:11-12); (15) He charges Timothy as a preacher with the obligation of charging men, in the sight of the Lord, that they "strive not about words to no profit, but to the subverting of the hearers" (2:14); (16) He urges upon Timothy the obligation to "Study to show thyself approved unto God, a workman that needeth not to be ashamed, rightly dividing the word of truth. But shun profane and vain babblings: for they will increase unto more ungodliness" (2:15-16); (17) He assures Timothy that the "firm foundation of God standeth sure," and that "the Lord knoweth them that are his. And, let every one that nameth the name of Christ depart from iniquity" (2:19-20); (18) He warns him to "Flee also youthful lusts: but follow righteousness, faith, charity, peace, with them that call on the Lord out of a pure heart" (2:22); (19) He warns Timothy to refuse foolish and unlearned questions that gender strife (2:23); (20) He exhorts Timothy, in spite of persecution, to "abide in the things which thou hast learned and hast been assured of, knowing of whom thou has learned them," and reminds him that "from a child thou hast known the holy Scriptures which are able to make thee wise unto salvation through faith which is in Christ Jesus" (3:14-15); (21) He reminds Timothy that "All Scripture is given by inspiration of God, and is profitable for doctrine, for reproof, for correction, for instruction in righteousness: that the man of God may be perfect, thoroughly furnished unto all good works" (3:16-17).

3. The circumstances and conditions gave great emphasis to the necessity both upon the part of Timothy and the church, for spiritual vitality and great evangelistic zeal. Perhaps nowhere in the letter is this more wonderfully and powerfully emphasized that in the final charge which Paul delivered in chapter 4:1-8. This passage of Scripture is the sad farewell and the glorious climax of a wonderful

service and of a very deep and abiding relationship that had endured between the great Apostle to the Gentiles and his beloved son in the Gospel, Timothy. It is an expression of complete and final assurance upon the part of Paul of his own salvation by the Lord in "His Heavenly Kingdom," and it voices the prayerful and loving desire that such assurance might also ever abide in the heart of Timothy.

STUDENT WORK

1. Why does this letter have special meaning? _____
_____

2. What were Paul's circumstances when the letter was written? ____
_____

3. What are the personal aspects of this letter? _____
_____
_____

4. About when was this letter written? _____

5. What are some of the needs of Timothy himself emphasized in the letter? (Cite passages.) _____
_____
_____
_____
_____
_____
_____

6. What exhortations particularly point out the needs of the church as apostasy threatened? _____
_____
_____
_____

7. What two essential characteristics did Paul charge Timothy to emphasize to the Church? _____
_____
_____

8. In view of what considerations were these great essentials to be so emphasized? _____
_____
_____

110

9. Explain the expression "In season and out of season." _____

_____

10. What hope did Paul express as he faced death in Rome? _____

11. Upon what basis did his own personal hope rest? _____

_____

Titus

A. The Background of the Letter.

Titus was written later than First Timothy. Both of them could be dated, probably, around 64 or 65 A.D. Paul had left Ephesus and had gone into Macedonia, from which place he had written the first letter to Timothy who had remained in Ephesus. In all probability, when he left Macedonia he sailed to Crete with Titus accompanying him. He had visited Crete before on his voyage to Rome. Upon this second occasion, he spent some time there and then left Titus to carry on and complete the work that had begun (1:5). Paul must have felt himself pressed for time, and refers to his purpose to send either Artemas or Tychicus to replace Titus in the work at Crete, so that Titus might join him at Nicopolis, for he had determined to spend the winter there (3:12).

The situation of the church in Crete was discouraging. The government of the church needed to be set in order, the careless behavior of its members needed to be corrected, and the church needed to be "grounded in sound doctrine" and stirred to "diligence in good works." Some of these needs arose in the dispositions of the Cretans (1:12-13). In addition to this, the Judaizing group that had followed Paul around disturbing the churches had some influence (1:14). These teachers did not emphasize the stringent observance of the requirements of the law and the traditions of the elders so much as "being unruly and vain talkers and deceivers, specially they of the circumcision: whose mouths must be stopped, who subvert whole houses, teaching things which they ought not, for filthy lucre's sake" (1:10-11). Titus, to whom this letter was written, had been a fellow-worker with Paul for 15 years or more. He was a Gentile, probably converted in the early days of the Gospel in Antioch. In the question that arose concerning the circumcision of Gentiles (Acts 15:1-5), Titus was made prominent (Gal. 2:1-3).

Titus evidently accompanied Paul on his third journey and acted as Paul's messenger to the church at Corinth (2 Cor. 7:1-16). He had gone among the churches with a Gentile element in them, probably because he himself was a Gentile, and had stirred them up to make a contribution to "the relief of the poor among the saints in Jerusalem (2 Cor. 8:6, 16-24). His work in this regard had the encouragement and the full approval of the Apostle Paul. Although he is not mentioned specifically anywhere by Luke in the Book of Acts, he must have been included in the references to "us" which Luke sometimes made (Acts 20:5). Paul's last reference to him is in 2 Timothy 4:17, which states that he had gone to Dalmatia. There is every indication that he was a very strong character and possessed great ability in meeting all opposition to the truth.

B. The Letter.

The general theme of Paul's letter to Titus could well be described as *"things which befit the sound doctrine"* (2:1). The discussion of this theme in the letter can well be seen in the following points:

1. The source of sound doctrine (1:1-4).
2. The means of furthering sound doctrine (1:5-16).

A. The appointment of qualified elders to oversee the function of the church (1:5-9). They were to be men especially "holding fast the faithful word as he hath been taught, able by sound doctrine both to exhort and to convince the gainsayers."

B. The necessity of exposing and stopping teachers of false doctrine (1:10-12). Their mouths were to be stopped (1:11); they were to be rebuked sharply (1:13) that they might be sound in the faith; they were to be condemned for turning others away from the truth, and for being defiled in both mind and conscience, and for believing nothing to be pure (1:14-15). They professed to know God, but denied Him in their works, "being abominable and disobedient and to every good work reprobate" (1:15-16).

C. The preaching of sound doctrine and its application to all classes within the church, such as aged men, aged women, young women, young men, and slaves (2:1-10).

D. God's grace providing salvation "to all men, teaching us that, denying ungodliness and worldly lusts, we should live soberly, righteously, and godly, in this present world; looking for that blessed hope, and the glorious appearing of the great God and Savior Jesus Christ; who gave Himself for us, that He might redeem us from all iniquity, and purify unto Himself a peculiar people, zealous of good works" (2:11-14).

3. The responsibility of Titus as a Gospel preacher was set forth in Paul's letter in the following exhortations:

A. "To set in order the things that are wanting, and ordain elders in every city" (1:5).

B. "But speak thou the things which become sound doctrine" (2:1).

C. "In all things showing thyself a pattern of good works: in doctrine showing uncorruptness, gravity, sincerity, sound speech, that cannot be condemned" (2:7-8).

D. "These things speak, and exhort, and rebuke with all authority. Let no man despise thee" (2:15).

E. "Put them in mind to be subject to principalities and powers, to obey magistrates, to be ready to every good work, to speak evil of no man, to be no brawlers, but gentle, showing all meekness unto all men" (3:1-3).

F. To remind them that God had richly poured out His mercy upon men, providing for their salvation through Jesus Christ, "not by works of righteousness which we have done, but according to his mercy he saved us, by the washing of regeneration, and renewing of the Holy Ghost; which he shed on us abundantly through Jesus Christ our Savior; that being justified by His grace, we should be made heirs according to the hope of eternal life" (3:5-7).

G. Paul charged Titus to "affirm constantly, that they which have believed in God might be careful to maintain good works . . . avoid foolish questions, and genealogies, and contentions, and strivings about the law; . . . . A man that is a heretic, after the first and second admonition, reject; . . . . let ours also learn to maintain good works for necessary uses, that they be not unfruitful" (3:8-14).

4. The elements of sound doctrine, as the theme of the Letter to Titus, can well be summed up in the following points:

A. The person of God (2:11; 3:6).

B. The manifestation of God's love and grace towards humanity in the giving of Christ for our sins and in the revelation of the Holy Spirit, — the Gospel of God's grace (2:11; 3:4).

C. The affirmation that our salvation emanates from God (2:10; 3:4).

D. That this salvation has been provided through Jesus Christ our Lord (2:13; 3:6).

E. That it has been revealed that we might be instructed concerning it through the Holy Spirit (3:5).

F. The Godhead consists of three persons, all of whom perform an agency in the salvation of man (3:5-6).

G. Redemption of sins made possible through the sacrifice of our Savior, Jesus Christ (2:13-14).

H. This salvation through Christ is for all mankind (2:11).

I. It is not by the works of man's righteousness, but has been provided by the grace of God (3:5).

J. It is offered unto men by the teaching of the grace of God through the Holy Spirit (3:5).

K. The Gospel provides for the sanctification (cleansing and separation from evil and dedication to the accomplishment of God's purpose) of His own people (2:12-14).

L. The hope of the second coming of Christ and the faithful inheriting eternal life (2:13; 3:7).

STUDENT WORK

1. About when was the letter to Titus written? _____

2. Why had Paul left Titus at Crete? _____

_____

3. What was the condition of the church in Crete? _____

_____

4. Who were "they of the circumcision" to which Paul refers? _____

_____

5. What does Paul say about the disposition of the Cretans? _____

_____

114

6. These false teachers were motivated by what? _____
_____

7. What did Paul say must be done about them? _____

8. Was Titus a Gentile or Jew? (See Gal. 2:3-4.) _____

9. What connection did Titus have with the relief to be sent to the poor saints in Jerusalem? _____
_____

10. What general theme is found in the letter to Titus? _____
_____
_____

11. What does the letter state to be the source of sound doctrine? ____
_____

12. How does Paul state "sound doctrine" should be furthered? (Cite passages.) _____
_____
_____
_____
_____

13. The responsibilities of Titus as a gospel preacher set forth in Paul's exhortations were. (Cite passages.)

   a. _____
   b. _____
   c. _____
   d. _____
   e. _____
   f. _____
   g. _____

14. List and give the verse cited for the elements of "sound doctrine".

   a. _____
   b. _____
   c. _____
   d. _____
   e. _____
   f. _____
   g. _____
   h. _____
   i. _____
   j. _____

k. _____

l. _____

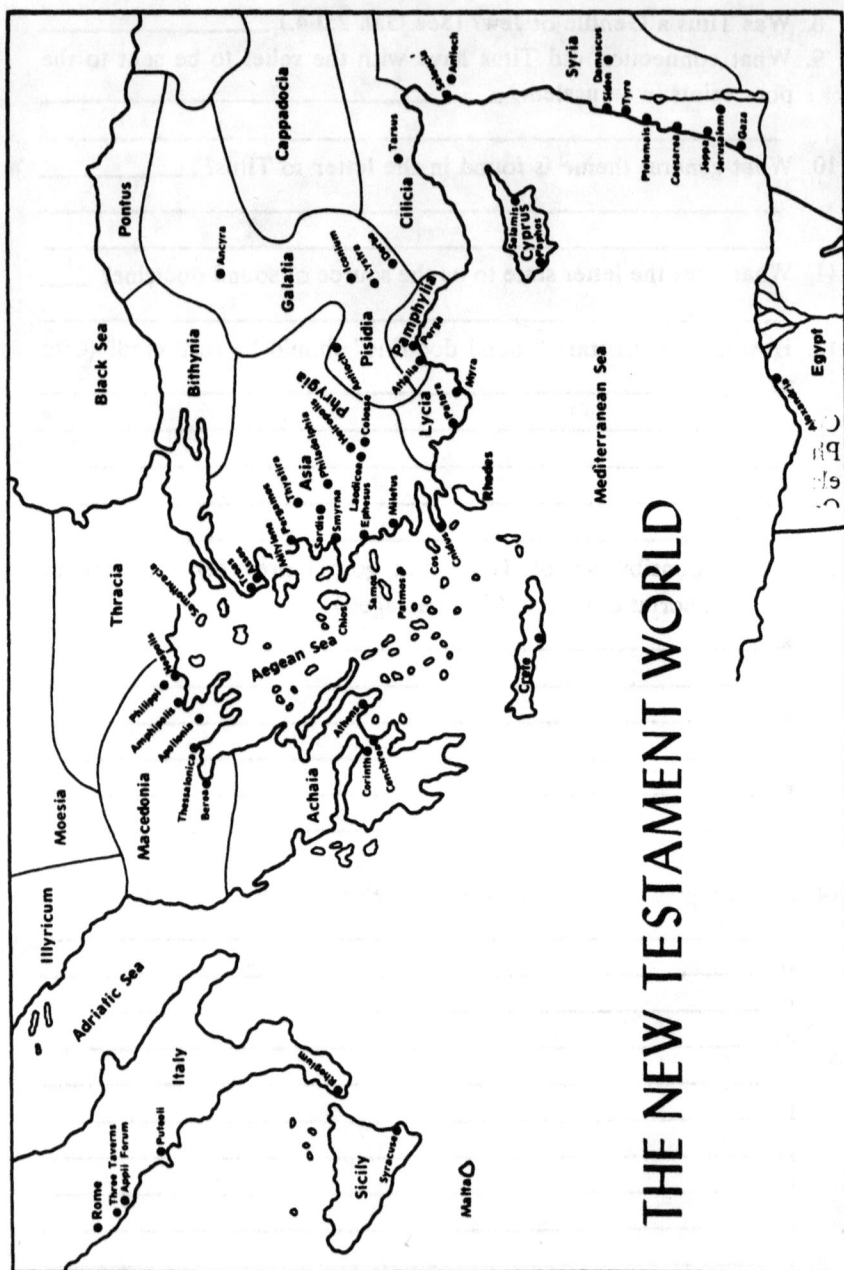

THE NEW TESTAMENT WORLD

Philemon and Jude

A. Philemon.

This is a private letter written to Philemon at Colossae. Paul wrote a number of personal or private letters, but this one alone has been preserved for us. This letter was sent by Tychicus and Onesimus to Philemon, along with the Colossian epistle.

1. *The Date.* Most of the scholars date the letter along with Colossians, about 60 or 61 A.D. The letter is closely associated with Colossians (Col. 4:10-17; Phil. 2:23-24).

2. *The Author.* The writer calls himself Paul three times in the Letter (Verses 1, 9, 19). Proofs of its early existence and genuineness are seen in references to it by several of the early writers, such as Ignatius, Tertullian, Origen, (who quotes verse 14 and attributes it to Paul), and Eusebius.

3. *The Background.* Philemon was evidently a resident of Colossae and the church seems to have assembled in his house (vs. 1). Philemon must have been converted by Paul either at Ephesus or elsewhere (vs. 19). He must have been a wealthy slave owner since Onesimus was his property and Paul refers to his benevolence towards the saints (vss. 5-7), and requests that he prepare for him a place to lodge (vs. 22).

Archippus may have been the preacher or evangelist as Paul exhorts him to "take heed to the ministry which thou hast received in the Lord, that thou fulfill it" (Col. 4:17).

It is commonly thought by many scholars that Apphia, to whom Paul also sent greetings (vs. 2), may have been the wife of Philemon.

Onesimus was a Phrygian slave belonging to Philemon. He had evidently run away from his master and had gone as far as Rome. There is some indication that he may have taken some of his master's property to aid him on his journey (vs. 18).

In Rome it is likely that he soon exhausted what he had and needed help. He was doubtless familiar with the name of Paul and eventually made contact with him. This may have been done through Tychicus or some other. Tychicus was an Asian and may have known Philemon and even Onesimus. At any rate, we learn from this letter that Onesimus had been taught the truth and converted by Paul while in prison (vs. 10). After his conversion, he had been very helpful to Paul. Paul wished that he might have remained with him to help him, but he could not do so without Philemon's consent (vss. 11-14). Onesimus had become a devoted follower and servant of the Lord (Col. 4:9).

4. *The Purpose Of The Letter.* This very heart-warming letter was written by Paul for the purpose of interceding for the runaway slave who had become a faithful Christian, and not only pleading for mercy for him from his master, but also to remind his master of his duty as a fellow Christian toward this penitent slave.

117

5. Characteristics and Contents.

(a). Slavery. This letter gives us a clear picture of social and domestic life in New Testament times. Slavery was one of the common practices of the ancient world. People then saw no more wrong in having slaves than in having domestic servants. Some authorities think that within the Roman Empire there were perhaps 60 million of these slaves. This grievous condition was so common it could not be uprooted immediately, so Christianity regulated it with such principles as to make righteous conduct toward it possible, while at the same time, making it very difficult to continue its inequities and be what Christians ought to be.

Paul besought Philemon to receive Onesimus back not as a slave but as a brother in Christ and to treat him as such (vss. 15-16). Paul was confident Philemon would do even more than he had requested him to do (vs. 21).

(b). This wonderful letter gives us insight into the inner life of Paul, the Christian, in the fact that he demonstrated the lowliness, sympathy and love that he had for Onesimus, by identifying himself with this runaway slave to the point of not only interceding for him with his master, but by offering to himself pay what he owed to his master (vss. 18-19). More than that, Paul treated him as, and referred to him as "brother," "son," and by also referring to him as "my own bowels" (vs. 12). This evidences the personal, tender and very great love and compassion that Paul had for him.

The letter suggests that social and inequitable evils in this world are not to be solved by revolution or violence but by Christian influence and teaching.

(c). This short letter demonstrates the power and influence of the Gospel. Onesimus was converted and faced again, with resolution, his obligations, determined to do his duty in spite of the cost. He could legally have been punished in any way his master chose, and could even have been put to death upon his return, but he was deterred to no degree by such a prospect, but rather placed his hope and faith in the Lord and followed the course He dictated.

(d). This simple story illustrates vividly that genuine repentence demands restitution to the fullest degree possible. Onesimus becoming a Christian laid upon him the necessity of returning to his master from whom he had run away, and settling his account somehow for what he had taken that did not belong to him.

(e). We can also learn from this letter from Paul of one Christian interceding for another and of his willingness to help "bear one another's burdens," by assisting him in paying even the debt that he owed.

(f). Further, the necessity of mercy and forgiveness by the master, Philemon, and proper treatment as a brother was as much an obligation as repentance and restitution on the part of Onesimus.

B. Jude.

1. *The Author.* The writer of the Epistle of Jude identifies himself as "Jude, the servant of Jesus Christ, and brother of James"

(vs. 1). Being a brother of James, who himself was a brother of the Lord (Mt. 13:55; Gal. 1:19), Jude would also be a brother of the Lord in the flesh. He along with the other brothers of Jesus in the flesh did not believe in Jesus during His early ministry (Jn. 7:5). His conversion must have occurred following the resurrection of Christ and we see him as participating in the meeting of the disciples for prayer and supplication following the ascension of the Son of God, as they had returned to the city of Jerusalem (Acts 1:13-14).

2. *The date of the Letter.* The general date of the letter written by Jude is indicated by the fact that it deals with the same problems, teaches the same truths, and makes to some degree the same arguments against those problems that are made in Second Peter. The indication, therefore, is that it was written about the same time as Second Peter and can be dated somewhere around 66 to 67 A.D.

Jude seems to rely greatly upon Old Testament examples, and makes many references to the persons and places of Old Testament history. It may be that he wrote largely, therefore, for the benefit of Jews who had been converted to Christianity.

3. *The Purpose of the Epistle.* This purpose is very definitely stated in verse 3 of the letter: "Beloved, when I gave all diligence to write unto you of the common salvation, it was needful for me to write unto you, and exhort you that ye should earnestly contend for the faith which was once delivered unto the saints." This statement evidently infers that while he had in mind writing a more general letter concerning their "common salvation," it became necessary for the tone of his letter to be changed because of the false doctrine and the danger of apostasy that characterized the church at the particular period when he wrote. While Second Peter was directed to Gentile Christians largely in the provinces of Asia Minor, as well as to Jews who had been converted to Christianity, Jude's letter seems to be directed to these converted Jewish brethren.

4. *Contents and Characteristics.* One of the strongest exhortations in the entire New Testament outlining perhaps the most important duty that any Christian owes unto the Lord is found in verse 3 of the epistle of Jude: "It was needful for me to write unto you, and exhort you that ye should earnestly contend for the faith which was once delivered unto the saints." This expression, "contend earnestly," comes from a term in the original language of the New Testament from which we get our English word, agonize. The Lord used this term when He said, "Strive to enter in at the strait gate" (Lk. 13:24). In this passage Jesus was exhorting people to "agonize" in the interest of their own salvation. However, in Jude 3 we have a prefix added to this term, "agonize," which increases the intensity of the word and makes it more emphatic, and therefore, lays upon the Christian a greater obligation. The most serious responsibility a child of God has, according to the meaning of this term and Jude's exhortation as he uses it, is to uphold, to contend earnestly for the faith of the Gospel. Jude points out that this contending earnestly for the faith is due to the fact that there were certain men, who under

false pretenses, sailing under false colors, were trying to lead the church of God and the people of God into apostasy, "turning the grace of our God into lasciviousness, and denying the only Lord God, and our Lord Jesus Christ" (vs. 4). He writes, therefore, as did Peter, to put them in remembrance of the word of God and its teaching that they might through this warning, remain faithful not only in their own lives, but in upholding the truth against such false teachers (vs. 5).

He reminds those to whom he is writing of how the Lord saved his people out of the land of Egypt and then afterward, when they became unfaithful, destroyed them for their unbelief (vs. 5): He also calls to their attention that the angels which did not abide within their state of submission and subjection to the will of God, but "left their own habitation, he hath reserved in everlasting chains under darkness unto the judgment of the great day" (vs. 6). He also recalls the example of Sodom and Gomorrah who "gave themselves over to fornication" and went "after strange flesh," and suffered "the vengence of eternal fire" (vs. 7). These false teachers of whom Jude was warning the brethren were also "filthy dreamers" which "defile the flesh, despise dominion, and speak evil of dignities" (vs. 8). He reminds them that even Michael the archangel when contending with the devil about the body of Moses, did not dare bring a railing accusation, but said, "The Lord rebuke thee." Vengence, therefore, is in the hands of God and judgment will be executed by Him (vs. 9).

Those who were teaching the false doctrine of Gnosticism that evidently Jude had in mind, along with Paul and Peter who dealt with this same false system of religion, were speaking "evil of those things which they knew not," and were living as "brute beasts," satisfying their natural and fleshly appetites and corrupting themselves (vs. 10). He pronounces "Woe upon them! for they have gone in the way of Cain, and ran greedily after the error of Balaam for reward, and perished in the gainsaying of Korah" (vs. 11). He suggests that these false teachers who were wrecking such harm to the souls of men and to the cause of Christ were like spots in a love feast, while they feed themselves without fear. In the midst of those who were Christians, they were to be compared with clouds without water, carried about by the wind, trees, whose fruit withered and fell off, and who were twice dead, plucked up by the roots (vs. 12). He eloquently describes them as "raging waves of the sea, foaming out their own shame; wandering stars, to whom is reserved the blackness of darkness for ever" (vs. 13). He refers to Enoch, the seventh from Adam, and said that he prophesied of these and promised, "Behold, the Lord cometh with ten thousands of his saints, to execute judgment upon all, and to convince all that are ungodly among them of all their ungodly deeds which they have ungodly committed, and of all their hard speeches which ungodly sinners have spoken against him" (vss. 14-15).

He classifies these false teachers as murmurers, complainers, walking after their own lusts, speaking great swelling words, seeking admiration and advantage from a personal point of view that they might receive by doing such (vs. 16). His exhortation is that those

120

who were his beloved should "remember ye the words which were spoken before of the apostles of our Lord Jesus Christ; how that they told you there should be mockers in the last time, who should walk after their own ungodly lusts. These be they who separate themselves, sensual, having not the Spirit. But ye, beloved, building up yourselves on your most holy faith, praying in the Holy Ghost, keep yourselves in the love of God, looking for the mercy of our Lord Jesus Christ unto eternal life" (vss. 17-21). He calls to their attention the need for compassion toward some, with a distinction to be made that others could be saved with fear and pulled out of the fire, hating even the garments that were spotted by the flesh (vss. 22-23).

And then, in the closing, he commends them unto Him who is able to keep them from falling and "to present you faultless before the presence of his glory with exceeding joy, to the only wise God our Savior, be glory and majesty, dominion and power, both now and ever. Amen" (vss. 24-25).

STUDENT WORK

Philemon.

1. Where did Philemon live? _____

2. Who were the messengers by whom the letter was sent? _____
_____

3. When was the letter written? _____

4. What other letter was sent from Paul at the same time? ____
_____

5. How do we know Paul was the author? _____

6. Where did Philemon live? _____

8. Who was Onesimus? _____
_____

9. What contact did Paul have with Onesimus? _____
_____

10. When Paul wrote Philemon concerning Onesimus was it to intercede (____); request that the runaway slave be allowed to go free (____); remind him to treat the returning runaway slave as a Christian brother (____). Check right one.

11. Why was Onesimus returning to his master after becoming a Christian? _____
_____

12. Why did not Paul condemn slavery as unchristian since it was so common in New Testament days? _____

II. Jude.

1. Who was Jude? Give Scriptures. _____
_____

2. What identifies the date this epistle was written? _____
_____

3. What use did Jude make of the Old Testament in this epistle?
_____

4. What was the purpose of the epistle? _____
_____

5. To whom was the letter more definitely directed? _____

6. Quote and cite the most fundamental exhortation in the
   epistle? _____
_____

7. What was the attitude of the false teachers who were leading
   the church into apostasy? _____
_____

8. What does he put them in "remembrance" of and what was his
   purpose? _____
_____
_____
_____

9. How does he describe these false teachers? _____
_____

10. What apostolic warning does he bring to their minds? Give
    Verse. _____
_____

11. Point out six different phrases with which he describes such
    false teachers?
    _____   _____
    _____   _____
    _____   _____

12. What does he admonish Christians to do to avoid apostasy?
_____

13. Give the expressions he uses in closing extolling God's power
    and greatness. _____
_____
_____

Hebrews

Introduction.

The Epistle to the Hebrews is peculiar and distinct in the fact that it is not in the class of the general epistles of the New Testament, but it is given as a summary of the transition from the Old Testament to the New. From the viewpoint of its doctrinal contribution to the New Testament scriptures, it is without a rival among the books of the New Testament. It shows that the change from the Old Covenant to the New Covenant was prefigured and prophesied in the Old Testament, particularly the change to a new priesthood, a new sacrifice, a new sanctuary, as a part of that New Covenant. Nowhere in all New Testament writings is the contrast between the Old Testament and the New made more vivid or marked out any more definitely. This epistle needs, therefore, very careful study and consideration in order that we may be able through it, to come to a better understanding of the place and purpose of both covenants and the differences between them.

A. The Author.

The question of who wrote the epistle to the Hebrews is perhaps the most vexing problem connected with this epistle. There is no name mentioned in it as to whom the writer might be, and another peculiarity of the letter is that the definite address of the letter, that is, to whom it was written, is likewise not identified within the letter itself.

Hebrews is not an anonymous epistle in the sense that the writer is unknown to the readers. They must have been acquainted with the one writing to them, from all indications in the epistle itself, but it is anonymous in the sense that the name is not indicated. The writer asks that they pray for him, that he may be able to visit those to whom he is writing (13:19), and expresses the hope that Timothy, who has been lately released from prison, might come with him (13:23). The writer of the letter must have been a Jew, since he frequently uses the first person plural in addressing his Jewish audience. Some of the possible authors suggested by the various scholars are Barnabas, Luke, and Apollos, but the predominance of the evidence that is available seems to indicate that the letter was most probably written by the Apostle Paul. He was a Hebrew among the Hebrews. No writer in New Testament days was any better acquainted with the Law of the Old Testament and the religion of the Jews with all of its ceremonies and their meanings than was Paul. Many of the early writers, the early "Christian fathers," as they are sometimes called, attributed the letter to Paul. According to Eusebius, Clement of Alexandria held that Paul wrote the letter in Hebrew and that Luke translated it into Greek. Eusebius also makes Pantaenus of Alexandria say that Paul wrote to the Hebrews. Origen repeatedly

123

cites it as by Paul. He further admits that men of old time have handed it down as Paul's. Athanasius included it among the 14 epistles of Paul, and from Athanasius onward the Greek writers universally ascribed it to Paul. Jerome and Augustine adopted the opinion of the East, and after that the authority of the epistle was established.

The internal evidence as to its authorship, although considered somewhat indefinite, yet has certain definite trends that ought to at least be accepted as worthy of notice and consideration. Among these, as suggested, is the reference to Timothy (13:23), Paul's long time associate; as well as the comparative statements, both in expression and thought, between various passages in Hebrews and the recognized Pauline epistles, such as: Hebrews 1:1 and Philippians 2:9; Hebrews 2:2 and Galatians 3:19; Hebrews 2:10 and Romans 11:36; Hebrews 7:18 and Romans 8:3; Hebrews 7:27 and Ephesians 5:2; Hebrews 8:13 and 2 Corinthians 3:11; Hebrews 10:33 and 1 Corinthians 4:9; Hebrews 11:13 and Ephesians 2:19; Hebrews 12:22 and Galatians 4:25-26. To these can be added the fact of the central Person and work of Christ in the Hebrew letter, as in all of the other Pauline epistles.

Although there are many differences that have been pointed out in the style of the Hebrew letter and the other Pauline epistles, these do not carry the weight of evidence that is sometimes given to them, as can be seen by the fact that Paul, as a highly educated individual, writing to a distinctly different people, and for a distinctly different purpose, was capable of adapting himself to the terminology as well as to the teaching that was particularly needed to accomplish his purposes.

If the question be raised as to why Paul did not give the same salutation in this letter that he did in all of the other letters written by him in the New Testament, and why his name is not mentioned in the book of Hebrews as it is most commonly in his other letters, there is perhaps a good explanation. Clement of Alexandria suggests that these were avoided that prejudice might not be aroused against the epistle. While there may be some doubt as to the authorship of the epistle, there is no doubt, in the mind of any of the scholars, that it is of Divine inspiration, and of its place in the sacred canon of the word of God. Mr. Westcott said that no book in the Bible is more completely recognized by universal consent as giving a Divine view of the facts of the Gospel, full of lessons for all time, than Hebrews.

B. To Whom the Letter Was Written?

The original title, Epistle to the Hebrews, was no doubt rightly given to the epistle. The author assumes an exclusively Jewish point of view in the minds of his readers as his major premise. Mr. Westcott says: "The arguments and reflections in their whole form and spirit even more than in special details are addressed to Hebrews." This view is sustained by the fact that there is no reference to Gentiles or to Gentile controversy in the epistle. Nothing is said

124

about circumcision, abstinence from things sacrificed to idols, or the equality of Jew and Gentile in the church. Abraham was given such prominence in 7:4-11, and in 11:11-12 as to indicate that the writer had those in mind who were the descendants of Abraham.

However, those to whom the letter was written were evidently disciples of Christ. This is indicated by a number of facts:

1. They had heard the Gospel from the disciples of the Lord (2:3).

2. They had witnessed the signs and the wonders and manifold power and gifts of the Holy Spirit, evidencing Divine revelation (2:4).

3. They had been made "partakers of Christ" and needed to hold fast the beginning of their confidence to the end (3:14).

4. They had engaged in the ministry to the saints (6:10). They had in former days, perhaps in connection with the persecution that had broken out when Stephen was stoned, endured suffering and persecution, although not unto blood, and had shown compassion toward those who were in prison (10:32-34; 12:4).

5. They had been believers for some time; their leaders had died (13:7), and they themselves should be teachers by the time the letter was written (5:12).

6. They had a good understanding of "the first principles of Christ" (6:1), but they had become dull of hearing (5:11), and sluggish in their conduct (6:12).

7. The writer feared that some of them were in danger of apostasy (6:4-8).

8. Their besetting sin was unbelief (3:12).

All of this indicates that the persons addressed in the letter were Christians who had been converted from Judaism.

The question is raised, however, as to what group of Jewish Christians the letter was addressed: Were they in a particular localtiy, or was it a general epistle to Hebrew Christians everywhere? The indication of the internal evidence points to the former. The various things said about them could not be true of all Hebrew Christians in the same way. Instances of this are found in Hebrews 2:3-4; 10:32-34; 13:7,19,23. The weight of the evidence seems to point most distinctly to Jerusalem and to those in its vicinity. All of them had held that the Temple at Jerusalem was the true center of worship, and it was among this group that the sentiment toward Judaism, in all probability, would have been the strongest.

C. The Occasion and Date.

The Hebrew letter was evidently written to second generation Christians. A considerable amount of time had elapsed since Christ had been here on earth. The close relationship that these Hebrew Christians, in the vicinity of Jerusalem, had with all of the rituals of Jewish worship and with the Temple itself, as well as with the Jewish community of that area; the growing difficulties that Rome had increasingly brought upon Christians in the persecutions afflicting them would likely have been great influences in the tendency of the

Jews of this area, converted to Christianity, to have become dull of hearing, sluggish in conduct, and to have grown weak in their faith and to be, therefore, in danger of apostasy. These conditions led to the writing of the epistle. It seems evident that the Temple had not yet been destroyed and that its service was still in progress. This meant that the letter had to be written before A.D. 70, probably about 66 or 67 A.D.

D. Purpose and Plan.

The principal aim of the Hebrew epistle very plainly was to establish the supremacy of Christ in the New Testament (1:1-10,18). The Apostle then points out to them that the demands of this truth requires their faithfulness to it and their refusal to turn away from it and to go back to the Old Covenant, and to be guilty, therefore, of apostasy (6:4-8; 10:19-39; 12:12-17). He exhorts them in the letter to make a complete break with Judaism (12:18; 13:17).

The writer argues throughout Hebrews for the superiority of Christ as Heaven's messenger; that God speaks to us today through His Son is the announcement of the epistle in the very beginning (1:1-4); and that this Son, the Christ, is the greatest messenger that Heaven could send. Because of the superiority of the messenger, it ought therefore to follow as a conviction that the message itself is superior to any former message that God ever gave, and ought to be given priority and preeminence in the minds and the hearts of those who had turned to God through Christ.

E. Contents and Characteristics.

1. In pursuit of the theme of the *superiority of the New Covenant over the old,* based upon the fact that it was brought from Heaven to earth by a superior messenger, the use of the term "better" is given quite frequent prominence in the Book of Hebrews. In fact, it becomes an outline of much of the contents of it, and ought to be looked for as we read the letter, and underscored in our Bibles as well as in our minds.

In the initial statement of the Epistle to the Hebrews, the writer calls attention to the fact that God, in times past, had delivered His message in many different ways, and in many different parts, or at many different times, and that He had spoken unto us through His Son. The Son, of course, is Heaven's greatest messenger. Paul sets forth the supremacy of the nature of Christ by pointing out a number of things: (a). That He is the heir to all things, as the Son of God; (b). That it was by Christ that God made the world; (c). That He is the brightness of God's glory and the express image of His Person; (d). That he upholds all things by the word of His power; (e). That when He had, by Himself, purged our sins through His sacrifice upon the Cross, that He ascended to the right hand of God, the Father, and sat down at the right hand of the Majesty on high (1:1-3).

The remaining part of chapter 1 and a good part of chapter 2 are devoted to showing the superiority of Christ over angelic messengers.

This was in direct contrast to the Law that God had given through Moses to Israel at Mt. Sinai, which had been ordained by the hands of angels. This points out that Christ is not only superior to all of the prophets of the Old Testament, because of the supremacy of His nature, but that He is also superior to even angelic messengers.

On the basis of the superiority of Christ over even the angels of God, Paul argues that we ought to give the more earnest heed to the message which God has delivered unto us through Him. He builds this argument around the fact that God's word was stedfast even when it had been delivered by the hands of angels, and since it was stedfast and under such a law every transgression and disobedience received a just recompense of reward, and today we have a greater message by a greater messenger, then certainly it is worthy of a more earnest heed and closer, more careful attention than was the Old, and is therefore more stedfast than the Old. If there was no escape from the penalty of the Old when it had been violated and set aside, his conclusion is, in Chapter 2, that there will certainly be no escape if we reject the message of Jesus Christ which is God's message to us today.

He points out that in delivering this message and becoming the Redeemer of mankind as well as God's messenger to mankind, Jesus was made a little lower than the angels; that He took upon Himself not the nature of angels but rather He took upon himself the nature of man, the seed of Abraham, that in all things He might be made like unto His brethren, and that in the midst of His brethren he might give praise unto God, and also that He might become because of being made like His brethren, a merciful and faithful High Priest in things pertaining to God, to make reconciliation for the sins of the people. This is emphasized in Chapter 2:5-18.

It is noticeable that after the various contrasts that Paul draws showing the superiority of the New Covenant over the Old that in each case, when his argument had been finished, it was followed by an exhortation. His exhortation in chapter 2, after pointing out the superiority of Heaven's messenger over the prophets, is found in 2:1-4. It is, "Therefore we ought to give the more earnest heed to the things which we have heard, lest at any time we should let them slip."

In chapters 3 and 4, the writer of Hebrews points out the superiority of the Son of God over Moses and over Joshua. The superiority of Christ over Moses is discussed in 3:1-6. Here it is pointed out that Moses was a *servant in God's house,* while Christ is the *Son over the house of God,* in complete control of the affairs of God's household in the Christian dispensation.

He points out that when the Law had been given through Moses and the Wilderness wanderings had begun because of their unbelief, they tempted God in the Wilderness in which they journeyed for 40 years; and that in their tempting God and displeasing God, they failed to enter into the rest that God had promised them at the end of the journey. All of this he attributes to unbelief, and if unbelief caused them to fall short of their goal and their final reward at the end of their journey under the leadership of Moses, then certainly unbelief would cause us to fail to receive the final rest that is prepared for the people of God at the end of our journey, if we fail to be faithful to Christ and God's message as it has been delivered through Him. He argues that the rest that God gave them was not in reality the final rest that God had in mind for His people, but rather a type of it. But if the rest that God promised to the Jews at the end of their journey to Caanan was forfeited because of unbelief, then the final rest that remains in Heaven for us can also be forfeited because of unbelief. He follows this reasoning by saying there remaineth therefore a rest for the people of God (4:9), and then he exhorts: "Let us labor therefore to enter into that rest, lest any man fall after the same example of unbelief" (4:11).

In chapter 5, he points out the fact of the superiority of the priesthood of Christ, arguing first of all in the latter part of chapter 4 that He had been qualified to become our High Priest, since He had come in the flesh and had been tested of life, and could be touched with the feelings of our own infirmities, "having been tempted like as we are yet without sin" (4:14-16). Then he contends that Jesus was qualified as our High Priest and as a perfect Savior by learning obedience by the things which he suffered (5:8). He continues: "And being made perfect he became the author of all salvation unto all them that obey him" and affirms that he was called a high priest after the order of Melchizedek (5:9-10). Having argued that Christ had been made perfect as our redeemer and having pointed out that He had been qualified to be our high priest unto God, Paul then argues the superiority of the priesthood of Christ over the Aaronic priesthood (chs. 5-7).

One of the things that the writer points out that emphasizes the superiority of the priesthood of Christ is the fact that Christ is a priest after the order of Melchizedek who was both king of Salem and priest of the most high God. The Old Testament prophets prophesied that Christ would be both king and priest upon His throne. So in this we find a very important point of comparison between Melchizedek and Christ (7:1).

Another point of comparison is the fact that Melchizedek had no predecessor. Nobody had gone before him in that line of priesthood and he was followed by no successor. In this fact he was "without father, without mother, without descent, having neither beginning of days nor end of life; but made like unto the Son of God; to abide a priest continually" (7:3). This refers not to the physical life of Melchizedek but to his reign as priest.

Paul then argues in this 7th chapter of Hebrews that Abraham paid tithes unto Melchizedek when he returned from the battle of the kings; that he gave a tenth of the spoils of the battle unto Melchizedek as a tithe. This is an indication, and Paul bases his argument upon it, that the lesser pays tithes to and is blessed by the greater, so Melchizedek was superior to Abraham. Since Melchizedek was himself superior to Abraham, and Christ is a priest after the order of Melchizedek, then the priesthood of Christ is greater even than Abraham, the father of the Jewish Nation. This argument is found in Chapter 7:4-10.

Paul continues by pointing out that if God had intended for the Levitical priesthood to have remained forever and if perfection had been possible under the Levitical priesthood, there would be no further need for another priest after the order of Melchizedek and not after the order of Aaron (7:11-12). The priesthood of Christ is not upon the earth; it was not possible while he was here upon the earth in His flesh for Him to be a priest (8:4). He came out of the wrong tribe to be a priest under the Law for He was of the tribe of Judah and under the Law nothing was spoken regarding a priest from the tribe of Judah. All the priests came from the tribe of Levi. So, the priesthood of Christ certainly was not, in any sense, under the Law of Moses. Paul argues that "there is a disannulling of the commandment going before for the weakness and unprofitableness thereof" (7:18), and that the Law made nothing perfect but the bringing in of a better hope by which we draw nigh unto God through Jesus Christ, our Lord, offering perfection (7:13-19). In this same connection, he argues that there being a change in the priesthood, there must have also, of necessity, been a change in the law.

The superiority of the priesthood of Christ is argued again by the fact that the priests under the Law of Moses were not suffered to continue by reason of death (7:23), but that Jesus would continue forever in an unchangeable priesthood, as a living priest, made so forever by the oath of God, whom "The Lord sware and will not repent, Thou art a priest forever after the order of Melchizedek" (7:21), and that we therefore have a high priest who is "holy, harmless, undefiled, separate from sinners, and made higher than the heavens" (7:26).

As another point of superiority over the Aaronic priesthood, Paul points out that the Aaronic priests had to offer up sacrifice for their own sins and then for the sins of the people, but that Jesus did this "once for all," not daily, when He offered Himself as a sacrifice for sins not his own, but the sins of the people (7:26-28).

In Chapter 8, he not only further emphasizes the ministry of Christ as our High Priest under the New Covenant, but he points out the fact that we have a better tabernacle, a spiritual ministration and a spiritual tabernacle, the Old serving as an example or a type of the New. In this connection, he suggests to us that God gave to us the pattern of the tabernacle through Moses in the mountain and charged him to build all things according to that pattern (8:5). The chief point, Paul says, is in this he is talking about a tabernacle that the Lord has pitched and not man (8:4).

He affirms that not only do we have a better ministry, "a more excellent ministry" in the Priesthood of Christ, but that He is the mediator of a "better covenant," which is established upon "better promises" (8:6). He reminds his readers of the prophecy in Jeremiah 31, in which God prophesied that He would give a New Covenant to

Interior of the Howland-Garber model reconstruction of Solomon's Temple. A study of 1 Kings 6 - 8 and Hebrews 9:1-10 (speaking of the tabernacle) with this photo before you would probably aid in understanding the construction and furniture of the temple.

the house of Israel and to the house of Judah, and that it would not be according to the covenant that was given to their fathers when He had led them up out of the land of Egypt. This is a specific reference to the Abrahamic covenant for the deliverance of Israel from Egypt and the giving of the Law of Moses on Mt. Sinai to guarantee the fulfilment of that covenant. He said that the reason that the Old was rejected, or that Israel was rejected, was because they continued not in His covenant and were unfaithful to Him under it. In pointing out the difference between the Old and the New Covenant which God promised, he suggests to them the superiority of the New in that its law would be written upon the hearts of men rather than inscribed upon tablets of stone; that instead of every man teaching his brother after he had entered into covenant relationship, that every man would be taught in order to enter into covenant relationship with God; that instead of their sins being remembered as they were under the Old Law, for animal sacrifices could not take away sin, that under the New Covenant was given remission of sins, the blotting out of sins, so that they would be remembered no more. He reminds them also that the expression, "Old Covenant," signified that it would "decay and wax old" and would therefore "vanish away" (8:13).

In Hebrews 9:1-7, Paul gives us a description of the Tabernacle

130

which was under the first Covenant, the tabernacle which Moses built after God had given him the pattern of it in the mountain. He refers to it as a worldly sanctuary, but affirms that it also had ordinances of Divine service. He. describes the tabernacle itself as of two parts; the first part called the sanctuary, is the part in which the candlestick, the table, and the showbread was situated; after the second veil the tabernacle had another part, which was called the Holiest of all (9:1-3). In this was the golden censer, the ark, the golden pot that had manna in it, Aaron's rod that budded, and the tables of the Covenant. These things were simply a shadow of the things to come (9:9; 10:1). In these ordinances under the Old Law there are some points that Paul suggests to us which become very important as a shadow of the things to come. He points out that while the priests went always into the first part of the tabernacle, the sanctuary, to carry on the. various ministrations which were ordained under the Law, yet the high priest alone went into the innermost part, the Holy of Holies, once a year. He did not enter it without blood or a sacrifice which he offered for himself and for the sins of the people.

In 9:8 Paul tells us that the Holy Ghost thus signified that the way into the Holiest of all, that is, Heaven itself, was not made manifest while this first tabernacle yet stood. It was therefore necessary that the first tabernacle be removed in order that the plan of human redemption, or man's opportunity to go to Heaven, might be provided by the grace of God and made known through the Gospel. Beginning with verse 11, he points out that Jesus Christ "being come a high priest of good things to come, by a greater and more perfect tabernacle, not made with hands, that is to say, not of this building." By this statement he contrasts God's spiritual dwelling place among His people today, the Church of our Lord, with the worldly sanctuary that existed in the days of the tabernacle service under the Old Covenant. Then, beginning with verse 12, he tells us that Jesus entered into the Holy place, having obtained eternal redemption for us and this He did by the sacrifice of Himself, by His own blood (9:12). Sanctification was not possible by the shedding of the blood of bulls and goats. Sins could not be remitted by the offering of animal sacrifices. This, Paul makes abundantly clear in Hebrews 10:4, when he said "that it is not possible for the blood of bulls and of goats to take away sins." The animal sacrifices under the Law of Moses could only sanctify to the purifying of the flesh (9:13), but the blood of Christ "who through the eternal Spirit offered himself without spot to God," purges our consciences from dead works that we might serve the living God (9:14).

Beginning with verse 15, Paul affirms that because it took the blood of Christ to provide for the remission of sins, for the redemption of the transgressions that were even under the first Covenant, as well as for ours, that it was thus necessary for Jesus to die. He points out that the Testament, or will of our Lord, providing for human redemption, could not take effect or force until the death of Him that made it. Just as Moses sprinkled blood upon the Law and upon the tabernacle and upon all of the vessels of ministry that were in the tabernacle, as well as all the people, sanctifying the Old Covenant and the people thereunder as the people of God, so Christ has entered into Heaven itself (9:24) to appear in the presence of God for us, and by His blood to sanctify the Gospel of the New Covenant, giving it force and effect by His death; sanctify the Church or the Temple of God today made up of living or spiritual stones as the dwelling place of God among His people, purchasing it with His own precious blood (Acts 20:28); cleanse and sanctify also the vessels of ministry by which the work of the Lord in the Church of the Lord is carried on, in harmony with His will, and in which everything is made Holy and acceptable in the sight of God; and in addition to all of this, by His blood He sanctifies also the people themselves when they come in contact with it. Concerning the blood of Jesus Christ which makes all of this possible, Paul affirms that He was once offered to bear the sins of many (9:28). He affirms also that it is not necessary that He should offer himself often, as did the high priest make a sacrifice every year with the blood of animals, but now "once in the end of the world hath he appeared to put away sin by the sacrifice of himself" (9:24-26).

In the 10th chapter of Hebrews the Apostle points out that under the sacrifices of the Old Law, *remission of sins* was impossible, but that there was a *remembrance of sins* made every year. But now that Christ has come into the world, a body having been prepared for Him (10:5-9), we, under the New Covenant, are sanctified through the offering of the body of Jesus Christ, one time for all time to come (10:10). In 10:9, he affirms that by Jesus coming in the flesh and dying upon the Cross, He took away the First Covenant in order that He might establish the Second Covenant. Nowhere in the New Testament is it made any plainer that we are living today under the New Testament, the will of Christ, the Second Covenant, and must serve God according to it, rather than under the First Covenant, the Covenant made with Abraham and established or enforced by the Law of Moses. Paul affirms the insufficiency of the sacrifices under the Old Covenant but the sufficiency and the finality, for all time to come, of the sacrifice of the Son of God under the New Covenant. He reminds his readers again that the Old Testament pattern (Jer. 31:31) prophesied of the fact that an offering would be made that would make it possible for their sins to be remitted and never remembered against them any more forever. He affirms that Jesus Christ by one offering, the offering of His own life upon the Cross for our sins, is able to perfect forever them that are sanctified (10:14).

The promise of God for a New Covenant having been fulfilled through the offering of the body of Jesus Christ, Paul exhorts his brethren that they should have "boldness to enter into the Holiest by the blood of Jesus, by a new and living way, which He hath consecrated for us, through the veil, that is to say, his flesh" (10:19-20). He further exhorts, "let us draw near with a true heart in full assurance of faith, having our hearts sprinkled from an evil conscience, and our bodies washed with pure water" (10:19-22). In this reference in the 22nd Verse, Paul affirms again, as he did in 9:13-14, that it is the sprinkling of the blood of Christ upon the heart of the sinner that cleanses and purifies his heart, but in 10:22, he connects this sprinkling of the blood of Christ, cleansing the heart from an evil conscience, with the body of man being washed with pure water, which is a very evident, plain reference to the act of baptism, which is the obedience of faith to the Gospel of Jesus Christ. Here again he follows the argument that we have a better sacrifice and a better tabernacle and a better promise, with an exhortation that we should "hold fast the profession of our faith without wavering" (10:23). He further exhorts that we are to provoke one another unto love and good works, "not forsaking the assembling of ourselves together," as some were doing, but we are to exhort each other so much the more as we see the day approaching. In this assembling of ourselves together, we have a reference very definitely to the practice of the New Testament Church meeting on the first day of the week to break bread in memory of the Lord (Acts 20:7; 1 Cor. 10:17). It is in this assembly of the saints and the observance of the Lord's Supper in remembrance of His death that we maintain communion with the blood of Jesus Christ and are kept cleansed and purified by our constancy in worship.

In connection with this exhortation to constancy in Christian worship, as the people of God come together to constitute the Spiritual body of Christ, the house of God, and to worship God in Spirit and in truth, Paul points out that when the Law of Moses was set aside and it had been established by the mouth of two or three witnesses that no mercy was extended but condemnation pronounced. He vividly emphasizes that fact that we will be punished with even a sorer punishment (10:29), if we are guilty of counting the blood of the covenant wherewith He was sanctified an unholy thing. He also suggests in verse 31 that it is a fearful thing to fall into the hands or under the judgment of the living God. He appeals to these Jewish brethren who were members of the body of Christ, that having suffered as they had and having shown the compassion which they had shown to Paul in his bonds or imprisonment, that they should not "cast away their confidence which hath great recompense of reward" (10:35) but that they needed to be patient after having done the will of God, that they might receive the promise (10:36). The life to which they had given themselves in obedience to the New Covenant and to the law of Jesus Christ announced in it required, even as obedience to God had always required, "the just shall live by faith," and that perdition awaits those who draw back and find no pleasure in faithfulness to the Lord (10:35-39).

Chapter 11 of Hebrews is a great chapter on faith. In fact, it is a chapter on the expression, "by faith." Paul gives a panoramic view of the faithful servant of God under the Old Law. He begins with Able, who offered a more excellent sacrifice, and brings us on down through Enoch, Noah, Abraham, Jacob and Joseph, Moses and

Aaron, Joshua and Caleb, and finally raises the question, "What more shall I say? for the time would fail me to tell of Gideon, and of Barak, and of Samson, and of the prophets" (10:32). The demonstration of faith by these Old Testament characters points out several principles that all who would serve God faithfully need to learn. The expression "by faith" necessarily implies: (1) that God has spoken. Nothing can be done by faith unless God says for it to be done, for Paul declares that faith comes "by hearing and hearing by the word of God" (Rom. 10:17); (2) Man must act. By faith, implies action upon man's part. Faith is a motive, and we are told in James 2 that faith without works, or faith that does not motivate obedience to the will of God is dead, being alone; (3) The thing which man does must be the thing which God has said if it is "by faith." No substitutes are acceptable; (4) The thing which man does in response to that which God has said must be done like God said do it. This is illustrated by examples in Hebrews 11. Noah had to build the Ark like God planned for him to build it. He would not have been saved had he not done so, Israel had to march around the city of Jericho according to God's plan. If they had not done so, the city would not have fallen. The same principle holds true in every other act of obedience which is cited; (5) In doing a thing "by faith," it must be done for the reason that God has assigned. In other words, Noah built the Ark to serve the purpose that God had planned for it to serve. This is true of every act of obedience "by faith" in the history of God's dealing with mankind, and it always will be true; (6) Then, there is the principle that in doing the thing "by faith," it must also be done just because God said do it. Not for the reason that it might seem reasonable, or that it might please me, or might be approved by my judgment or wisdom, but for the reason that it is God's will, taught in the word of God, and becomes therefore the duty of man, and faith in God requires that we act upon it.

Paul concludes this great chapter on faith by pointing out that in spite of all of the worthies of the Old Testament endured by faith and in obedience to the will of God, "they received not the promise: God having provided some better thing for us that they without us should not be made perfect" (11:39-40). If justification had been offered under the Old Covenant when that Covenant included only the seed of Abraham, then God would have been a respecter of persons and left those outside of the seed of Abraham without justification at all.

Paul concludes the Book of Hebrews in chapters 12 and 13, having presented his argument of the superiority of the New Covenant over the Old with an exhortation to faithfulness and Godliness, and to various other duties concerning their manner of living, and to the performance of their duty under the New Covenant, as the people of God.

The key word in this main argument that runs throughout the Book of Hebrews, setting forth the comparison between the Old and the New Covenant and showing the superiority of the New, is the word "better." You can follow it all the way through the Book of

Hebrews as it is applied by Paul to many different things, such as: (a) better revelation (1:1-4); (b) better hope (7:19); (c) better priesthood (7:20-28); (d) better covenant (8:6); (e) better promises (8:6); (f) better sacrifices (9:23); (g) better possessions (10:34); (h) better country (11:16); (i) better resurrection (11:35). Thus, by the use of this term repeatedly, the Apostle Paul emphasizes how foolish it would be to turn away from a better covenant with better hopes and better promises to go back to the Old Covenant.

2. This Book impresses us with the fact that following his arguments concerning the superiority of the New Covenant, Paul *filled the Book of Hebrews with exhortations.* The common form that this exhortation takes in its introduction, are the two words, "let us." This expression, in connection with the exhortation offered, is found in a number of passages: *(a)* Let us fear (4:1); *(b)* Let us therefore give diligence to enter (4:11); *(c)* Let us hold fast our confessions (4:14); *(d)* Let us draw near to the throne of grace (4:16); *(e)* Let us press on unto perfection (6:1); *(f)* Let us draw near (10:22); *(g)* Let us hold fast the confession of our faith (10:23); *(h)* Let us consider one another (10:24); *(i)* Let us lay aside every weight (12:1); *(j)* Let us run the race (12:1); *(k)* Let us have grace (12:28); *(l)* Let us therefore go forth unto him (13:13); *(m)* Let us offer up sacrifice of praise (13:15). All of these exhortations are exhortations to a higher state of spiritual perfection. The bulk of these exhortations occur in the concluding chapters, the last 3 chapters of the Book of Hebrews. The other 5 are connected with severe warnings for the purpose of offering a word of encouragement.

3. One of the subjects more fully treated in the Book of Hebrews is *the priesthood of Christ.* To the Jew under the Law of Moses the priest represented access to God. This is the particular function that Christ performs as priest for those who are children of God today under the New Covenant. Through Him, God approaches man, and by Him every Spiritual provision is made. In Him, and through Him alone, can man approach God and find the grace to help in every time of need. The Aaronic priesthood under the Old Law by its sacrifices and its intercession ministered to the people of God. Christ under the New Covenant is a more perfect priest. Paul affirms that He came into the world to qualify Himself by being tempted in all points like as we are. He is able therefore to understand our needs and to extend not only complete understanding, but sympathy and compassion to men. He has offered the necessary sacrifice for our sins that makes it possible for us to draw nigh unto God. He ever lives as a priest to intercede for us at God's right hand.

4. Another very significant expression that is found repeatedly in the Book of Hebrews is the expression, *"He was made."* The instances of the appearance of this expression, sometimes in slightly varied form, are: *(a)* 1:4 — "made so much better than the angels; *(b)* 2:7 — "thou madest him a little lower than the angels"; *(c)* 2:9 — "but we see Jesus who was made a little lower than the angels for the

suffering of death"; *(d)* 2:17 — "made like unto his breathren"; *(e)* 5:9 — "being made perfect he became the author of salvation to all them that obey him"; *(f)* 6:20 — "made an high priest after the order of Melchizedek"; *(g)* 7:17 — "made after the power of an endless life"; *(h)* 7:22 — "made the surety of a better covenant."

These passages all affirm that under the New Covenant, in harmony with the will and plan of God from eternity, Jesus occupies a place in the scheme of human redemption that He did not occupy until He gave Himself up in order that man might be redeemed.

STUDENT WORK

1. What major transition in God's place does Hebrews emphasize?

_____

2. Do you believe Paul wrote the Hebrew epistle? Give the reasons why you do or do not believe so. _____

_____

_____

_____

_____

3. What good reason can you give for his name not being mentioned? _____

_____

_____

4. To whom was the letter written? _____

_____

5. Relate the facts that indicate that the people to whom this epistle was written were Christians and not just Hebrews religiously? _____

_____

_____

_____

_____

_____

_____

_____

_____

6. When do you think the letter was written? _____
   Why? _____

_____

_____

7. State the principal purpose of this epistle. _____

_____

_____

8. In the introduction of Hebrews what characteristics of Christ emphasize his being Heaven's greatest messenger? Heb. 1:1-4. _____

_____

9. What argument or theme is indicated by the occurence of the word "better" in the epistle? Cite some of the "better" things in the New Covenant. Give passages: _____

_____

_____

_____

10 In comparing the two covenants to show the superiority of the New, why would the writer need to show the superiority of Christ over the angels as a messenger? _____

_____

11. Why should we give the more earnest heed to the message through Christ? Give passage. _____

_____

12. When was Christ, who was superior to the angels "made a little lower than the angels"? State why. _____

_____

13. When the writer made an argument showing the superiority of the New Covenant over the Old Covenant, what always followed?

_____

14. In Chapters 3 and 4, what argument is made based upon the failure of Israelites to enter into the land of Caanan at the end of their journey? _____

_____

_____

_____

15. What warnings does the writer base upon this O. T. history? Give the passage expressing the warning. _____
_____
_____

16. We have in the New Covenant a "better" priest in Christ. Why? Give passages. _____
_____
_____
_____
_____

17. Who was Melchizedek and how is Christ a priest after his order?
_____
_____
_____
_____

18. How does the writer argue that Christ is superior to Abraham?
_____
_____
_____

19. What passage shows that God did not intend for the Aaronic priesthood to endure forever? _____
_____

20. Why could not Christ be a priest on earth? _____
_____

21. What did a change in priesthood require? _____
_____

22. The Aaronic priests offered sacrifices not only for the sins of the people but also for their own, why did not Christ have to do the same? _____
_____

23. The old tabernacle was a type of *the church*: (Give passages. _____) How many points of comparison in this type can you find? _____
_____
_____
_____

24. Our "better covenant" is better in what respects? Give passages.

_____

_____

_____

_____

25. What passage tells us that the "way into the holiest of all" could not be made known while the first tabernacle yet stood? _____

26. What can cleanse our hearts from evil consciences that we may serve God? Give passages. _____

_____

27. Why is the sacrifice which sanctifies the New Covenant a "better sacrifice" than the animal sacrifices under the Old Covenant? ____

_____

28. How is faith defined? Give the two elements that make up saving faith. _____

_____

29. Point out what the expression "by faith" means. _____

_____

30. How many times does the writer begin an exhortation in this epistle with the expression "Let us" _____

31. How many times with reference to Christ does the expression "He was made" occur? _____ What is the significance of it?

_____

_____

32. What should the priesthood of Christ mean to us? _____

_____

_____

James

Unlike the letters written by Paul, which were directed either to individual Christians or congregations of Christians in some particular locality, the Epistle of James is one of the general epistles of the New Testament, addressed to no particular individual and to no particular congregation, but to the church which had been dispersed. In the epistle the address James uses to designate those to whom he is writing is "the twelve tribes which are scattered abroad," or "which are of the dispersion, Greeting" (1:1).

The Epistle of James is of an intensely practical nature and is primarily concerned with the ethics of Christian living and service. With the writer of this epistle religion was not a matter of theory and speculation, as was true of many of the false religions in New Testament days, but it was a matter of revealed truth which was intended to be the guide for the life of the individual. The book emphasizes truth as it is meant to be expressed in Christian living and in the performance of Christian duty. It has been called by some "the gospel of common sense."

A. The Author.

At the beginning of the letter the writer identifies himself as "James, a servant of God and of the Lord Jesus Christ" (1:1). This does not, however, identify the author in a very definite way. In the New Testament there are at least four men by the name of James:

1. The brother of John, the son of Zebedee, was called James (Mt. 4:21). He was killed by Herod Agrippa I early in the history of the church (Acts 12:1-2).

2. Another of the disciples of Jesus bore the name of James (Mt. 10:3), and he is further identified as the son of Alphaeus.

3. There was then a James, who was the father of Judas, another one of Jesus' disciples (Lk. 6:16). This Judas is distinguished from Judas Iscariot who betrayed the Lord (Lk. 6:16).

4. There was James who was the brother of Jesus, being one of the four brothers of our Lord (Mt. 13:55).

It is not likely that the Epistle of James was written by James, the son of Zebedee and the brother of John, for the reason that this James met an early death, earlier perhaps than the writing of the letter. Neither is it likely that James, the son of Alphaeus, could have written the Epistle, or did write it, because we know very little about him and he is rather obscure in New Testament history except for his identification as one of the Apostles. The probability is, and it is commonly accepted, that James, the brother of our Lord, is the author of the Epistle of James.

This James is very prominent in New Testament history. He was probably with some of those who sought an interview with Jesus

140

somewhere in Galilee (Mt. 12:46). He probably also went with Jesus to Capernaum (Jn. 2:12). Later he joined in the attempt to persuade Him to go to Judea for the feast of tabernacles (Jn. 7:3). He himself went up to the feast but he was an unbeliever at the time (Jn. 7:5-10). We are told in 1 Corinthians 15:7 that after the resurrection Christ appeared to James also. This probably was the thing that convinced him to believe in Jesus and made out of him a disciple of our Lord. He is next seen among the Lord's brethren waiting for the coming of the Holy Spirit (Acts 1:14). About A.D. 35 or 36, this James was still in Jerusalem and had a visit from Paul when the latter returned from his three year stay in Damascus and Arabia (Gal. 1:18-19; Acts 9:26).

By the time Peter was imprisoned in Jerusalem, about A.D. 44, James seems to have become very prominent as a leader in the Church at Jerusalem (Acts 12:17). He had a very prominent part in the council concerning circumcision in the city of Jerusalem (Acts 15:13, 19; Gal. 2:1,9,10). He is mentioned again in the New Testament in Acts 21:18-25 in connection with the contribution that was made by the churches of Macedonia, Achaia and Galatia and brought to Jerusalem for the relief of the poor saints (Acts 21:18-25).

Josephus tells us that James was stoned by the order of Ananias, the high priest, but Eusebius said that he was thrust down from the pinacle of the Temple and then beaten to death with a club. These are traditions concerning the end of his life as a servant of the Lord, and we do not know whether or not they are true.

It is evident from Paul's reference to James, the writer of this epistle, that he was not only a brother of the Lord, but he was also one of the Lord's Apostles. In Gal. 1:18-19 Paul said, "after three years I went up to Jerusalem to see Peter, and abode with him fifteen days. But other of the apostles saw I none, save James the Lord's brother." This explains to us the reason for the fact that the epistle is written with a note of authority. It is in no sense characterized by an autocratic spirit, and yet, nearly every other verse in the epistle contains an imperative. The writer frequently addresses his readers as brethren.

B. To Whom the Epistle Was Addressed.

Because James addressed his letter "to the twelve tribes which are scattered abroad" (1:1), there has been a great deal of controversy about to whom the Epistle of James was actually directed. There are many who think that it was directed only to Jews and that it properly, therefore, belongs in reality in the Old Testament canon rather than being a part of the New Testament. Chief, perhaps, among the proponents of this idea was Martin Luther. Martin Luther had initiated the doctrine of justification by faith alone. He considered this to be the very theme of both Romans and Galatians. When he came to the Book of James and the argument that James presented (Jas. 2:14ff.) against the idea of justification by faith only and in emphasis of the fact that a man can be justified only by the faith that motivates obedience to the will of God, he found such a great conflict that he was unable to amend either his own understanding of the teaching of the Scriptures and correct his false impression, or accept the Epistle of James as a part of the Gospel of Christ because of what he considered to be a serious conflict between its teaching and other parts of the New Testament. Therefore, he classified it as a Jewish Epistle and called it the "Epistle of straw." Along with him, other proponents in the denominational world, among even the scholars, who have their minds so centered upon the doctrine of justification by faith only, think that the Epistle of James was written largely to either Jewish Christians, or to just Jews that had been scattered among the nations of the world. However, a careful study of the New Testament will convince us of the fact that James was not writing to Jews nor just to Jewish Christians, but that his letter was addressed to the Church of the Lord generally which had been "scattered abroad" from Jerusalem and throughout the nations of the earth under very severe persecution.

The problem of whom he meant by the "twelve tribes which are scattered abroad" is not a great problem at all when we take into consideration the remaining part of New Testament teaching. In Galatians 3:28 the Apostle Paul tells us who Jews are, and who Israel is, under the New Covenant. He said in verse 28, "There is neither Jew nor Greek, there is neither bond nor free, there is neither male nor female: for ye are all one in Christ Jesus. And if ye be Christ's then are ye Abraham's seed, and heirs according to the promise." Along with this passage, in Romans 2:28 we hear Paul saying, "For he is not a Jew, which is one outwardly; neither is that circumcision which is outward in the flesh: but he is a Jew, which is one inwardly; and circumcision is that of the heart, in the spirit, and not in the letter; whose praise is not of men, but of God."

In Matthew 19:27-28, when the disciples came to Jesus with Peter as the spokesman, and raised the question, "We have forsaken all to follow thee; what shall we therefore have?," the record says, "And Jesus said unto them, verily I say unto you that ye which have followed me, in the regeneration when the Son of man shall sit on the throne of his glory, ye also shall sit upon twelve thrones, judging the twelve tribes of Israel." The twelve tribes of Israel here mentioned were the twelve tribes over which the Apostles would have authority. But the Apostles exercised no authority over fleshly Israel, hence the Lord is not talking about fleshly Israel. In the period of regeneration, which is when men are being born again and becoming new creatures in Christ, the Apostles are exercising the authority of Jesus Christ, through the Gospel, over all the Church. They have authority over the twelve tribes of Spiritual Israel. Jesus gave it to them. He said, "Whatsoever you bind upon earth shall be bound in Heaven and whatsoever you loose upon earth shall be loosed in Heaven" (Mt. 18:18). The Church in its entirety is subject to the authority of the Apostles of Jesus Christ our Lord. The twelve tribes of fleshly Israel constitutes all of fleshly Israel. The twelve tribes of Spiritual Israel constitutes all of Spiritual Israel, and this is the Church of God. It had been dispersed from Jerusalem under persecution and they had gone everywhere preaching the word (Acts 8).

The only Israel that God knows or recognizes then, under the New Covenant, is Spiritual Israel. Paul tells us in Romans, "And he received the sign of circumcision, a seal of the righteousness of the faith which he had yet being uncircumcised: that he might be the father of all them that believe, though they be not circumcised; that righteousness might be imputed unto them also: and the father of circumcision to them who are not of the circumcision only, but who also walk in the steps of that faith of our father Abraham, which he had being yet uncircumcised" (Rom. 4:11-12). In this passage it is simply affirmed that Abraham is the father of all who exercise toward God the same faith that characterized him, whether they be Jew or Gentile. There is no distinction under the New Covenant in the Church of the Lord between Jew and Gentile, but all are one in Christ. James, therefore, was simply writing to Spiritual Israel, not to fleshly Israel, and his letter written to the Church that had been "scattered abroad" is a general Christian epistle for the benefit of Christians wherever they might be in all of the world.

Within the letter itself there are several distinct references that identify the letter as a general Christian epistle, without any sort of Jewish flavor, or connection.

1. *James 1:18:* "Of his own will begat he us with the word of truth, that we should be a kind of firstfruits of his creatures." This is a suggestion of the plan of salvation under the Gospel of Jesus Christ, begotten by the power of the Gospel, under the influence of the Holy Spirit, and led to become the children of God, or the firstfruits of His creatures. This identifies the letter as directed to men and women who were Christians, not Jews.

2. *James 2:1,* "My brethren, have not the faith of our Lord Jesus Christ, the Lord of glory, with respect of persons." Here again is identified those to whom James wrote, that is, the men who believed in Christ. They were believers in Christ.

3. *James 2:7:* "Do not they blaspheme that worthy name by the which ye are called"? The "worthy name" is a very evident reference to the name of Christ which had been given to the followers of Christ under the New Covenant.

4. *James 5:7:* "Be patient therefore, brethren, unto the coming of the Lord." This refers to the coming of the Lord Jesus Christ. Whether he meant in judgment upon the Jewish nation because of their rejection, or whether it is a reference to the eventual coming of the Lord at the end of time, the reference certainly identifies Jesus Christ coming either in judgment or coming to receive His own, and marks the letter, as we have suggested, as a general Christian epistle. We need then to recognize that it belongs to the canon of the New Testament, that it is a part of the Gospel of the Son of God in spite of all of the opinions of critics colored by the doctrine of justification by "faith only" and prejudiced against the truth that James teaches when he says that this doctrine is not true (Jas. 2:24).

C. The Date of the Epistle.

Josephus fixes the death of James at about 62 A.D. If he is the author of this letter, then, of course, it must have been written prior to that time. There are several other things that give us an idea of the time of its writing. If it was written after the Jerusalem conference (Acts 15) and after the issue concerning whether or not Gentiles had to be circumcised in order to obey the Gospel and the great dissension between Jews and Gentiles in the Church of the Lord had such a prominent place in the writing of other New Testament Scriptures, it is rather remarkable that James made no reference to such. He does say that the faith of our Lord Jesus Christ is not to be held with the respect of persons, but this is about the only reference in the Book of James that could even indirectly be construed as a reference to the Gentile controversy that characterized the Church at about the time of the Jerusalem conference. So, many of the scholars tell us that James must have written prior to that Jerusalem conference.

The scholars in general seem to hold that the Epistle of James was one of the earlier parts of the New Testament written, one of the earlier epistles, and that it could have been written as early as 45 or 50 A.D. The persecution that arose in Jerusalem that began with the death of Stephen and which was headed by Saul of Tarsus, was the persecution that dispersed the Church. It made havoc, (Acts 8:3-4) the record says, of the Church in Jerusalem and they were scattered abroad, and went everywhere preaching the Word. It may have been that in order to encourage those Jewish Christians who had thus been driven out from their homes and who had been under severe persecution that had tested and tried their faith in the Lord Jesus Christ, that James was directing his letter and that he wrote it shortly after this general dispersion of the Church under this persecution of which we read in Acts 8. This could have been the case, but there is no way to definitely fix the date of his letter. Some of the scholars place the date of the letter, however, near the end of James life, early in the 60's of the first century.

D. Contents and Character.

The general theme of this letter, which is so practical in its nature, is "pure and undefiled religion," suggested by the text in James 1:26-27, "If any man among you seem to be religious, and bridleth not his tongue, but deceiveth his own heart, this man's religion is vain. Pure religion and undefiled before God and the Father is this, "To visit the fatherless and widows in their affliction, and to keep himself unspotted from the world." The discussion of pure and undefiled religion takes the form in the letter of a contrast, and it is interesting for us to read the Epistle of James, and as we read through it to mark the passages on the one hand that set forth the elements and characteristics of what James calls "pure and undefiled religion," and then on the other hand to list those characteristics that make our religion vain. He talks about a religion

144

that is pure and undefiled, and a religion that is vain. That means, of course, that vain religion is exactly the opposite of pure and undefiled religion. Vain religion does not accomplish its purpose. The purpose of religion is nullified by those characteristics that make it vain or void, empty, and meaningless in the sight of God. So, we suggest that a fine way to study the Epistle of James is to make a list of the elements that go to make up and that characterize pure and undefiled religion and the elements that will make our religion vain, void, empty and meaningless in the sight of God. We suggest, partially at least, a list of this sort:

1. *The characteristics of pure and undefiled religion.* *(a)* Joy and patience in the midst of trails (1:2-4); *(b)* Unwavering faith and singleness of mind (1:5-8); *(c)* Acceptance of the providential allotments of life and contentment with them (1:9-11); *(d)* The endurance of temptation (1:12); *(e)* The recognition of the sources of temptation, the nature of it, and the consequences of yielding thereto (1:13-15); *(f)* The recognition of the Divine source of all blessings, God as the giver of every good and every perfect gift (1:16-18). The consequence of this recognition, of course, is a knowledge and awareness of our dependence upon Him; *(g)* Spiritual hearing, deliberation and speech, and patience under provocation characterize pure religion (1:19-20); *(h)* The necessity of forsaking all evil, purging it from our lives, and our hearts, and in meekness receiving the truth which is able to save our souls (1:21); *(i)* Searching after the truth and practicing it (1:25); *(j)* The practice of generosity and benevolence towards others, and purity in life and character are essential elements of pure and undefiled religion (1:27); *(k)* The works of faith. The demonstration of faith as a motive by the fruit that it bears in our lives in the works of obedience to the will of God (2:18); *(l)* The necessity of faith performing the will of God as a means of perfecting our faith (2:21-25). In this Abraham is offered as an example in the offering of Isaac, his son, in obedience to God's will, as the means of perfecting his faith in God.

2. *The marks or characteristics of vain religion.* *(a)* Carelessness and forgetful hearing of the word of God (1:22-24); *(b)* The profession of religion nullified or made vain by an unbridled tongue; the misuse of this member of the body, and along with that of course, the misuse of any other member of the body would be included (1:26); *(c)* Respect of persons toward brethren or among brethren, honoring the rich and despising the poor (2:1-9); *(d)* Partial obedience to the law (2:10-12). This, of course, points out that when a man is not willing to respect the authority of all of the law or the authority by which all of it is given, that he does not respect any of it because of the authority by which it is given. There is no selective obedience which faith in God and in the Word of God allows. We either seek to yield ourselves fully in obedience to the will of God or not at all, and thus express our lack of faith; *(e)* An unmerciful disposition toward others makes our religion vain (2:13); *(f)* A mere profession of faith, unaccompanied by acts of mercy and help toward

145

others which evidences our faith (2:14-16); *(g)* An inactive faith. A faith that does not motivate and produce the works of obedience to the will of God, but which makes out of our religion a mere game of "make believe" (2:17-18); *(h)* A mere intellectual assent or agreement to truth, without any change in life and character in submission to truth (2:19-20); *(i)* The failure to control and to keep our tongues bridled, which allows them to become destructive in their influence and to be misused, and makes our religion vain (3:1-8); *(j)* When blessings and cursings proceed from the same mouth, hyprocrisy is evidenced and vain religion is the case (3:9-12); *(k)* Envy, strife, and following the wisdom which is earthly, sensual and devilish, which therefore emanates from Satan, makes our religion vain (3:14-16); *(l)* When we give ourselves to discontent· and to unholy passions, our religion is made vain (4:1-2); *(m)* Unanswered prayer, because of our lustful desires and our selfish attitudes and worldliness in the lives of those who are God's children, evidences unfaithfulness to God, and is branded as spiritual adultery, and this of course makes our religion vain (4:3-4); *(n)* Pride in our hearts, stubbornness of spirit, impurity of heart and soul, will nullify religion and make it void in the sight of God (4:5-9); *(o)* speaking evil of others and being uncharitable in our judgments of them nullify our religion and our relationship with God (4:11-12); *(p)* Presumption in arrangement of future business enterprises, or leaving God out of our plans (4:13-16). Every plan concerning the future as well as the present, needs to be made and carried out with the condition in mind and the view always before us of whether or not the grace and the mercy of God and the will of God will allow it; *(q)* When a man neglects what he knows to be right and violates his conscience by not doing what he understands to be his duty, his religion is made vain and void (4:17).

3. *Warnings, exhortations, and instructions. (a)* A warning to those who put their trust in the riches of this earth concerning the misery that would come upon them as a consequence (5:1-2); *(b)* A warning concerning hoarding wealth and unjustly withholding the wages due the poor (5:3-4); *(c)* A warning concerning seeking pleasure and the persecution of the righteous (5:5-6); *(d)* Exhortations in view of the coming of the Lord. *(1)* to be patient and stedfast, refrain from murmuring against one another (5:7-10), *(2)* to emulate the example of the prophets and Job in patient endurance (5:10-11), *(3)* that it is wise to refrain entirely from oaths (5:12); *(e)* James closes the letter with a final exhortation and instruction respecting prayer, a willingness to confess their faults to one another and pray for one another, and the importance and necessity of engaging in the winning of the souls of the lost. *(1)* prayer in time of trouble and for the sick, indicating genuine reliance upon God and His help and our dependence upon Him (5:13-15), *(2)* the confession of faults and intercessory prayer one for another (5:16), *(3)* effectual prayer, illustrated in the case of Elijah, which example from the Old Testament demonstrates that the power of prayer cannot be measured and what it can accomplish cannot be definitely known;

146

only the will and power of God limits it (5:16-18), *(4)* the duty of winning souls and turning them from the error of their way in order that the multitude of their sins might be covered up by the mercy and the grace of God in forgiveness (5:19-20).

4. *The discussion of the relation of faith and works is one of the paramount and classic passages that characterize the Book of James.* In fact, it is true that this passage is outstanding in all of the Scriptures on this theme. James raised the question in James 2:14, "What doth it profit, my brethren, though a man say he hath faith, and have not works? can faith save Him"? The faith of which James speaks in this verse and the question that he raises is whether or not a professed faith, separated from any works of obedience to the will of God, can be the means of justification. Nowhere in the Bible is "justification by faith only" and its truthfulness any more clearly raised than in this passage. In the paragraph that begins with verse 14, James points out to us a number of things about "faith only." He says that "faith only," that is, faith without the works of obedience, and we need to keep in mind that is the kind of works James was discussing in this paragraph, means that we have a "dead faith." Just as the body without the spirit is dead, so faith without works is dead, being alone (2:17,20,26). In this same paragraph James points out that a faith unaccompanied by the works of obedience is not only dead but he points out also that such a faith is barren and unfruitful; that it produces no benefit and results in no good. He uses a very apt illustration of this unfruitfulness of faith without works in 2:15-16. It is merely professed and is not productive of any good at all. Then, in the same paragraph, he points out that mere conviction, that is, merely being convinced alone of the identity of Jesus characterized even the devils. They knew His identity. They believed and trembled (2:19). So, faith without the works of obedience is no better than the mere conviction concerning the person of Christ which the Devils possessed.

He further illustrates the importance of faith and its relationship with the works of obedience by showing that Abraham was justified by works, not by faith only, when he offered Isaac, his son, upon the altar. That his faith wrought or *worked with his works,* and that *by his works* was his faith made perfect (2:21-22). He further suggests to us that the Scripture which said, "Abraham believed God and it was imputed unto him for righteousness, and he was called the friend of God," was a prophecy upon God's part concerning the fact that when He called upon Abraham to make the sacrifice of faith and the offering of his son, that he would faithfully perform that which God asked him to do, that his faith would obey. He says that this Scripture was "fulfilled" when Abraham offered Isaac upon the altar. That means that until he offered Issac upon the altar, it was unfulfilled, and if it was unfulfilled, it was merely a prophetic statement upon the part of God, made because God's wisdom knew what Abraham's faith would do when it was put to the test. The significant statement of this

147

entire paragraph and one that needs to be underscored in our Bibles and in our minds, is James 2:24: "Ye see then how that by works a man is justified, and not by faith only."

5. Another theme that is of great importance that is suggested to us in the Epistle of James and needs to be carefully studied, is *the contrast in two different kinds of wisdom*. James says earthly wisdom descended not from above, but is earthly, sensual and devilish (3:15). He raises the question, (3:13), "Who is a wise man and endued with knowledge among you"? Let him show or demonstrate his wisdom, he says, out of a good manner of life showing his works with meekness of wisdom. He continues, "if ye have bitter envying and strife in your hearts, glory not, and lie not against the truth," because such wisdom comes from Satan and not from God. He warns that where envying and strife is, there is confusion and every vile deed. Contrasted with this wisdom that is earthly, sensual and devilish in its nature and Satanic in its origin, is the wisdom that is from above, and it is "first pure, then peaceable, gentle and easy to be entreated, full of mercy and good fruits, without partiality, and without hypocrisy" (2:17). The wisdom of this world and the wisdom of God lead in opposite directions. One of them points downward. The other points toward Heaven and eternal life. We need to rely upon the wisdom that is from above, and this is the message of James in the last part of chapter 3.

6. *Still another important discussion in the practical Epistle of James concerns temptation.* He affirms that true faith is not wrecked or injured by temptation; that when we endure temptation and our faith is strong enough to help us withstand it,.that our faith becomes more able to endure and that it becomes stronger, and he exhorts that we are to "let patience have her perfect work that ye may be perfect and entire, lacking in nothing" (1:4). This is done when the trying of our faith "worketh patience" (1:3). By enduring trials, he suggests to us that our faith is proven and maturity of character is developed (1:3-4), and that such patient endurance holds the promise of the Crown of Life after a while (1:12). An analysis of what James teaches concerning temptation and its relationship to sin and the life of the Christian discloses: *(a)* Temptation does not come from God (1:13), but it originates within the uncontrolled desires of the individual (1:14); *(b)* it lures the individual, appealing to his own desires. This is the approach of temptation (1:14); *(c)* It entices the individual as a bait ensnares a fish or an animal (1:14); *(d)* It conceives, or takes hold, finds lodgment within the individual's heart and brings sin to a reality in his life (1:15); *(e)* As full grown sin, it results in death, separation from God (1:15).

Finally, we call attention to the fact that James is outstanding in the practical wisdom that is called to the attention of Christians wherever they are and by which their lives need to be guided. The teaching, in addition to that which has already been suggested on the nature and the use of the tongue (3:1-12), the recognition of the nature of life (4:17), and the necessary and essential place of prayer

148

in Christian living (5:13-18), are all examples of the very vital and very practical and very necessary nature of the instruction that fills this general epistle and which every Christian can use in his every day life.

STUDENT WORK

1. Why is the epistle of James called a "general epistle"? _____

2. Why has it been described as "The gospel of common sense"? ____

3. Who was the author? _____

4. How many James are mentioned in the New Testament? _____

5. What does the New Testament tell us about the James who wrote the book? _____

6. What writer tells us that this James was also an apostle? _____

7. To whom did James address this epistle? _____

8. What was Martin Luther's concept of the epistle of James? Why?
_____

9. To what twelve tribes did James direct this epistle? _____
_____ Give some passages that show who is the Israel of God in the New Testament? _____
_____

10. Give some of the passages that show the epistle to be written to Christians.

(1). _____ ; (2). _____ ;

(3). _____ ; (4). _____

11. What evidence do we have that indicates the date of the epistle?
_____

12. What is the general theme of the epistle? _____
_____

13. What sort of a contrast runs all the way through the letter? _____
_____

14. Give some of the Characteristics of "pure and undefiled" religion and give passages:

(a) _____ _____

(b) _____ _____

149

(c) _____ _____
(d) _____ _____
(e) _____ _____
(f) _____ _____
(g) _____ _____
(h) _____ _____
(i) _____ _____
(j) _____ _____
(k) _____ _____

15. What are some of the marks of "vain" religion? Give citation.

(a) _____ _____
(b) _____ _____
(c) _____ _____
(d) _____ _____
(e) _____ _____
(f) _____ _____
(g) _____ _____
(h) _____ _____
(i) _____ _____
(j) _____ _____
(k) _____ _____
(l) _____ _____

16. List some of the warnings and instructions of the epistle and give citations.

(a) _____ _____
(b) _____ _____
(c) _____ _____
(d) _____ _____
(e) _____ _____

17. Discuss the relation of faith and works as set forth in James.

18. Contrast the two kinds of wisdom James sets forth.

_____
_____
_____

19. What does James teach about temptation and the origin of sin?

_____
_____
_____

First Peter

A. The Author, Simon Peter.

We first call your attention to a sketch of the life of the author. Peter was also called Simon, or Simeon (Acts 15:14; 2 Pet. 1:1), was born at Bethsaida (Jn. 1:44). His father's name was Jonas (Mt. 16:17), or John (Jn. 1:42), with whom he and his brother, Andrew, carried on the trade of fishing at Capernaum, and where he afterward resided (Mt. 8:14), where his wife's mother also lived (1 Cor. 9:5). Andrew, his brother, was responsible for bringing him to Christ and Jesus gave him the name, Cephas (Jn. 1:40-42). This was his first call. It was a call to discipleship, and upon this first call, he was given a new name. This new name meant "a rock," and it was a prophecy by the Lord of the change that would come about in his character that would make him very stable and dependable, a solid and faithful disciple. The second call came for him to become a constant companion with Christ (Mt. 4:19; Lk. 5:10), and this, of course, meant that new associations were to be his. Instead of following his old occupation, he was to be made a fisher of men and they were to become the objects of his energies. A third call, which was the call to become an Apostle of the Lord (Mt. 10:2; Mk. 3:14-16), gave to him a new vocation. Jesus called him so that he might be with Him and to send him out "to preach, and to have authority to cast out demons."

Peter's ardor, earnestness, and courage made out of him from the very first a leader among the disciples. His name always appears first in the list of the Apostles (Mt. 10:2; Mk. 3:16; Lk. 6:14; Acts 1:13), and he was also one of the three in the inner circle of disciples, including also James and John along with Peter. The Catholic doctrine of the primacy of Peter, however, has no foundation in the Scriptures. They base it primarily on the record in Matthew 16, where, when he confessed, "thou art the Christ, the son of the living God," Jesus answered him, saying, "Blessed art thou Simon Barjona: for flesh and blood hath not revealed it to thee, but my Father which is in heaven. And I say also unto thee, That thou art Peter, and upon this rock, I will build my church; and the gates of hell shall not prevail against it. And I will give unto thee the keys of the kingdom of Heaven; and whatsoever thou shalt bind on earth shall be bound in heaven; and whatsoever thou shalt loose on earth shall be loosed in heaven." This, however, does not justify the conclusion that Peter was given any primacy among the Apostles. Upon his acknowledgement of the Divine truth of the Sonship of Jesus of Nazareth, Jesus simply stated that this was the rock, the great ledge of rock, upon which the Church would be founded. The Apostle Paul tells us in 1 Cor. 3:11, "For other foundation can no man lay than that which is laid, which is Jesus Christ," which of course removes any possibility of doubt that the church is founded upon the fact that Jesus Christ is the Son of God, rather than upon the Apostle Peter. Furthermore, in the statement that He would give unto the Apostles authority to bind and loose, Jesus included not only Peter as an Apostle, but He included all of the other Apostles in the bestowal of the same authority. In Mt. 18:18, Jesus said, "Verily I say unto you, Whatsoever ye shall bind on earth shall be bound in heaven; and whatsoever ye shall loose on earth shall be loosed in heaven." This was directed, according to the context, to all of the Apostles and not just to Peter, so all of them had the same authority so far as binding and loosing is concerned. Then in 2 Cor. 11:5, Paul was discussing his rights as an Apostle of our Lord, and said, "For I suppose I was not a whit behind the very chiefest apostles."

Peter's life could well be divided into two different parts for the purpose of studying it, — before Pentecost, and after Pentecost. During the former period, Jesus healed his mother-in-law (Mt. 8:14ff), gave to him a great draught of fishes (Lk. 5:1-11), and called him as an Apostle (Mt. 10:2). When Jesus came to the disciples walking on the sea, Peter attempted to walk likewise (Mt. 14:28); he confessed Jesus as the Christ upon two occasions (Jn. 6:68-69; Mt. 16:13-17) Peter witnessed the raising of Jairus' daughter (Mk. 5:37), and the transfiguration (Mt. 17:1-5), and benefited by the miracle of the tribute money (Mt. 17:24). At the Last Supper, he at first objected when Christ wanted to wash his feet (Jn. 13:1-10). He boasted of his devotion to Christ (Lk. 22:31-33), but Christ predicted that he would deny Him thrice (Mt. 26:31-35).

Peter was one of the three allowed to follow Christ into Gethsemane (Mt. 26:36-46). He drew the sword and cut off the ear of the servant of the high priest (Jn. 18:10-12). At the trial of Christ he denied Him thrice: but he also repented genuinely (Mt. 26:56-75). He accompanied John to the tomb (Jn. 20:1-10); the angel directed the women to tell His disciples "and Peter" that Jesus went before them into Galilee (Mk. 16:7); the Lord appeared to him (Lk. 24:34; 1 Cor. 15:5); and he was fully restored to the task that had been assigned him and recommissioned to that task (Jn. 21:15-19). He was a witness to the Lord's ascension (Acts 1:9,10). When the disciples returned to the city of Jerusalem, Peter led in the process of choosing of Mathias to take the place of Judas, as one of the twelve Apostles (Acts 1:15-26).

The second period of the life of the Apostle Peter runs from the day of Pentecost through chapter 12 of the Book of Acts. On the day of Pentecost he preached the sermon that is recorded in Acts 2:14-41. In company with John he healed a man who was lame from birth at the gate Beautiful of the Temple (Acts 3:1-10); he preached a second sermon in the city of Jerusalem (3:11-26); he and John were arrested, tried, and released (4:1-22). He administered the rebuke to Ananias and Sapphira whom God disciplined with sudden death as the result of their seeking to deceive the Holy Spirit (Acts 5:1-11). He was arrested with the other Apostles and miraculously released, tried, beaten, and dismissed (5:12-41). He along with John was sent by the Apostles to those who had believed and obeyed the Lord in Samaria to bestow upon them the gifts of the Holy Spirit (Acts 8:14-25). While in Jerusalem, Paul paid Peter a brief visit (Gal. 1:18). After this, he left Jerusalem to visit in various parts of Judea and Samaria. He healed Aeneas at Lydda and raised Dorcas at Joppa; he saw a vision and preached to the conversion of Cornelius and his household at Caesarea (Acts 9:32 through 10:48). In Jerusalem again, he gave an account of his mission to Cornelius to the Jewish brethren (Acts 11:1-18). He was imprisoned by Herod Agrippa and miraculously released (Acts 12:1-17); then it is said he went to "another place" (Acts 12:17). He was present at the Jerusalem conference about circumcision and took a leading part in it (Acts 15:1-21; Gal. 2:6-10). When he came to Antioch a little later he withdrew from the Gentile Christians and the association that he had with them because of the presence of Jewish brethren, and for this dissimulation was rebuked by Paul (Gal. 2:11-15). We know little more about him, actually, except that he traveled extensively, being often accompanied by his wife (1 Cor. 9:5). He may have paid a visit to Asia Minor, especially to the provinces of Pontus, Cappadocia and Bithynia, where Paul did not visit; and he probably made a longer trip to Babylon on the Euphrates.

The internal evidence of First Peter sustains the evidence externally that Simon Peter himself is the author. Once, he refers to himself as Peter (1:1). He shows himself to be well acquainted personally with the life of Christ and with the teachings of Jesus. The words, "be clothed with humility" (5:5), seem to refer to the time when Christ girded himself with a towel as a demonstration of the humility that ought to characterize the disciples, when he washed their feet (Jn. 13:3-5). The admonition to "feed the flock of God" (5:2), reminds one of Christ's words to Peter, "feed my lambs," "feed my sheep" (Jn. 21:15-17). He was probably recalling some of the things that he had heard the Lord say in such expressions in the epistle as "if ye be reproached for the name of Christ, happy are ye" (4:14), "casting all your care upon Him" (5:7), "be sober, be vigilant" (5:8), etc. He claims to have been a "witness of the sufferings of Christ" (5:1), and in 3:18 as well as 4:1, we notice the force of the impression that was thus made upon him by having witnessed these sufferings. In 2:19-24, he describes the person of Christ in His sufferings and admonishes his readers to remember that they are partakers of the sufferings of Christ (4:13).

The similarity of Peter's speeches in the Book of Acts and his words in this epistle are to be noted also. Such comparisons can be made between Acts 10:34 and 1 Pet. 1:17; Acts 2:32-36; 10:40-41 and 1 Pet. 1:22; Acts 4:10-11 and 1 Pet. 2:7-8.

The external evidence concerning Peter's authorship in the early Church of this epistle is seen in the fact that it was universally recognized as written by him. No book has earlier or stronger evidence than First Peter. Second Peter 3:1 is the earliest acknowledgment of First Peter, for even those who deny the genuineness of that epistle admit that it is an early book. There are possible references to First Peter in various other early writings, such as the Epistle of Barnabas, Clement's Epistle to the Corinthians, and the Testaments of the Twelve Patriarchs. Polycarp quotes 1:8; 3:9; 2:11 in his Epistle to the Philippians, and makes other references, but he nowhere mentions the author by name. These early references, and the general acceptance of it is evidence of its genuineness and its authenticity.

B. To Whom the Epistle Was Written.

The epistle is addressed to the elect who are *sojourners of the dispersion* "in Pontus, Galatia, Cappadocia, Asia, and Bithynia" (1:1). The word, "elect," as well as the entire epistle indicates that the readers were Christians. The question is sometimes raised as to what *"sojourners of the dispersion"* means. It becomes clear from the letter itself that Peter was writing to Christians, including both Jews and Gentiles. He refers to the former state of his readers, "the time of your ignorance" (1:14), and reminds them of "him who hath called you out of darkness into his marvelous light: which in time past were not a people, but are now the people of God: which had not obtained mercy, but now have obtained mercy" (2:9-10). He also says, "For the time past of our life may suffice us to have wrought the will of the Gentiles, when we walked in laciviousness, lusts," etc. (4:3-5). All of these references evidence that at least many of the people to whom he was writing were Gentile Christians.

They were "sojourners of the dispersion" evidently in the sense that they were strangers and sojourners upon earth (2:11 cf. Heb. 11:13-16; 13:14). He looked upon the Christians as dispersed among the heathen nations of the world. It is also likely that because of the persecution in Rome, led by Nero, many Christians had been forced to seek safety in the provinces, Asia Minor being a likely place for them to flee.

He refers specifically to Pontus, Galatia, Cappadocia, Asia, and Bithynia. This is an indication that the letter was probably intended for all of the churches of Asia Minor. There is no indication that any of the churches in Pontus, Cappadocia and Bithynia had been established by Paul, for there is no record that he ever visited these provinces. They may have been founded by some of Paul's converts from Galatia and Asia. On the other hand, we read in Acts 2:9 that there were people in Jerusalem for Pentecost from the provinces of "Cappadocia, in Pontus, and Asia." I is altogether probable that some of those who were present upon Pentecost from this area were converted and returned to establish Christianity in their home territory.

C. Date and Purpose of the Epistle.

To begin with, in the history of Christianity there was not too much conflict with the Roman government. In the early part of the First Century Christians had left a favorable impression upon the

154

Roman authorities. Paul stood on his rights as a citizen on at least two occasions and demanded recognition for them (Acts 16:36-39; 22:24-29). But he could also say that he had never been guilty of subversive activity or of causing any insurrection or rebellion against Rome (24:12). The church had peacefully penetrated the society of the Roman Empire with the Gospel of Christ.

Eventually, however, Christians had been separated distinctly from Judaism, were recognized as a different group, and their firm adherence to belief in an invisible God and a risen Christ excited the suspicion and the opposition of the public, while their talk of a coming judgment and the overthrow of the existing world created perhaps misunderstanding and hatred. This all reacted against them in Rome under Nero and persecution was the product of this dislike. It was activated by Nero's accusations. The close of the letters to Timothy and Titus show that Paul's death marked a turn in the policy of the government of Rome from tolerance to severe and extreme condemnation and persecution.

When the Churches began to recognize this change in attitude upon the part of the Roman government, they became fearful of what the consequence would be. They had no organized resistance to withstand it, for this would be a violation of their own principle of peaceful obedience to the government and would only arouse further persecution against them. The question of whether or not they faced extinction and complete suppression no doubt occurred, and in their minds was raised the question of what the outcome would be. They wondered if the brutality of Nero would be duplicated in the provinces. They were looking to their teachers and leaders for answers to these questions.

First Peter was written in reply to this situation and under these circumstances as it affected the churches of northern Asia Minor and the provinces of Pontus, Galatia, Cappadocia, Asia, and Bithynia.

We learn something about the state of these churches from the epistle itself. We observe, for example, that they were under "elders" (5:1; cf. Acts 20:17-35). Some sort of persecution was evidently going on (3:17; 4:12-19). There is no record, however, of martyrdom, of imprisonment, or of demands of Emperor worship. The persecution seems to have taken the form of slanderous attacks against the Christians (4:14-15). They were ridiculed for withdrawing from the licentious and sinful practices of the heathen (4:4-5); they may have even been accused of disloyalty to the state (2:13-17). There may also have been tendencies in the churches to fall in with the heathen way of living that caused Peter to write (2:11,12,16; 4:1-5), and a greedy or domineering spirit among the elders (5:2-3). The persecutions under Nero in Rome may have emboldened and encouraged persecution in the provinces in Asia Minor, and Peter wrote at this particular point or period of time to prepare the Christians against the persecutions they were being called upon to withstand, as well as more severe persecutions that probably would come thereafter. The date of the epistle then likely would be around 64 or 65 A.D.

In 5:13 Peter refers to "Babylon," and sends salutations unto the saints to whom he was writing, so that we get the impression that Peter was in Babylon when the letter was written. A great deal of speculation has been engaged in as to whether or not this was literal Babylon, the city on the Euphrates River, or whether the term, Babylon, symbolically refers to the city of Rome. It seems possible, although there is no positive evidence, that Peter may have visited Rome, from the writings of men like Ignatius, Papias, Clement, Haggesippus, Clement of Alexandria, Origin, Dionysius of Carthage, Tertullian, Jerome and others. But if Peter was in Rome he evidently got there after the history of the Book of Acts closed, for there is no reference made to him, either in the Book of Acts or in the prison epistles that Paul wrote. Furthermore, in the salutations that were written by Paul or sent by Paul to the Roman saints, in which a number of individuals were mentioned personally, Peter was not included.

There were a great many Jews at Babylon and for a while they had prospered. Caligula, according to history, persecuted the Jews at Babylon and as a result, many of them migrated to the rising city of Seleucia, about forty miles distant. However, when the persecution relented it is probable they returned to their homes in Babylon and that the number increased. Mr. Alford, an eminent scholar along with Erasmus, Calvin, Hort, Gregory, Mayer, Morehead and a number of others, holds to the idea that the city of Babylon is a literal reference to Babylon on the Euphrates River, and that Peter from this place wrote his first epistle. Mr. Alford's reason for accepting this view is a very good one. He thinks that "we are not to find an allegorical (figurative) meaning in a proper name thus simply used in the midst of simple and matter-of-fact sayings."

The very dark shadow of persecutions was the occasion for the writing of this letter. "Suffering" is one of the keynotes of the epistle, being mentioned no less than sixteen times. The references to "hope" occur five times in the letter, and by its prominence Peter gives the proper perspective to the Christians that were enduring the persecution. In addition to these two elements the letter was designed to remind believers of their obligation to exercise obedience and patience in whatever circumstances they found themselves (2:13-17,20).

D. Contents and Characteristics.

The chief value of First Peter is that it shows Christians how to live a redeemed life in the midst of a world contrary and hostile to them. It also points out that salvation may involve suffering but that this can be patiently endured because of the hope which the grace of God has made possible for the Christian and because God's grace is supplied to him to help him endure it.

1. *It is apparent that the major theme in 1 Peter is suffering;* that is, suffering as Christians and how we are to bear that suffering triumphantly. As a general view of this suffering, that

Christians are called upon many times to endure, Peter does not suggest that there is any special merit in suffering. Neither does he suggest that suffering is necessarily inevitable (1:6). Rather, he points out that the will of God is that we be allowed to suffer (4:19). He also suggests at the same time we are not to view suffering as abnormal when it comes (4:12). We must also remember that suffering is not an indication of Divine displeasure since Christ himself suffered and died for our redemption (3:18; 4:1). Peter reminds these Christians to whom he writes that to share the sufferings of Christ is a privilege and that they should do so with joy (4:13-14).

2. Peter reminds the Christians to whom he is writing that *their faith is to be tried by the suffering that they are called upon to endure* and that this "trial of your faith being much more precious than gold that perisheth, though it be tried with fire;" that the very purpose of it is that they "might be found unto praise and honor and glory at the appearing of Jesus Christ" (1:7).

3. In view of the suffering that was to be endured Peter was interested in pointing out *the attitude that the believer ought to have toward that suffering. (a)* It is to be borne patiently for the sake of Christ, as it was His lot to suffer for us (2:24). *(b)* Suffering is intended to produce positive effects in the Christian life (5:10). *(c)* It is to be viewed in light of the second coming of Christ and the hope that is ours at His coming (1:7,13; 4:13).

Furthermore, the Apostle points out the effects of suffering when it is properly borne by the Christian and the benefits that can be derived from enduring it properly. *(a)* it affords an opportunity to give evidence of their faith and of a Christian's faith in general. It evidences the readiness to answer those who ask a reason of the hope which the Christian possesses which makes it possible for him to so patiently endure the suffering that is brought upon him (3:13-16). *(b)* It has a purging or purifying effect (3:17-22). *(c)* It produces a watchfulness upon the part of the Christian as he confronts sin all around and as he faces the approach of the end of all things (4:1-11). *(d)* The suffering which a Christian endures emphasizes the provisions of God's grace to help him endure it. Five of the ten occurrences of this word in the First Epistle of Peter are linked with God. Grace is an attribute of God or an expression of His character (5:10). Grace is given by God to the believer in order that he may endure and be faithful (4:10; 5:5,12), and it is suggested in 3:7. Furthermore, grace is an attitude of God toward those who suffer for His sake (2:19-20). Peter further reminds these Christians who are enduring persecution that God's grace is bountiful in its nature (4:10).

Peter points out in this connection also the difference that is to be noted between suffering as a Christian and suffering as the result of our own wrong doing. We are not to be ashamed if we "suffer as Christians" (4:12-16), but if these sufferings are for our own misconduct or wrongdoing, then we are to be ashamed that it is brought upon us. In 4:12 Peter indicates that even greater suffering is in store for them, when he tells them "think it not strange concerning the fiery trial which is to try you, as though some strange thing happened unto you."

4. After the salutation of the epistle, Peter brings to the attention to the Christians to whom he is writing *the salvation which they enjoyed*. He describes it as a glorious, heavenly inheritance (1:3-5), as a life of faith and love subject to severe testing and refinement (1:6-9), and as the theme of the Old Testament prophets (1:10-12). Following this discussion of the theme of the salvation which they enjoyed, Peter then makes a plea for holiness (1:13-21) and for mutual love one for another, based on regeneration (1:22-25). The Christian is likened to a growing infant insomuch as they feed on the milk of the Word (2:1-3). and are called living stones built upon the risen Christ to constitute a spiritual house of God's habitation (2:4-10).

5. *Peter appeals to these Christians as pilgrims to be blameless in the eyes of men (2:11-12)*, submissive to government or authority (2:13-17). In all of the relationships of life they are to conduct themselves as Christians in harmony with the will of Christ. Slaves are to be subject to their masters, encouraged by the example of Christ's own conduct under mistreatment (2:18-25). Wives also have an obligation of submission to their husbands (3:1-6), and husbands have the duty to deal considerately and gently with their wives (3:7). Christians were to be governed by the spirit of love and tenderness in order that a Divine blessing might be insured (3:8-12). If such conduct brought suffering at the hands of the world, Divine vindication would be extended, as there was for Christ, the crucified and exalted one (3:13-22). They must not indulge in their former sins (4:1-6). Prayer, hospitality, and good works were to accompany and occupy the saints (4:7-11). Believers must always be ready to suffer for the sake of Christ, for this is God's will (4:12-19). Leaders are to care for the flock of God with due humility (5:1-5). All of the saints are urged to find their refuge and strength in God as they resist the evil one (5:6-11).

6. The Epistle of Peter is *intensely practical in its nature*. This is shown by quite a number of commandments stated as imperatives, beginning in the very beginning of the letter and extending all the way through it. For example: *(a)* "be ye sober" (1:13); *(b)* "hope . . . for grace" (1:13); *(c)* "be holy" (1:15); *(d)* "pass the time . . . in fear" (1:17); *(e)* "love one another" (1:23); *(f)* "desire the sincere milk" (2:2); *(g)* "submit yourselves to every ordinance of man" (2:13); *(h)* "Honor all men. Love the brotherhood. Fear God" (2:17); *(i)* "Servants, be subject to your masters" (2:18); *(j)* "wives, be in subjection" (3:1); *(k)* "husbands, dwell with wives . . . (3:7); *(l)* "be ye all of one mind . . ." (3:8); *(m)* "fear not" (3:14); *(n)* "neither be ye troubled" (3:14); *(o)* "sanctify . . . in your hearts" (3:15); *(p)* "arm yourselves" (4:1); *(q)* "be ye sober" (4:7); *(r)* "think it not strange" (4:12); *(s)* "rejoice" (4:13); *(t)* "let none of you suffer" (4:15); *(u)* "let him not be ashamed" (4:16); *(v)* "let him glorify God" (4:16); *(w)* "let

them . . . commit their souls" (4:19); *(x)* "submit yourselves unto the elders" (5:6); *(y)* "be clothed with humility" (5:5); *(z)* "humble yourselves" (5:6); *(aa)* "be sober" (5:8); *(bb)* "be vigilant" (5:8); "resist . . . the devil" (5:9).

These imperative commands give the epistle a directness and an informality which resemble a sermon. Peter was speaking from his heart and not simply writing a final essay. These all indicate the stronger and better qualities that he had developed in his maturity as a Christian. It is Peter at his full stature seeking to "strengthen the brethren," as the Lord had commanded that he should do when he was converted (Lk. 22:32).

7. Another theme that is given a good deal of attention in First Peter is *the obligation of the Christian to so live that his life might have the proper influence on the unsaved in the world about him.* This, of course, is an application of the teaching that Jesus gave his followers, that they are the salt of the earth and the light of the world. Peter points out the right conduct will offset prejudice (2:12); and ignorance (2:15); that it may prove to be more potent than discussion or argument (3:1); and that it will put to shame those who revile the saints (3:16). He also shows that even where it may seem ineffective as a means of spreading the gospel, it will serve the cause of Divine justice by testifying against those who have belittled (4:4-5).

8. *Peter gives a good deal of emphasis to Divine truths concerning God.* He points out that God is holy (1:15), that He is to be recognized as Father (1:17) and the God and Father of our Lord Jesus Christ (1:3), the creator of men (4:19), and the judge of all mankind (4:5), the shepherd of His people (2:25), and that He is the ultimate object of faith and our expectation (1:21; 3:18).

9. *Peter gives a good deal of attention also to the Doctrine of Christ.* He points out that He was intended as Savior of the world before even the foundations of the world were laid and that he was manifested in God's own due time (1:20). He is sinless (2:22), yet He suffered (2:21), and offered Himself as the lamb whose blood is a ransom for the lost (1:18). His redeeming death (2:24) is also for us (3:18).

The various phases of His triumph are outlined. *(a)* the resurrection (1:3,21; 3:21), *(b)* His ascension (3:21), *(c)* his position at the right hand of God (3:22), *(d)* His victory over hostile powers (3:22). He emphasizes that Christ deserves and receives the title of Lord (3:15). That He was the stone rejected by man but approved of God (2:4), the precious cornerstone for the saints (2:6-7). He emphasizes further that He will be revealed in glory to consummate the Divine purposes of God (1:7,13; 4:13; 5:1).

10. *The Holy Spirit is pictured as active in God's plan for human redemption* through the Old Testament prophets as He prophesied the sufferings of Christ and the glories that would follow them (1:11), and as effective in the guiding of men who now proclaim the Gospel (1:12), as setting apart believers unto God (1:2), and dwelling in the church habitation of the Almighty (4:14).

11. *Concerning the saints Peter writes that they are chosen of God (1:2) and called (1:15), born anew (1:23).* No mention is made of the church by name but believers constitute the living stones in the Temple of God (2:5). They are described as a holy and royal priesthood (2:5-9). They are the people of God (2:10), the flock of God (5:2). They were saved by the agency of water in the act of baptism in fulfilment of the Old Testament type seen in Noah's salvation (3:21).

12. *Peter also emphasizes the second coming of our Lord.* He points out that the coming of Christ is sufficient reason for maintaining a watchful alertness (1:13; 4:7); that it will bring recompense for suffering (4:13), and for faithful service (5:4). The glorious inheritance that is reserved in heaven for the saints will be received at that time (1:4-5). Through all of these references to the second coming of the Lord, Peter points out to these suffering Christians that at the horizon of their lives, in spite of that which they were enduring, the glorious hope of the coming of Christ would give them encouragement to continue their endurance and finish their pilgrimage.

STUDENT WORK

1. Identify the author as to birthplace, family, work. _____

_____

2. What is meant by his having three calls? Distinguish between them. _____

_____

3. How do you account for Peter's prominence among the disciples?

_____

4. Did Jesus indicate that Peter would be the foundation of the church in Mt. 16:18? Discuss. Who is the foundation of the church? (1 Cor. 3:11). _____

_____

5. Did Christ give binding and loosing authority only to Peter or to all of the Apostles? (Mt. 16:18-19 and Mt. 18:18; 2 Cor. 11:5). ____

_____

_____

6. Tell what you know of the life of Peter before Pentecost. _____

_____

7. Give the history of his life after Pentecost. _____

_____

8. How do we know Peter is the author of 1 Peter? _____

_____

9. Who are the elect? _____

10. What does "sojourners of the dispersion" mean? _____

_____

11. In what provinces were these sojourners? _____

_____

12. How does Peter describe the former state of his Gentile readers?

_____

13. Who had brought many of these Christians into Asia Minor from Rome? _____

_____

14. Who had established these churches in these provinces? _____

_____

15. When was the epistle written? _____

_____

16. Why had Christians aroused the dislike of the Romans? _____

_____

17. What do you learn about the state of these churches from the epistle itself? Give references. _____

_____

_____

18. Where was Peter when he wrote the letter? Had he ever been to Rome? Be able to discuss. _____

_____

19. What is the main purpose and theme of the letter. _____

_____

20. Is suffering to be regarded as an indication of God's displeasure?

_____

161

21. What is the goal when our faith is "tried as by fire"? _____

_____

22. With what kind of attitude should Christians bear suffering? _____

_____

23. What effect should Christians have when suffering for Christ is to be endured? _____

_____

24. What is the difference in attitude between suffering for our own wrongs and as a Christian? _____

25. How does Peter describe the salvation which Christians enjoy?

_____

26. What appeals does Peter make to these Christians. Give passages.

_____

_____

27. Point out the practical nature of the epistle from the impractical commands given as to their conduct. _____

28. What effect will Christian conduct have on influence? Give passages. _____

_____

_____

29. What truths concerning God does Peter emphasize? Give passages. _____

_____

_____

30. What truths does he emphasize concerning Christ? Cite passages.

_____

_____

31. What passages emphasize the triumphs of Christ? _____

_____

_____

32. What work does the writer ascribe to the Holy Spirit? Give passages. _____

_____

33. How does Peter describe the saints? _____

_____

_____

_____

34. Point out the passages in 1 Peter that mentions what the 2nd coming of Christ will mean to Christians. _____

_____

Second Peter

A. The Author.

A great deal of speculation has been raised by the scholars and the critics concerning whether or not the Epistle of Second Peter was really written by the Apostle Peter. Many of them reject it as having been written by Peter. The letter is brief and lacks the mention of any specific destination. It is regarded by many as a late work, but it needs to be remembered that it was adopted by the church councils of the Fourth Century, the one in Laodicia in A.D. 363 and the one of Carthage in A.D. 397 as genuine, and this fact ought not to be discounted.

Internal evidence for Peter's authorship is strong. In his address the writer calls himself "Simon Peter, a servant and an apostle of Jesus Christ" (1:1). It is rather unreasonable to think that the writer's name is either an interpolation or that it was forged for there is no evidence to support either charge. It is said, "there is no Christian document of value written by a forger who uses the name of an Apostle" (Dods). Again, it is said "it is almost inconceivable that a forger, writing to warn against false teachers, writing in the interest of truth, should have thus deliberately assumed a name and experience to which he had no claim" (Lumby).

In the letter Peter testifies to his association with Christ on the Mount of Transfiguration (1:16-18). His affection for Paul is referred to in 3:15-16. In the letter there are certain personal references that indicate Peter's authorship. He refers, for example, to his approaching death as something that will occur suddenly (1:14), apparently recalling the Lord's prophecy concerning him (1:18). He pledges that the purpose of his writing is that after his death the readers may have help in remembering the things that he has taught them (1:15).

There are certain other distinctive items of the epistle's vocabulary that are found in the reported speeches of Peter recorded in Acts of the Apostles: (1) "obtained" (2 Pet. 1:1; Acts 1:17). The word occurs besides in only two other New Testament passages. (2) "godliness" (2 Pet. 1:3,6,7; 3:11; Acts 3:12). Aside from these references the word is found only in the letters written by Paul to Timothy and Titus. (3) "lawless" (2 Pet. 2:8; Acts 2:23). This word is little used elsewhere. (4) "wages of iniquity" (2 Pet. 2:13,15; Acts 1:18). No other New Testament passage has this same form of expression. (5) "the day of the Lord" (2 Pet. 3:10; Acts 2:20). These comparisons between the expressions found in Second Peter and the speeches delivered by him in the Book of Acts of the Apostles and recorded under the direction of the Holy Spirit form valuable evidence as to the authorship of Second Peter.

Then, there are points of similarity to be noted between Second Peter and First Peter. (1) "grace to you and peace be multiplied."

These words occur in the salutation of both epistles. *(2)* "precious" is a catch-word in both epistles (1 Pet. 1:19; 1:7; 2:6-7; 2 Pet. 1:4; 1:1). *(3)* "virtue" or "excellence" is used of God (1 Pet. 2:9; 2 Pet. 1:3), and of man (1:5). It occurs in only one other New Testament passage (Phil. 4:8). *(4)* "putting off" appears only in 1 Pet. 3:21, and 2 Pet. 1:14. *(5)* "cease from sin" (1 Pet. 4:1; 2:14). *(6)* "eye witness" (1 Pet. 2:12, 3:2), used as a participle; 2 Pet. 1:16 has the noun. This is an uncommon word; the root is not found elsewhere in the New Testament. *(7)* "supply" (1 Pet. 4:11; 2 Pet. 1:5, 11) with the preposition, "used," in composition with the verb. The verb is rare in the New Testament. *(8)* "love the brethren" (1 Pet. 1:22; 2 Pet. 1:7). This is used three other times in the New Testament. *(9)* "manner of life" (1 Pet. 1:15,18; 2:12; 3:1,2,16; 2 Pet. 3:14; 2:13). These, and others that could be added to them, are evidences of the fact that the two letters must have been written by the same author.

B. The Date of the Epistle.

If Peter was martyred around 67 or 68 A.D., as tradition indicates and many of the scholars believe, then this second epistle must have been written before his martyrdom and could be dated somewhere around 65 to 66 A.D. Some writers, however, think that First Peter was written after Second Peter, and that Second Peter should be dated early in the 60's.

The recipients of the letter are not designated as they are in the First Epistle of Peter. However, in 2 Pet. 3:1, there seems to be a reference very definitely to the First Epistle. If this is correctly interpreted, then the destination of the two letters are the same; otherwise, to whom Peter wrote in the second letter is not known.

C. The Purpose of the Letter.

Gnosticism had crept in among the believers in these particular Provinces of Asia Minor and was creating a great deal of disturbance. Paul had dealt with it, John deals with it in his epistles and Peter directed some of the things in the second epistle particularly toward this false religion that was characterized by its intellectual and lawless nature (2:1-10). This Gnosticism was characterized by a definite immoral tendency. It was already active in some places (2:11,12,17,18,20; 3:5,16), and Peter was able to foresee that it would soon be even more widespread (2:1,2; 3:3). Peter declares that he had made known unto them "the power and coming of our Lord Jesus Christ" (1:16) and therefore, he feels some responsibility for them (1:1-14). This concern for their faithfulness to the truth led to the writing of this epistle.

Perhaps the clearest statement of the exact purpose that Peter had in mind in writing this letter is found in this expression: "This second epistle, beloved, I now write unto you; in both which I stir up your pure minds by way of remembrance: that ye may be mindful of the words which were spoken before by the holy prophets, and of the commandment of us the apostles of the Lord and Savior" (3:1-2). We find another reference to his purpose in these words: "But grow in grace, and in the knowledge of our Lord and Savior Jesus Christ" (3:18). And a third statement like wise reveals his purpose: "Wherefore I will not be negligent to put you always in remembrance of these things, though ye know them, and be established in the present truth" (1:12).

D. The Contents and Characteristics.

The epistle can well be divided into three sections, fairly well identified by its division into chapters. The first chapter emphasizing knowledge, a knowledge of the truth, the importance of a correct understanding of it, and a retention of it in their minds. The second chapter, a warning against false teachers, with a description of their characteristics, their unlawful deeds, their disregard for the Lord, and for His Word, and the disasterous effects of being influenced or misled by them. The third chapter, emphasis placed upon the hope that belongs to the child of God concerning the second coming of our Lord. This third' chapter is more wholly devoted to this second coming of the Lord than any other chapter in the New Testament. He strengthens the hope of the Lord's coming by calling their attention to the fact that God is faithful in keeping His promise, and emphasizes the fact that they are to prepare themselves for the coming of the Lord which God has promised, as a means of realizing that hope.

1. In the first chapter of the epistle, Peter reminds them of the fact that they *have obtained like precious faith with the Apostles* through the righteousness of God and our Savior Jesus Christ (1:1). He calls to their attention also that they have been made partakers of this like precious faith through the knowledge of him that "hath called us unto glory and virtue" (1:3). He also reminds them that they had been made partakers of the Divine nature through the "great and precious promises" that are given in the revelation of the Gospel (1:4). The emphasis in chapter 1 is placed upon the word, knowledge." It occurs in 1:5; 1:8; 1:12, and in a number of other passages in the other two chapters of the epistle. Based upon this common faith which they enjoyed through Divine revelation, he encourages them to grow in certain Christian graces: "Add to your faith virtue; and to virtue, knowledge; and' to knowledge, temperance; and to temperance, patience; and to patience, godliness; and to godliness, brotherly kindness; and to brotherly kindness, charity" (1:5-8). He assures them that if these virtues are developed in accordance with the knowledge of Divine truth, or as he expresses it, "in the knowledge of our Lord Jesus Christ" (1:8), that they will not be barren or unfruitful, but that they shall enjoy eventually an abundant entrance into "the everlasting Kingdom of our Lord and Savior Jesus Christ" (1:11).

After assuring them that their eternal salvation depended upon the development of these Christian graces in their lives and characters and that such would bring about the proper fruit and give

166

According to textual scholars the Alexandrian manuscript of the New Testament was copied in the fifth century. It is now in the British Museum. This photo shows the end of 2 Peter 3 and 1 John 1:1 through 2:9.

them assurance of eternal salvation, he calls to their attention to the fact that this is the purpose for which he is writing, and then assures them that the Gospel which he had preached and that he was writing to them about and which they needed to remember, having learned, was not a Gospel following "cunningly devised fables." This was evidently a reference to the origin of Gnosticism and to its foundation, for it was based upon the cunningly devised fables of human wisdom. He then goes ahead to tell them that as an Apostle of Jesus Christ that he was an eye witness of the Lord's majesty and glory; that he had heard the acknowledgment of God in Heaven upon the occasion when Jesus was transfigured, at which time Peter, James and John were present; that they not only beheld His glory, but they heard the acknowledgment of the Father, "This is my beloved son in whom I am well pleased. Hear Ye him."

He claims, as the result of being an eye and ear witness of the Lord, and having seen His glory in the mount, and being therefore a qualified witness, able to testify accurately concerning the Lord, guided by the Holy Spirit both in his remembrance and in the very words he spoke (1:21), that "the word of prophecy" (1:19) by the testimony of the Apostles had been made "more sure," and that they would do well to take heed to it, "as unto a light that shineth in a dark place, until the day dawn, and the day-star arise in your hearts" (1:19). In this connection he calls to their attention the fact that the prophesies of the Old Testament and none of the other utterances of God's revealed will should be interpreted or applied except in the light of all else that God had said (1:20). He reminds them of the fact that the prophesies of the Old Testament had been inspired. "Holy

167

men of God spake as they were moved by the Holy Ghost" (1:21); and that since these prophesies were inspired, they must be understood in the light of all the truth that inspiration had revealed and that they were not to be understood or applied without taking into consideration all else God had said. This very pointedly emphasizes the fact that Old Testament prophecy can be understood only in the light of New Testament revelation, and this is an important principle in the study of the Word of God.

2. In chapter 2, the Apostle Peter is *dealing with false prophets*. He not only points out that there were false prophets in the Old Testament period, but that there will be, and there were, false teachers in the New Testament period. He says that there are false teachers among you "who privily shall bring in damnable heresies, even denying the Lord that bought them, and bring upon themselves swift destruction" (2:1). He further warns them that "many will follow their pernicious ways" (2:2), and that because of them the way of truth "shall be evil spoken of" (2:2). He calls attention to the fact that they would be moved by covetousness, which is idolatry according to New Testament teaching, and with vain words they would "make merchandise" of the very people whom they pretended to be trying to save (2:3). He reasons that if God "spared not angels that sinned," but condemned them into hell and reserved them unto eternal judgment, and if He "spared not the old world" because of its sin but destroyed it by the flood, and if the cities of Sodom and Gomorrah in their wickedness and in their rebellion against God had been utterly destroyed, that all of these should be "an ensample" to those that were leading ungodly lives even then (2:4-6).

He points out that God's deliverance of Lot from the destruction of Sodom and Gomorrah is a demonstration of the fact that God knows how to "deliver the godly out of temptation;" but that it is also, in all of these instances impressed that God knows also how "to reserve the unjust unto the day of judgment to be punished" (2:7-9).

As a further description of these false teachers, he characterized them as *(a)* "walking after the flesh" (2:10); *(b)* "in the lust of uncleanness" and without regard for authority (2:10); *(c)* "presumptuous" and "self-willed" and hesitating not "to speak evil of dignities (2:10); *(d)* that they were living as natural "brute beasts" and speak evil of things that they understand not" (2:12); *(e)* that they will "receive the reward of unrighteousness" (2:13); *(f)* that they "count it pleasure to riot in the daytime" (2:13); *(g)* that they are "spots and blemishes" upon the Church, the body of the Lord (2:13); *(h)* that they sport themselves "with their own deceivings while they feast with you" (2:13); *(i)* that they have "eyes full of adultery, and that cannot cease from sin; beguiling unstable souls," and exercise their souls "with covetous practices" and are therefore "cursed children" (2:14); *(j)* that they had "forsaken the right way, and gone astray, following the way of Balaam . . . who loved the wages of unrighteousness" (2:15); *(k)* he compares these false teachers to "wells without water, clouds that are carried with a tempest", and states that to them "the mist of darkness is reserved forever" (2:17); (l) that "they speak great swelling words of vanity, they allure through the lusts of the flesh, through much wantonness" those who had escaped from unrighteousness, and while promising them liberty, they actually enslaved them in sin and error and made out of them "servants of corruption" (2:18-19); (m) he warns that "if after they have escaped the pollutions of the world through the knowledge of the Lord and Savior Jesus Christ," they become again entangled in such and are overcome therein, "the latter end is worse with them than the beginning" (2:20); (n) he states further that in such a condition as he describes, if they were led into apostasy, it would be "better for them not to have known the way of righteousness," than after knowing it, to turn away from the Lord and the Lord's will. He compares these people to the old proverb that the "dog is turned to his own vomit again; and the sow that was washed to her wallowing in the mire" (2:21-22).

3. *In chapter 3, Peter stirs up "by way of remembrance" their minds concerning the promise of the coming of the Lord (3:1-2).* He reminds them that they are to keep themselves aware of the words spoken by the Holy prophets and of the commandments of the Apostles and the Lord and Savior (3:2). He calls to their attention the fact that in the last days scoffers would come "walking after their own lusts," and raising the question of whether or not God had been unfaithful in the keeping of His promise of the second coming of the Lord, since it had been delayed for such a long time, and there seemed to be no indication that it was about to be fulfilled (3:3-4). He suggests that these scoffers are willingly ignorant of the fact that God had once destroyed the world by water in the days of Noah, and that it was God's plan that the world would be destroyed the second time by fire, and that it is thus reserved unto the destruction by fire in the day of judgment (3:5-7).

He reminds them that God does not reckon time as men reckon it, and that man's system of reckoning time cannot be bound upon God (3:8). He further assures them that the Lord is not slack concerning His promise as men are, but that the delay in the fulfilment of the promise of the second coming of our Lord ought to be construed as an extension of grace and mercy and long-suffering upon the part of God Almighty to give men an extended opportunity and a better chance to be prepared for the day of the Lord (3:8-9). He then gives the assurance that when the day of the Lord will come that it will come in an unexpected moment, "as a thief in the night" (3:10); that in this day of the Lord the heavens "shall pass away with a great noise, and the elements shall melt with fervent heat, the earth also and the works that are therein shall be burned up" (3:10). He assures them that this material universe will "be dissolved, and the elements shall melt with fervent heat" (3:11-12). He assures them that our hope as Christians, based upon the promise of the Lord, is that there will be "new heavens and a new earth," wherein only

169

righteousness will be allowed to dwell (3:13). He then exhorts that because at the coming of the Lord the universe will pass away, the earth and its works will be burned up, and the heavens shall pass away with a great noise, that we ought to look forward to the coming of the Lord and to the end of this material universe of which we are a part; therefore, to the end of time and the end of opportunity, and see the importance as living as God has instructed us to live so that in holiness, without spot and blameless in His sight, that we might be prepared to enter with the Lord into the final rest that He has prepared for the saints (3:13-15). He reminds them that the ignorant and the unstedfast will wrest the things that had been written to their own destruction and warns them against being "led away with the error of the wicked" and from their "own stedfastness" (3:17). He closes the letter with a final admonition, "grow in grace, and in the knowledge of our Lord and Savior Jesus Christ" (3:18).

STUDENT WORK

1. Be able to discuss the evidence against Peter as the author of 2 Peter.

2. When did Peter die according to tradition and what is the date usually assigned for the writing of 2 Peter? _____

3. What false teaching received some attention from Peter in this epistle that also claimed much attention from Paul and John? _____

4. In what part of the epistle does he particularly describe these false teachers? _____

5. What passage particularly sets out the definite purpose of this epistle? _____

6. What sections does the contents of the epistle logically divide into as to subject matter? State each division and its subject matter. (1) _____ (2) _____ (3) _____

7. With whom did they share this "like precious faith"? _____ How had they received this faith? _____

8. What is emphasized in chapter 1? Cite passages. _____

9. What graces did Peter exhort those disciples to grow in? _____

10. What did he point out as the result of growth in these graces?

_____ Passage: _____

_____ Passage: _____

_____ Passage: _____

11. How does Peter make known the origin and authority of the Gospel preached by him? _____

_____

Give passages: _____

12. How did the Gospel preached by the Apostles make the "word of prophecy more sure"? What comparison does he make between the revelation of the Old Testament and the New Testament? ____

_____

13. What restriction does he make of the use of Old Testament prophecy? _____

_____

14. What were the results of the teaching by the false teachers described in chapter 2? _____

_____

15. What examples does the author cite to show God's condemnation of false teachers? _____

_____

_____

16. What example shows that God knows how to "deliver the godly out of temptation"? _____

What will God do with the "unjust" until the judgment? _____

_____

17. List the characteristics of these false teachers in chapter 2.

_____   _____   _____

_____   _____   _____

_____   _____   _____

_____   _____   _____

18. What does he compare these apostates to? _____

19. In chapter 2 what promise made by the Lord (John 14) does Peter discuss? _____

_____

20. How and when will the world and the universe be destroyed? ____
_____

21. Why has the coming of the Lord been delayed? _____
_____

22. What statement shows that men do not know when the Lord will come again? _____
_____
_____

23. What statement shows that God is not bound by man's system of reckoning time? _____
_____

24. What great exhortation is based upon the second coming of our Lord? _____
_____
_____
_____

First John

A. The Author.

There is very little question in the minds of scholars in general about who wrote the Epistle of First John. Many of the early Christian writers quoted from it and attributed it to John the Apostle, such as Polycarp, Iraeneus, Clement of Alexandria, Tertullian, Cyprian, Origin, Dionysius of Alexandria and Eusebius.

In addition to the common acceptance of the letter as written by John there is a great deal of internal evidence that also points to John, the Apostle, as its author: *(1)* The author represents himself as an eye witness of Christ (1:1-4; 4:14). The plural simply refers to the other Apostles who also had seen the Word of Life, and had come into personal contact with the Lord while he was here upon the earth, and were personal disciples of Jesus. *(2)* The writer seems to have sustained such a relationship to his readers or to those whom he wrote (1:2-3), as to have made it unnecessary for him to identify himself. Such would have been entirely superfluous for the reason that his thoughts, the things that he taught, his language, and the emphasis of what he wrote were too well known to those whom he had taught. There is so much similarity between the Gospel of John and the Epistle Of First John that the opinion of the scholars is practically unanimous that the one who wrote the Gospel wrote also the Epistle. Many expressions are common to both. We list just a few of them: *word, life, eternal life, Lord, new commandment, abide, lay down one's life, take away sins, works of the devil, overcome the world, murderer, pass from death unto life, water and blood, Savior of the world, begotten of God, joy fulfilled, and bear witness.* Both books were written in the Hebrew style, used the same Hebrew parallelisms, and had the same simplicity of sentence construction. For all of these reasons, there seems to be practically no question at all but that the Apostle John, who wrote the fourth Gospel, also wrote the First Epistle of John.

B. The Date of the Epistle.

The exact time and place of the writing of First John cannot be determined, but the general view is that this epistle was written by John for the Churches of Asia toward the close of the First Century. Most of the scholars are also inclined to the view that First John was written after the Gospel of John had been written, and there are some specific reasons why this opinion is generally accepted. He had been released from the Isle of Patmos and had in all probability returned to Ephesus, from which place the letter was likely written.

In comparing First John with the Gospel of John in his introduction (1:1-4), and especially in verse 2, we gain the impression

173

that a summary is being given of the message already conveyed through the writing of the Gospel. We gain the impression that the aim of the Epistle is to recall to those to whom it is directed that which has already been taught, but perhaps not completely understood, and that John is writing in order that they might be more deeply grounded in those fundamental truths of the Gospel which had already been known unto them.

C. To Whom the Epistle Was Written.

There are several things that indicate to us from a reasonable point of view that John was writing to the churches of Asia Minor. In the first place, in the Revelation given to him by Jesus, he specifically addressed seven of the churches of Asia. In the second place, he had been associated with the church at Ephesus. In the third place, it was the churches of Asia who were being stirred by the false religion of the Gnostics with which John deals at length in the first letter. It was not written, apparently, to any particular local church, but had in mind likely a group of churches. The fact that John warned against idols (5:21), combined with the fact that there is little reference to the Old Testament in the epistle, is an indication that the readers were perhaps largely Gentile Christians.

The early Christian writer, Irenaeus, represents John as residing in Ephesus during the latter days of his life. In the first place he calls him "the disciple of the Lord," and in the second, he refers to him in the following way: "Then, again, the church in Ephesus, founded by Paul, and having John remaining among them permanently until the time of Trajan, is a true witness of the tradition of the apostles." So, it is only natural that we reach the conclusion that the first epistle was evidently addressed to the disciples of this particular area in which John had been situated and with which he had had such close relationship.

D. The Purpose of the Epistle.

The best statement of the purpose of the First Epistle of John is found within the letter itself in these words, "These things have I written unto you that believe on the name of the Son of God; that ye may know that ye have eternal life, and that ye may believe on the name of the Son of God" (5:13). This purpose in the epistle is best served by the effort that John makes to define the nature of Jesus Christ as the Son of God, that He may be set forth correctly in the face of heresies or false teachings which were afflicting the church near the end of the First Century. The general name given to this system of false doctrine was Gnosticism. It was a combination of religion and philosophy and basically, was characterized by the idea that only Spirit is good and that matter, or flesh and things material, are altogether evil. As in all other Greek or Oriental religions the Gnostics believed that one must free himself from the material world and be occupied alone with Spirit. Their means of solving this

174

problem was in the exaltation of superior knowledge, or human wisdom. They thought by learning the mysterious secrets of the universe that they could obtain freedom. Their reliance upon the things that claimed that they knew, the knowledge that they possessed, is the source of their name as a sect. The term, "Gnosis," in the Greek, means "to know." They were Gnostics because they claimed to know, or thought they knew. But what they thought they knew and their entire system of philosophy was in conflict with Christianity at almost every point.

This conflict, however, was more pointed with reference to the person of Christ than at any other point. The question was raised as to whether or not the Son of God, Diety, could have anything to do with the flesh or with the material body. A complete union of the two, from the viewpoint of Gnostic philosophy, was completely impossible. In their efforts to solve this problem they proposed two solutions: Either the Christ was not actually made flesh, but just appeared to be so, or else the Spirit of the Christ did not actually inhabit the human body of Jesus. At least, not until after He had been baptized, and that it must have departed from him before His death on the Cross. The first attempted solution was referred to as Docetism, from the word "Dokeo," meaning "to seem." The latter was called Cerinthianism because it was advanced by Cerinthus, who was its chief advocate in the First Century.

It can readily be seen that either of these proposals would have been fatal to the Gospel and completely destructive to what it revealed. The first theory made the human Jesus simply a ghost, an illusion, that seemed to appear to man but that had no real existence. Cerinthian Gnosticism would make a strange contradiction out of the personality of Jesus. It would be impossible to know where to tell whether the human Jesus or the Divine Christ — Spirit, — was speaking or acting. This would make a sort of "Dr. Jeckel and Mr. Hyde" out of the person of Christ. Throughout the letter, therefore, you find the Apostle John dealing with the reality of the incarnation; that is, Jesus in human flesh. God with us: the reality of the guilt of sin because of the errors and the mistakes of the flesh as well as of the heart; the exhortations to be separate from the world; the proof of salvation, the evidence of redemption; the way of distinction between truth and the spirit of error in discerning the Anti-Christ, and the assurance of salvation.

E. Contents and Characteristics.

When we are able to understand the false doctrines that John was combatting in his first epistle, many of the statements that are made in it take on new meaning and significance to us.

1. *In 1 John 1, in order to offset Docetism, John insists on the reality of the humanity of Christ.* He affirms that "that which was from the beginning, which we have heard, which we have seen with our eyes, which we have looked upon, and our hands have handled,

of the Word of Life; (for the life was manifested, and we have seen it, and bear witness, and show unto you that eternal life, which was with the Father, and was manifested unto us" (1:1). In this language John simply affirms that he was an eye witness of the humanity of Christ; that he had seen and heard and come into personal contact with God in human form, with Diety in the flesh, and that Christ, the Son of God, therefore had been incarnated, or had been made flesh to dwell among men.

2. *He then addresses himself to the proposition of fellowship with God and with Christ and with the Holy Spirit.* He declares that the Gospel which had been preached unto them bore testimony of the Lord which the Apostles had been eye and ear witnesses of, and that this testimony had been borne, or delivered unto them in order that they might have fellowship with the Apostles. He declares that this fellowship is with the Father and with His Son, Jesus Christ. He further states that he was writing in order that their joy in this fellowship with God and with Christ might be fully realized (1:3-4).

3. *He then lays down some of the conditions upon which this fellowship with God and with Christ, through the Gospel preached by the Apostles, might be enjoyed.* He affirms that the man who claims fellowship with God, while he walks in darkness, is a liar and does not the truth (1:5-6).

"Light" is one of John's favorite expressions: *(a)* God is light, and in Him is no darkness at all" (1:5); *(b)* "If we walk in light, as he is in the light" (1:7); *(c)* the darkness is past, and the true light now shineth" (2:8); "He that saith he is in the light, and hateth his brother, is in darkness even until now" (2:9); "He that loveth his brother abideth in the light" (2:10).

If we walk in light and have fellowship with God, we must confess that we sin (1:8). If we deny that we have sinned we make God a liar (1:10). God will cleanse us, if we confess our sins (1:9).

4. *John's testimony concerning Jesus.* *(a)* He was from the beginning and is therefore eternal (1:1; 2:14). *(b)* Jesus is the Son of God and we must so genuinely believe (4:15; 5:5). *(c)* Jesus Christ is the Messiah (2:22; 5:1). *(d)* Jesus Christ came in the flesh (4:2-3; 1:1-3; 5:6; 3:16). *(e)* All divine manifestations of Christ: *(1)* His coming, *(2)* His dwelling in flesh, *(3)* His death, *(4)* His resurrection, *(5)* and His ascension combine to make Him able to take away our sin. Jesus was without sin (3:5) while man is a sinner (1:8-10).

In order that He might take away our sins John declares that He does three things: *(a)* He is the propitiation for our sins (2:2; 4:10), and *(b)* He is our advocate with the Father (2:1), *(c)* His blood cleanses us from all sin (1:7).

Jesus is therefore Savior to all men who believe in Him (4:14; 4:9; 5:11-12). By the revelation which the Spirit has made and the testimony which He has given, we can be sure that God dwells in us and we in Him (3:24; 4:13).

5. *One of the big problems created by Gnostisism and that demanded solution then and does now is the Christian's relationship*

176

with the world. This John sets forth boldly: *(a)* The whole world lieth in wickedness (5:19). *(b)* The world does not know the Christian, because it knew not Christ (3:1). *(c)* The world hates the Christian because it hated Christ (3:13). *(d)* The false teachers and their doctrines were of the world (4:4-5). *(e)* The Christian cannot love the world (2:15). *(f)* The world is the subject of destruction (2:17).

6. Assurance of salvation based upon God's provisions and promises are emphasized: *(a)* Assurance of fellowship with God when we walk in the light (1:6-7); *(b)* Assurance that we know Him if we keep His commandments (2:3-4); (c) We can know we are in Him if we keep His word (2:5); *(d)* We abide in Him. if we walk as He walked (2:6); *(e)* By loving the brethren (2:9-11; 3:14-19); *(f)* By keeping His commandments and loving one another (3:23-24); *(g)* By believing that Jesus Christ has come in the flesh (4:1-3); *(h)* We prove that we know God when we are willing to hear and accept the testimony of the Apostles (4:6); *(i)* By loving one another we prove that we love God (4:7-12; 4:20-21); *(j)* Love is keeping God's commandments (5:2-3); *(k)* Our faith evidences that we have overcome the world (5:4-5, 10).

7. *Born of God.* By combining 3 verses we learn what John means when he talks about being "born of God." *(a)* 5:1, "whosoever believeth that Jesus is the Christ is born of God;" *(b)* 4:6, "everyone that loveth is born of God;" *(c)* 2:29, "every one that doeth righteousness is born of Him."

8. *Righteousness. (a)* Sin is the transgression of the law (3:4); *(b)* To be righteous we must do righteousness. *(c)* sin identifies the children of the devil (3:8); *(d)* doing righteousness, that is, continuing in the practice of the righteousness evidences that we are "born of God," and that the nature of our Father remains in us (3:9).

STUDENT WORK

1. Give some of the reasons why this epistle is attributed to the Apostle John as its author? _____

   a. _____

   b. _____

   Cite passages _____

   c. _____

   d. Name some of the expressions in this epistle that are also found in the Gospel of John. _____

   _____

   _____

   _____

2. What about the date of the epistle? _____ To Whom?

   _____

3. What passage best states the purpose of the letter? _____
_____

4. What false religious philosophy was disturbing the churches in Asia particularly? _____

5. Name some of the characteristics of this false teaching? _____
_____
_____
_____
_____
_____

6. What doctrines of truth did John emphasize to combat this false doctrine? _____
_____
_____
_____
_____

7. What does John affirm both in his Gospel and in this letter concerning the reality of the humanity of Christ? _____
_____
_____
_____
_____

8. Through what means is it possible for men to have fellowship with God, Christ, and the Apostles. _____
Verse: _____

9. What conditions are stipulated in order for this fellowship to be enjoyed? _____
_____ Verse: _____

10. What does John testify about Jesus?
   a. _____ Verse: _____
   b. _____ Verse: _____
   c. _____ Verse: _____
   d. _____ Verse: _____
   e. _____ Verse: _____

1. What are the manifestations of the diety of Christ?
   (a). _____ (b). _____ (c). _____
   (d). _____ (e). _____

178

12. How was it possible for Christ to take away our sins? (3:5; 1:8-10).

   (a). _____ Verse: _____

   (b). _____ Verse: _____

   (c). _____ Verse: _____

13. How does John counteract the false concept of Gnosticism about the Christian's relationship to the world?

   a. _____ Verse: _____

   b. _____ Verse: _____

   c. _____ Verse: _____

   d. _____ Verse: _____

   e. _____ Verse: _____

14. What assurance does the Christian have of salvation?

   a. _____ Verse: _____

   b. _____ Verse: _____

   c. _____ Verse: _____

   d. _____ Verse: _____

   e. _____ Verse: _____

   f. _____ Verse: _____

   g. _____ Verse: _____

   h. _____ Verse: _____

   i. _____ Verse: _____

   j. _____ Verse: _____

15. How does John define the expression "Born of God"?

   a. _____ Verse: _____

   b. _____ Verse: _____

   c. _____ Verse: _____

16. How is righteousness manifested that we may know we are the children of God? _____

   a. _____ Verse: _____

   b. _____ Verse: _____

   c. _____ Verse: _____

   d. _____ Verse: _____

Second and Third John

Second John

1. *The background of 2 John is very similar to 1 John.* The false philosophy of Gnosticism and its teachers is still the major problem with which this epistle deals. The first letter has no definite intimation as to whom it is written, while 2 John is personal in its salutation. This second letter has more to do with the practical side of the right attitude to take toward Truth, false doctrine, false teachers and faithful brethren.

2. *To Whom Addressed.* There is great diversity among the scholars as to whom the letter was really addressed, some think "the elect lady, and her children" meant a particular Christian woman and those who met in her house to worship God. Some even contend that "Electa" was her name. Perhaps as Westcott says, "the problem of the address is insoluble with our present knowledge," but that John was writing to a particular group of Christians in Asia Minor where the false system of Gnostic teaching had taken such deep root and had led many astray and divided the people of God (1 Jn. 2:19) seems altogether reasonable. To speak of a church under the figure of a "Lady and her Children" is in no sense unlikely and it is probably in this sense such address was used by the writer.

3. *The Author.* John refers to himself as "the elder" not in the sense in which that word is synonymous with bishop in a local church but in the primary sense of an older or aged person. While John does not use his name in the epistle, it is generally accepted by the scholars that the writer is the same as the writer of the first and third epistles and of the Gospel that bears his name.

4. *Purpose and Contents.* (a) John expresses his joy at the fact that many of "thy children" are walking in truth as they had been commanded of God.

This was a cause for joy when so many were being led astray by false teachers. They had been taught to love the truth (2 Thess. 2:10-12). That truth had to be discerned and they must continue to walk in it lest they lose those things already accomplished such as their forgiveness from sin and the hope of eternal life (vss. 8-9) that their joy might be made full (vs. 12).

(b). John also exhorts to walk in love (vs. 5). Truth not only taught them to love God and His truth but that walking also required walking in love (vs. 6). Their love had to include loving one another because they loved God and His truth.

(c). John warns that many false teachers who loved only self had come into the world and had to be withstood and avoided lest they lose all they had wrought (vss. 7-8).

(d). The truth must be limited to the truth of Christ and we dare not go beyond for that would separate us from both God and Christ (vs. 9). The "doctrine of Christ" here is not the "doctrine about Christ" revealed in the Gospel (objective genitive) but the doctrine emanating from Him and belonging to him (subjunctive genitive) or the doctrine which we taught. To go beyond that forfeits all connection with both God and Christ (Gal. 1:6-12; 2 Cor. 4:13; 1 Cor. 4:6).

(e). Adherence to the truth revealed by Christ meant rejecting, refusing to fellowship by encouraging or supporting those teachers who teach any other doctrine. When we fellowship false teachers we become as guilty as they of disloyalty to the truth (vss. 10-11).

(f). John closes the epistle with the hope that he might again see them face to face to further teach and encourage them and with a salutation from other Christians in a sister congregation to them.

Third John

The third letter, like the other two, deals with their love for the Lord, His Word, and their love one for another from a very practical point of view and shows what it will produce in spiritual achievement in the believer who continues to walk in truth. It also shows on the other hand how those who do not properly walk in the Lord and His Word will conduct themselves. In this way genuine believers may be discerned from professed believers. All three letters furnish an index to the Christian of his personal spiritual achievement so he can know whether or not he is a true believer.

All of these epistles draw a sharp line of distinction between truth and error righteousness and unrighteousness, light and darkness and love and hatred. The Christian must distinguish and discern these differences both in teaching and practice (Phil. 1:9-11).

This letter is addressed to "Gaius, the beloved whom I love in the truth" (vs. 1). We do not know which Gaius (cf. Acts 19:29; Acts 20:4; Rom. 16:23; 1 Cor. 1:14). Some writers mention a Gaius, not referred to in the scriptures, who had been ordained a "bishop" of Pergamos by John but we do not know that such is reliable.

Contents. Trouble had arisen in the church of which Gaius was a part, travelling preachers, perhaps sent by John, had visited the church. Diotrephes, had appeased them, spoken against the Apostle John and had stood against those who had received them.

The only reason given for his conduct was that he "loved to have the preeminence." John condemned this haughty and selfish ambition and the envy and jealousy it stirred up in his heart as reflected in his wicked treatment of both John and other brethren.

Rejection of Apostolic authority and instruction is a destructive attitude and alienates a man from God (1 Jn. 4:6).

John expresses his love for Gaius (vs. 1), assures him of his prayers (2), tells him his joy over his standing for the truth (3,4), commends him for his hospitality and fellowship toward faithful brethren (5,6), encourages him to continue to do so in spite of Diotrephes (6,8).

He informs him of his intended visit to deal with Diotrephes

(9,10) commends Demetrius to him (11,12), and gives him assurance that he intended to visit him and talk with him face to face and tell him many things he could not write.

This letter, as John's other epistles, was evidently written close to the end of the first century and gives us a view of life in a congregation at that period.

STUDENT WORK

Second John

1. How does John refer to himself in both of these short letters? _____ In what sense is this term used? _____

_____

2. What is the background of 1 John? _____

_____

3. What does 2 John deal with on the practical side and what are the four places discussed? _____ _____

_____ _____

4. What is the most reasonable conclusion as to whom this letter is addressed? _____

_____

_____

5. What fact brought John joy concerning those to whom he wrote?

_____

6. John also exhorts them to walk in _____
7. To walk in truth requires also walking in _____
8. How is it evidenced that we walk in love? _____

_____

9. What does John warn against? _____
10. How was it possible to lose all they had accomplished? _____
_____ Give Verse: _____
11. What is the penalty in going beyond the doctrine of Christ? _____

_____

12. What does the expression "doctrine of Christ" mean? _____

_____

13. What obligation accompanies adherence to the "Doctrine of Christ"? _____

_____

14. What hope does John express concerning them? _____

182

Third John

1. How is our love for God, His word, and for one another best demonstrated? _____

   _____

2. What kind of conduct will be the result of failing to walk in the truth and in love one for another? _____

3. Give an example of such conduct on the part of a character in 2 John? _____

   _____

4. What is characteristic of true faith? _____

5. What emphasis is laid down concerning truth and error, righteousness and unrighteousness, light and darkness, and what is the Christian's obligation? _____

   _____

6. To whom does John address this letter and what does John say about him? _____

   _____

   _____

7. Who was causing the trouble in this church? _____

8. What was this man's principal problem? _____

   _____

9. How did he defy the authority of the Apostle John? _____

   _____

10. In what manner did he mistreat the brethren? _____

    _____

11. What did John say about Demetrius? _____

    _____

12. What did John say about dealing with Diotrephes? _____

    _____

    _____

Revelation

This brings to a close the New Testament and its history. It completes and perfects the divine revelation of God's scheme for human redemption. It is final in its thought and places endorsement upon all that has been revealed and a divine prohibition of any alteration or deletion (Gal. 1:6-11; Jude 3; Rev. 22:16-19).

While all of the Bible constitutes a revelation from God to man, this book in a particular way is a special revelation, given in a special way, and with a special message. The word "revelation" comes from "apokalupsis" (Greek) and means "to reveal, or unveil." In this book our Lord has drawn back the veil through this revelation given through John that the early church, and all of those to come, might not only see more clearly the forces at work against God and human redemption, but might also have a glimpse of what the future would hold for those who are His followers.

The kind of a revelation that it contains required the manner in which it was given, that is, that it would belong to the category of "apocalyptic" literature. The prophetic element predominates and the book highly abounds in figurative language, signs and symbols, which makes it comparable to the prophetic books of the Old Testament and particularly to the books of Daniel, Ezekiel, and Zechariah. These prophecies expressed in such symbolic and figurative language, as vehicles to convey its message to those to whom it was directed, served the purpose of making known to them in language with which they were familiar, especially the Jewish element in the churches, its message and yet, withholding it from the multitude of the people and especially the enemies of the Lord. In that particular it is comparable to the parables taught by the Lord (Mt. 13:10-15).

A. Its Genuiness and Authenticity.

The external evidence of the genuiness and authenticity of this book is as strong as it need be for any unprejudiced mind. If indeed, it is of late origin as to time and was not written until the close of New Testament revelation, there is some reason for it not coming into use and recognition quite as early as some of the other books in the New Testament.

There are some possibilities of its having been referred to by such early writers as Barnabas, Ignatius and others. Justin Martyr says that the Apostle John prophesied certain things quoted from Revelation. Irenaeus also quotes from it and attributed it to John, the Apostle. In his writings he quotes from nearly every chapter in the book. Tertullian states that the Apostle John saw the visions contained in the book and also quotes from almost every chapter in the book. Hippolytus is another early writer that assigns the book to the Apostle John as its author.

The eastern writers of an early date such as Clement of Alexandria, Origen, and Victorinus, who wrote the earliest commentary on the book that has been preserved for us, attributes it to John. Alford, the great commentator, says that Syrus, the greatest writer in the Syrian churches, repeatedly cites this book as a part of divine revelation and as written by John.

Some early manuscripts leave out the entire book and among the reformers, such as Luther, Zwingli, and Erasmus, some rejected the book as non-apostolic. In the existence of so much other testimony of an earlier date, we have good reason to reject their opinion. Four times the writer calls himself "John" (1:1,4,9; 22:8).

The writer named John states that he was in exile on "Patmos." Early history confirms that John, the Apostle, was banished to the island. Clement of Alexandria says that he returned from this island; Eusebius says that he returned after the death of Domitian; and Irenaeus says that he remained in Ephesus after his return until the times of Trajan.

B. Date of Writing.

The majority of recent scholars such as Alford, Swete, Milligan, Orr, Moffatt, and Zahn assign the date of 95 or 96 A.D. to the book. They base their conclusion on the fact that Irenaeus, Clement of Alexandria, Eusebius, and others testify that the banishment to the island of Patmos and John's reception of the visions took place in the latter part of the reign of Domitian as emperor of Rome. Domitian reigned from 81 to 96 A.D. This is further supported by history that points out to us that Domitian's persecution of Christians was based upon and provoked by the demand that all in the Roman empire worship him as "Lord" and to so confess him, which faithful Christians throughout the empire refused to do (see vision — 13:1-18). The church everywhere received the book, *when it was written, as inspired. This indicates the early date is erroneous.*

C. To Whom Addressed.

It is thought by historians that John came to Ephesus probably as early as 69 or 70 A.D. He probably made Ephesus his home but worked through the province of Asia Minor and was well acquainted and therefore very concerned with the churches addressed as the "Seven Churches of Asia." According to Eusebius, he was imprisoned on the island of Patmos in the fifteenth year of Domitian, and returned in the beginning of the reign of Nerva. Clement of Alexandria also accepts these dates and facts, "For when on the tyrants death, he returned to Ephesus from the isle of Patmos, he went away, being invited, to the contiguous territories of the nations, here to appoint bishops, there to set in order whole churches, there to ordain such as were marked out by the Spirit."

There can be no dispute that the book of Revelation was primarily addressed to the seven churches mentioned in the

185

Revelation several times (1:4,10,11; chs. 2,3). The number 7 indicates the whole of the thing under consideration, it is used in this manner elsewhere in this book and this would indicate that the Revelation was not in any sense exclusively directed to just these seven churches but to all the churches of the Lord throughout the whole world and for all time (1:3).

D. The Purpose and Nature of the Letter.

This book was written at the direct command of the Lord. John asserts this in the introduction of the book (1:10-13). The book may also have been prompted in a measure by the knowledge of the needs of these churches by information which John may have received through messengers from these churches, who visited him on the island of Patmos. However, the letters were commanded to be written and were dictated by the Lord himself.

The condition of these seven churches, and the Lord's concern for them and message to them is only a part of the consideration, as we shall see. As far as these particular churches are concerned severe persecution had already begun. In the letter to Smyrna the "things thou are about to suffer" and tribulation to come were mentioned (2:10). In Pergamum, Antipas had already been killed for the sake of his faith and this was the place of "Satan's throne" (2:13). "Great tribulation" was the warning to Thyatira (2:22). In the letter to the Church at Philadelphia "that hour which is to come upon the whole world" (3:10) indicates that such persecutions as these churches were to suffer were to be general upon the church throughout the whole world and the promise of protection to the faithful (3:10) likewise was general.

The conflict between Christianity and atheistic heathenism was increasing rapidly and the lives of the people of God were endangered throughout the Roman Empire. Many would be called upon to die for the sake of their faith in Christ as they refused to confess the emperor as Lord. History has confirmed that this occurred. In the first thirty years of its existence the church had enjoyed freedom and peace in the Roman Empire that came to an end abruptly and to be a Christian took courage almost unimaginable to us. In its early days the church was regarded only as a sect of Judaism but beginning in the reign of Nero dangers multiplied and difficulties increased and to be faithful as a Christian often meant the giving of one's life as well as perhaps his entire family and all of his possessions. Nero blamed the burning of Rome on Christians (64 A.D.). There were local persecutions and there were others that descended upon the church and those who faithfully followed the Lord throughout the empire.

This revelation was given to unveil to the people of God what they would be called upon to suffer for the sake of Christ, encourage them to faithfulness, and to renew to them the promises of God's providential care over His own, and of the ultimate triumph of truth and righteousness over the forces of error and evil. In it is the intense

186

despair of present circumstances but even a more intense hope of divine intervention in the future. The fact of God's overruling sovereignty and providence to overcome and even employ celestial and demonic powers as messengers and agents to fulfill His divine purposes is very clearly emphasized. It makes certain to the believer God's judgment of the wicked and their destruction and the glorious triumph and reward of the righteous and faithful.

This book makes clear the growing hostility between the forces of atheism, infidelity, and paganism as exemplified in the Roman state and the glorious church for which Christ died. It was a message of encouragment to Christians everywhere who were feeling this growing conflict and as a warning to them not to be overcome by the enemies of the Lord and His people but through their faithfulness to overcome. It was God's last warning to those who were negligent and careless and tempted to take the easy way out for themselves by forsaking the Lord and the interest of their own souls and the hope of eternity.

E. Methods of Interpretation.

1. Preterist. This method of interpretation includes those who try to understand the book by making the symbols and visions of the book relate only to the events of the day in which it was written and who therefore believe the book in its entirety was fulfilled by the

The agora (marketplace) of ancient Smyrna. The agora was built on three levels, one below ground, one on ground level, and a third one built on top of the columns. The citadel of the city can be seen in the distance. This city which was mentioned in Revelation 2 is now the modern city of Izmir, Turkey.

destruction of Jerusalem (70 A.D.). This necessitates the conclusion that the book was written at an early date.

2. Historist. Those who approach the book with this method believe that its visions form a complete historical outline of the entire course of history of the church from the beginning to the second coming of the Lord.

3. Futurist. This approach is made by those who believe that the first three chapters were fulfilled in the day in which it was written or else that the seven churches of Asia represent seven different epochs or periods of church history covering the history of the church from the Apostles of Christ to the second coming of our Lord.

4. Idealist. This represents the approach to the understanding of this book by those who believe in making a spiritual application of the various visions and symbols of the book. They believe that the book becomes a symbolic picture of the struggle between Christ and Satan, the church and the world, truth and error, righteousness and sin, Christianity and its enemies ending in the ultimate triumph of Christ and His Church over all the forces of error and sin.

F. Some Things for the Student and Teacher to Keep in Mind.

1. Whatever your approach to the study of Revelation may be, it is well to remember that *the blessing is pronounced upon "he that readeth, and they that hear the words of this prophecy, and keep those things which are written therein."* This necessitates an open mind, a willingness to hear and study without prejudice or a closed mind. If there is any part of God's revelation that should be approached in all humility with an open mind, this is certainly one.

2. *Whatever God wanted those who read and study the book to understand without any doubt or uncertainty, He has in this book made unmistakably clear and positive.*

a. The source of the revelation that we might reverence it, "the Revelation of Jesus Christ, which God gave unto him, to shew unto his servants things which must shortly come to pass; and he sent and signified it by his angel unto his servant John" (1:1).

b. The message which John was to write concerned those "things which thou hast seen, the things which are, and the things which shall be hereafter" (1:19). Some things in the vision were being fulfilled and some things were "hereafter." How much time "hereafter" embraces no man knows and no man can find out. Only God knows when the end will come (Mt. 25:34-39; Acts 1:6-7; 2 Pet. 3:1-15; Mt. 24:50; 25:13).

3. *Avoid speculative guessing in your efforts to understand this book.* What is not plainly made known avoid being dogmatic about. Christian humility demands this attitude.

4. *Some things which are figurative in the book God has disclosed the significance or meaning:* ("the fine linen is the righteousness of the saints" 5:8; "The seven stars are the angels of the

seven churches: and the seven candlesticks which thou sawest are the seven churches" 1:20). We can be certain of such plain declarations.

5. *One of the primary rules of interpretation of any literature of any kind is to avoid giving the language under consideration a figurative meaning unless it is demanded by the context or for some other reason.* In the midst, however, of a visionary scene full of symbolic representation we must be careful about making a literal interpretation. As an example, in chapter 20: evident figures are *(a)* an angel with a chain in his hand; *(b)* the dragon, that old serpent, *(c)* souls seated upon thrones.

This whole martyr scene is concerning those who in chapter 6 were crying out from beneath the altar where their blood had been shed for the faith of Christ. Whereas they were beneath the altar crying out to God to avenge their blood, now in chapter 20, they are envisioned as seated upon thrones reigning with Christ. In other words their blood has been avenged and the cause for which they have died has been triumphant and they are seen as having a part in that triumph. This is entirely a spiritual scene and all of it is expressed in figurative language. "The first resurrection" is a spiritual resurrection rather than a bodily resurrection or a literal, physical one. The thousand years is likewise figurative rather than literal. God does not reckon time as we reckon time, and hence, literal periods of time cannot be bound on God (2 Peter 3:8).

Several things are read into this passage by premillennialists that simply are not there: *(a)* the second coming of Christ is not mentioned; *(b)* the reign of Christ upon this earth is not mentioned; *(c)* resurrected bodies are not mentioned. When we read and study this book we must not inject into it our own thoughts and attribute them to God's word for this is condemned (Rev. 22:18-19).

6. *The expression "shortly come to pass" does not justify that the things which John wrote were to be considered necessarily imminent or that their fulfillment would necessarily immediately begin.* Second Peter 3:8, as we have pointed out, shows that time as man reckons it cannot be bound on God. The New Testament abounds in expressions that represent the coming of the Lord as near at hand but 1900 years and more have passed since these passages were written and it has not occurred yet (1 Thess. 4:16-17; Phil. 4:5; Jas. 5:8; 1 Pet. 4:7). We are taught to watch and pray and be ready, for He may come at any time (Mk. 13:31-37; 1 Thess. 1:9-10; Rom. 13:11-12; Tit. 2:13; Heb. 9:28).

7. *It is very simple to discern whether a symbol, whether just a figurative expression or a vision, represents good or evil.* We may not be able to determine just what some of them do represent, but there is no difficulty in determining whether they represent good or evil from this much of its meaning can be determined.

8. *Read the book carefully; study it prayerfully; understand and believe that which has been clearly revealed; do not speculate upon that which God has not plainly pointed out but determine whether it*

189

represents good or evil; hear its warnings of God's judgments upon those who are "overcome" and believe in your heart that the sovereignty of God, the Gospel of Christ, and the church of our Lord, with all who are faithful will ultimately win the victory and you will receive from the book the promised blessing of God which it contains.

G. Contents and Characteristics.

The real message of Revelation does not depend upon human theories concerning the book or the particular method adopted for its interpretation but the right attitude of those who study it and in the contents and character of the book itself. The general themes which characterize this book run all the way through it and are easily discerned.

1. *The absolute sovereignty of God.* John emphasizes in the initial statement (1:1) of the book that the revelation which it contains was given by God unto Jesus Christ. So it emanates from God. Jesus never laid claim to a message of His own but to one received from the Father (John 3:34; 7:16; 8:26-29; 12:49; 16:13; 17:6-8; John's vision of the throne of God: Rev. 4:2-11 - 5:1-10; 6:14-17; 7:9-12; 11:15-19; 15:3-4; 19:1-6).

All of the above passages emphasize that the "earth is the Lord's and the fulness thereof;" that God rules over the affairs of men; that by His good providence and power He will overrule and accomplish His purposes and will among the nations of the world.

2. *"The revelation of Jesus Christ" (1:1) is the beginning of the book and one of its most prominent themes.* This expression denotes that not only is Christ set forth in and by this revelation but it has come through Him and by His authority. Christ is the central figure in the book.

a. He is represented as the "faithful witness," "the first begotten from the dead," and "the prince of the kings of the earth." He has faithfully borne to men the message received from His Father; He has died because he loved us and would have us cleansed from our sins by His blood; He has been raised from the dead as the "first born" from the dead and has taken his place by the will and power of the great God of heaven and earth as ruler over all the kings of the earth — "King of Kings and Lord of Lords" (1:5-6; 17:14). It is promised that He "cometh with clouds: and every eye shall see Him" (1:7). He is "Alpha and Omega, the beginning and the ending;" He "was, is, and is to come" and is therefore the Eternal One, ever existant (1:8). This self existant and eternal nature of God and His Christ is often affirmed in this revelation.

b. Christ is in the midst of His churches. He is to be glorified in the church forever, world without end (Eph. 3:21). He inspects, reproves, and counsels His churches as "head over all things to the church, which is His body" (Eph. 1:19-23; Rev. 2:1). His authority over the church, therefore, is absolute and exclusive.

190

c. He is "the Lamb" with the right to administer judgment under the authority of the "sealed book," having acquired this right by his redemptive work (5:4-7).

d. He is revealed as "conqueror," riding upon a white horse at the head of a triumphant procession as the Roman Emperors did with their victorious armies (19:11-16; 17:14; 11:15; 15:3-5; 7:9-17; 5:9-14).

All of the foregoing passages and others that could be listed reveal Jesus Christ as "King of Kings and Lord of Lords." They do not prophesy that He will become King at His second coming but John's vision of Him reveals that he is King now with all authority over the Kingdom of God and the nations and rulers of the earth.

3. *The Office and Work of the Holy Spirit is Revealed.*

a. John was under the power and guidance of the Holy Spirit in all of these visions which he describes and what he testified about them (1:10; 4:1-2; 17:1-3; 21:9-10). All of these four great cycles of visions are begun with the assertion "in the Spirit." That assures that these visions were not just imaginary dreams or hallucinations but true revelations by the Lord and that they were recorded in all of the testimony concerning them by John under the direction of the Spirit.

b. In all that he wrote to the seven churches of Asia he reminds them of their obligation to "hear what the Spirit saith unto the churches," (2:7; 2:11; 2:17; 3:6; 3:13; 3:22).

c. In 22:17 John affirms that the revelation he had given in this book had been given by the Holy Spirit.

4. *The church as the bride of the Lamb of God is revealed.* This is a common figure in the New Testament, (Eph. 5:22-33; Rom. 7:1-4; Jn. 3:29). In Revelation this figure is used to reveal the relationship between Christ and His church (19:7-9; 21:9). At His coming He will receive her unto Himself as His chosen bride and will escort her into the presence of the Father and dwell with her in the eternal city of God forever. She shall partake in eternity of His everlasting glory (2 Thess. 1:7-12). One of the major conflicts in this Revelation is that between the Great Harlot and the Bride of the Lamb (17:1 - 21:9).

5. *The everlasting conflict until the end between Christ and Satan and the Kingdom of God and the Kingdom of Darkness.* The Kingdom of God and Christ (Eph. 5:5) has been engaged in conflict with the forces of evil from its beginning. In its everlasting struggle with the enemies of righteousness the Kingdom of God has met in every generation the same opposition and its enemies have been the same. At some periods, some of this opposition has no doubt been stronger than in others, but all of them have been there in every generation and have been incessant in opposition to the reign of Christ in the hearts of men. Satan tires in his struggle against truth and righteousness and is constantly using all of his wiles.

In the first eleven chapters we find not only the messages of the Lord to His churches, but as a matter of encouraging them to persevere, there is given a series of visions of God's might and power, The worthiness of the Lamb, the glory of the reign of Christ through

Ruins of the gymnasium at the acropolis of ancient Pergamum. The church at Pergamum was addressed in the book of Revelation (2:12-17).

His kingdom, the church, and the ultimate triumph of the redeemed who faithfully follow Him.

In chapter 12, the great red dragon is identified as "that old serpent called the Devil, and Satan" and who persecuted the woman "clothed with the sun, and the moon under her feet, and upon her head a crown of twelve stars." She gave birth to a man child which the dragon sought to devour. The man was destined "to rule all nations with a rod of iron (Ps. 2:9; 110:1-4). This man child was caught up into heaven and in his struggle in the heavens between Satan and Michael and his angels, the dragon and his angels failed to prevail but he was cast out unto the earth to deceive the nations of the world. The woman fled into a place which God had prepared and was sustained and nourished by the good providence of the Father. The dragon continued to make war with the seed of the woman. This is a direct picture of Satan's attempt to prevent and then overthrow the reign of Christ.

In chapter 13, the first beast came up out of the sea and had seven heads, and ten horns, and upon his horns ten crowns, and upon his heads the name of blasphemy. This beast was given power by Satan (13:4). He was given a "mouth speaking great things and blasphemies." This spirit of blasphemy belongs to the antichrist and vividly pictures heathenistic unbelief. This came to a peak in opposition to Christ and His church when Rome demanded of the entire world over which she ruled that they recognize the head of the

192

Roman civil state as "Lord" and so confess him and burn incense unto him. This beast made war against the saints and destroyed the faith of man and ruled over all men except those "whose names are written in the book of life of the Lamb" (13:5-8).

In verse 11 of this chapter another great beast came up out of the earth who had two horns like a lamb and he spake as a dragon, exercised all of the power of the first beast, caused all the earth to worship him, and "doeth great wonders . . . and deceiveth them that dwell on the earth by those miracles which he had power to do" (13:11-18). This beast suggests to us another enemy of Christ — false religion — identified first by religious Rome and the false prophet. False religion since the very beginning of the Kingdom of Christ, both in Roman Catholicism and protestant denominationalism, has been the true enemy of truth and has deceived the hearts of countless millions of the earth.

In chapter 17:1-5, "the woman arrayed in purple and scarlet colour and decked with gold and precious stones and pearls, having a golden cup in her hand full of abominations and filthiness of her fornication; and upon her forehead was a name written, MYSTERY, BABYLON THE GREAT, THE MOTHER OF HARLOTS AND ABOMINATIONS OF THE EARTH," was revealed to John sitting upon the beast that had come up out of the sea (13:1). Evidently this is a picture of *seduction to evil, ungodliness and lasciviousness* as it combined with the other enemies of Christ.

These three enemies, pagan atheism and heathenism, false religions, and the spirit of lasciviousness and ungodliness are the sources from which destruction has been so widely wrought upon the souls of men and that have contested and opposed truth and righteousness all of the time and all of the way.

6. *The Parallelism of the book.* The last two sections of the book are parallel to each other: 17:1 - 21:8 depicts the destruction of the world system of evil represented by the harlot, Babylon; 21:9 - 22:5 pictures the final appearance of the bride of Christ, the New Jerusalem.

These two sections are parallel by way of contrast as well as by similarity. Each show the consummation of a purpose: one, the end of the trend away from God; the other, the end of redemption. Both are introduced by one of the "seven angels that had the seven bowls."

The first section introduces a harlot, the latter a bride. The former sets a wilderness scene (17:3); the latter, on a mountain (21:10); the former says that on the harlot are written the names of blasphemy (17:3); the latter tells us that the names of the twelve tribes and of the twelve apostles are inscribed on the Holy City (21:12-14); the former presents Babylon, the city of corruption and judgment (17:6); the latter describes the New Jerusalem which comes down out of heaven pure and chaste (21:10); the former perished in dire judgment; the latter endures in eternal light; the former is cursed; the latter is blessed.

7. *Judgment.* The scene of judgment centers around the throne of God, once again emphasizing the absolute sovereignty of God. This judgment scene reveals that the final civilization on this earth will be a highly prosperous one, culturally advanced and utterly godless (18:1-5). The last act of organized humanity is an armed rebellion against God and His Christ (20:7-10). The picture of the final doom of sin is terribly drawn (20:15).

Three series of judgment are in the second vision — the seven seals, the seven trumpets, and the seven bowls. These give a terrible picture of the judgments of God upon those "that dwell upon the earth." Yet, in spite of these terrible judgment, man remains unrepentant (6:15-17; 9:20-21; 16:9,11,21).

With the defeat of the forces of evil God reigns supreme. The chief enemies of the Lord *(a)* the dragon, *(b)* the first beast, *(c)* the second beast and the false prophet, *(d)* the scarlet woman riding upon the beast, all fail in their "war against the Lamb" and are overcome and consigned to their doom (19:19-21). Satan is finally defeated and shares their fate (20:10).

The very heart of the message of this book is found in 17:14 in which we are assured with great certainty of the final triumph of the Lamb of God and the forces of righteousness over the forces of evil and error. This is the message the world needed then and now.

STUDENT WORK

1. What peculiar and distinctive place does this book have in the New Testament? _____

_____

2. What does "Revelation" mean? _____
Name some characteristics of Apocalyptic Literature and name some other books in the Bible of like nature. Characteristics:

_____

_____

Other books similar: _____
3. Why did God give such a revelation? _____

_____

4. What are some of the evidences of the genuineness and authenticity of this book? _____

_____

_____

194

5. What evidences indicate that the Apostle John wrote it? _____

_____

6. When was it written? _____ Give your reasons for this date? _____

_____

_____

7. To whom was this book written particularly? _____

Who was addressed, generally? _____

8. By whose authority did John write the book? _____

9. With whom did it originate? _____

10. Where was John when he wrote it and why? _____

11. What was the purpose of the revelation? _____

_____

12. Name and describe briefly the different methods employed by some in their effort to understand the book.

(1) _____

_____

(2) _____

_____

(3) _____

_____

(4) _____

_____

13. List some important things to keep in mind in studying this book?

_____

_____

14. What is the connection between the scene in Chapter 6:9-11 and the scene in Chapter 20:4-5? _____

_____

195

_____

_____

_____

15. What are some of the things that some read into Chapter 20 that are not mentioned there? _____

_____

_____

16. How do we know that "shortly come to pass" does not necessarily mean bound to occur very soon? _____

_____

_____

17. What does the Bible teach us about the time of the coming of the Lord and what our attitude should be concerning it? _____

_____

_____

18. What distinction between the visions and symbols of this book is easily made? _____

_____

_____

19. List some of the great themes that run all the way through the book.
    (1). _____
    (2). _____
    (3). _____
    (4). _____
    (5). _____
    (6). _____

20. What are some of the revelations concerning Christ?
    (1). _____
    (2). _____
    (3). _____
    (4). _____

21. What main admonition is given as our obligation to hear the message of this book? _____

_____

_____

22. What are some of the things emphasized in the first eleven chapters? _____

_____

_____

_____

_____

23. What forces are pictured as the enemies of truth and righteousness and in constant conflict with them in every generation? _____

_____

_____

_____

24. What are some of the contrasts between The Great Harlot and the Bride?

(1). _____
(2). _____
(3). _____
(4). _____
(5). _____
(6). _____

25. What series of judgments does the book picture against the earth? _____

_____

_____

_____

26. Did these terrible judgments upon rebellious humanity bring men to repentance?_____

27. Do the closing scenes indicate a utopian age for mankind upon this earth?_____

28. What is the final picture of mankind upon the earth? Cite passages.

_____ Passage: _____
_____ Passage: _____
_____ Passage: _____

29. What passages picture the ultimate doom of the enemies of Christianity? _____

_____

197

30. What passage particularly expresses the main theme of the book
— the ultimate triumph of Christ and His Church — truth and
righteousness against the forces of error and evil? _____